The Body's Perilous Pleasures

Dangerous Desires and Contemporary Culture

Editor

MICHELE AARON

EDINBURGH
University Press

© The contributors, 1999

Edinburgh University Press
22 George Square, Edinburgh

Typeset in ITC–New Baskerville
by Pioneer Associates, Perthshire, and
printed and bound in Great Britain by
Cromwell Press, Trowbridge, Wiltshire

A CIP record for this book is available from
the British Library

ISBN 0 7486 0961 X

Contents

Contents

Acknowledgements

I WOULD LIKE TO THANK the Centre for Language and Cultural Theory, 1995–6, at the University of Southampton for their support of the Cutting Edge Seminar Series, Linda Ruth Williams for her encouragement and counsel regarding the series and the proceeding publication and Jackie Jones at Edinburgh University Press for her enduring enthusiasm for the project. I would also like to thank all those who participated in the inspiring seminars and, especially, the contributors to this book for their patience and commitment.

Thanks, finally, to Monica Pearl – for everything.

Tanya Krzywinska's chapter is a shorter version of an article published in Jack Sergeant (ed.), *Suture* (London: Creation Books, 1998).

Introduction

Michele Aaron

THIS COLLECTION AROSE FROM a seminar series held at the University of Southampton's Centre for Language and Cultural Theory, entitled 'Cutting Edge: The Body's Perilous Pleasures'. Papers had been invited that addressed those pleasures of the body that were dangerous socially, legally or politically. When first publicised within the University, a problem arose and, although it was overcome, its implications provide a poignant statement on the central preoccupation, and significance, of this collection. In the original publicity for the group, the list of themes to be covered ended in paedophilia. The sentence that followed stated that the purpose of the series was to establish a 'network of researchers working in similar areas'. A complaint by one graduate student as to the general tone of the series became concentrated, by several key members of the Arts Faculty, into a problem with the proximity of the words paedophilia and network. Fears for the University's reputation became bound up with fears that they were supporting a paedophile ring.

While I do not wish to underplay public concern at paedophilia – and over the course of producing this collection there have been several paedophilia-related scandals from the Dunblane murders to the 'questioning' of public figures in Belgium and Britain – this problem perhaps perfectly discloses the trouble or danger with the subject (and possibly its appeal). This is the clouded area of the difference between what one studies and what one practises, what one fantasises about and what one condones, what one watches or reads and what one does, in many ways the difference between theory and practice. This is not a field where Empiricism rests assured.

This collection aims to intervene in this tangle of association and to question the identity of this 'one', who watches and reads, in which we are all endlessly implicated. However, rather than demarcate or freeze the boundaries of this state of implicatedness, it aims to allow for the essential discussion of complicity – of the fragile positions of removal, of the 'safe' distances or neutrality of the reader, the viewer or witness – by both indulging and unweaving this web of implication. Thus, the range of chapters negotiates the different perspectives on this sensitive area through interrogating the representation of perilous pleasures in contemporary Western culture. These representations include the cinematic or fictional display of dangerous desires, such as risky sex, vampirism or violence, but they betray the more pervasive, yet less explicit, risks for the individual enjoying these texts, such as voyeurism, masochism or an implicated homosexuality. Perilous pleasures, then, refer to the blatant activities or images of horror, suspense and eroticism on the screen or page, but they also pertain to the consumer of these representations, whose desires are met or activated by them, whose desires determine their production and popularity. These are the perilous pleasures *in* film and fiction, but, most importantly, the perilous pleasures *of* the reader or viewer and *of* society in general. Thus, this collection is about the gap between culture's overt flirtation and exploitation of the danger-tinged image – the thrill and quick fix of risk – and the unnamed, unacknowledged, subliminal elicitation of other perilous pleasures that are either contained within this elicitation or exist within those images that are supposedly safe.

The issue of the 'body' in all its interdisciplinary splendour has been a particular interest within the academy since the mid-1980s. In its ability to hold, store and generate meaning, the body has been addressed and charged with multifarious potential. Seminal feminist works have claimed it as a site for political struggle and change, its applications ranging from the investigation of sexuality, to the interrogation of history, to the 'more' subversive approaches more recently in which the body can be read as the 'queer' interface of 1990s culture. However, the focus of this discussion is not the body and its place in contemporary theory, but rather the body as the vessel for the experience of pleasure, the affirmation of presence and of participation in cultural representations that depend upon this pleasure. The chapters are about the pleasuring of the body in 1990s culture. That is not to say that all bodies or

2

all desires are the same. Like recent publications' attention to oppositional bodies, this collection challenges the authoritative stand on a universal body, its sexuality and corporeal identity. It similarly undermines the presentation of a neutral, unmarked and unsexy body.[1] Thus, the question of identity and identification, within these 'dangerous' representations, is a critical and recurrent theme, as are the issues of gender and sexuality; after all, desire is dangerous in different ways for different people. For example, a gay romance in a Hassidic community is quite different from a gay romance on Old Compton Street, and cinema's threat of male violence for the thriller film fan might mean something quite different if she is a battered wife.

The danger-tinged image pervades Western society. Successful advertising, the film industry, performance art and the fashion world exploit the frisson of eroticism, of risk. Eroticism sells, but it is a distinctly dangerous eroticism with more than a hint of aggression, of threat as promise. The 'sex-crime industry' – the ever-expanding trade surrounding real-life sex killings consisting of both theory, feminist and other, and entertainment forms (films, books, magazines) – revels and grows in this cultural desire for the consumption of dangerous pleasures,[2] but this cultural desire demands the problematic positioning of the public within questions of responsibility or cultural consciousness. After all, the 'sex-crime industry', for example, depends upon an 'appreciation' of unconscionable activities. In many ways this problem is reconciled through the fact that the representation of perilous pleasures often incorporates the representation of cultural anxieties. This collection might be about the pleasuring of the body in 1990s culture, but this body is also laden with the anxieties of 1990s life. What is at stake here is the extent of culture's sanctioning and solicitation of the body's perilous pleasures and how these pleasures offer a reflection upon society itself. The degree to which cultural anxieties are dealt with in the representation of perilous pleasures varies. Horror depends upon them for its charge of fear. Suspense seems to draw upon a ubiquitous fund of tension. Yet, at the same time, these representations are about placating anxieties, albeit in more or less overt ways. In Monica B. Pearl's chapter, for example, fears about AIDS are worked through in the most unexpected places. At the same time, brushes with perilous pleasures provide the necessary 'threat' against which we build up our natural resources, as Anna Powell writes: '[b]y supporting the process of reality-testing, Art assists in the maintenance of psychological wholeness and thus is instrumental in maintaining both subjective and societal cohesion'.

The 'marketability' of the body's perilous pleasures is of prime importance in these chapters. The commercialism and exploitation of dangerous desires for the 'risk'-hungry Western audience delineates those desires that are sanctioned, to reveal how they implicate and yield those that are not. Rather than celebrating transgression for transgression's sake, a steady scepticism is necessary to evaluate the truly liberatory potential of these 'risky' behaviours and images, to distinguish subversity from fashion or from a final restoration of hegemonic order. This scepticism underlies the collection, with many authors questioning the popularity of the perilous pleasures that they discuss. For example, for Paul Sweetman, the issue is precisely about fashion and distinguishing tattooing and piercing from this more passing enterprise. For Tanya Krzywinska, the seemingly irrefutable subversity of the explicit sex film is shown to serve a more conservative function. In my own chapter, lesbian chic is revealed as a combination of faddishness and conservatism. The prevalence of piercing on the street, and the fact that lesbian chic and devilish children (Julian Petley's chapter) are currently media favourites, are reminders of the transience of 'subversity', but that is not to say that they always relinquish their dangerous or transgressive potential. A preoccupation of many of the recent counter-narratives on the body has been the shift of the marginalised 'body' to the centre and the, albeit transitory, replacement of the fringe by the 'more' subversive. As Judith Squires has asked in the editorial to *Perversity*, perversity sells but is it then still subversive?[3] The purpose here is not to separate out the margin's influence on the centre or its passage there – the margin and the centre are not so clearly delineated – but to scrutinise the production and the exploitation of dangerous desires throughout the cultural marketplace. Thus, transgressive interpretations of traditional or popular imagery combine with a critical contextualising of subcultural forms.

In 1984 the book *Pleasure and Danger: Exploring Female Sexuality* 'expressed the ambivalent and contradictory extremes women experience in negotiating sexuality'.[4] Here, while maintaining a concern with gender and sexuality, the reader or viewer's ambivalent relationship to pleasure and danger resounds with broader application. While not specifically about the body or transgression, *The Body's Perilous Pleasures* attends to the stormy relationship

4

between pleasure and danger, these overlapping, rather than contradictory, forces so prevalent in our Western culture. The synchronicity between pleasure and danger, the relationship between the on-screen delights and the off-screen dangers, varies but has provided the division of the chapters into three parts. These trace the different degrees or forms of interaction between represented (perilous) pleasures and their incumbent risks. They reflect not only different concerns but the different levels of 'bodily' involvement or wittingness. Running through them, however, is a stream of similarly themed perilous pleasures that challenge the 'safe' boundaries between life and death, pain and pleasure, and sexuality and gender, and include necrophilia and vampirism, transsexuals, cyborgs and piercees.

There are many interconnections between the chapters, not only in their critical investments, but in their overlapping vocabulary and imagery. In addition, in this collection, academics in Britain enter what is perceived to be a predominantly North American debate. They carry with them the experience of a culture markedly similar to the USA – indeed, one that enjoys the same set of representations – yet with different cultural reactions to, and stages of development of, social phenomena such as the 'sex-crime industry', gun culture and youth-drug culture. Several of the chapters provide specifically British contexts to their engagement. The recent success of the film *The Full Monty* (Peter Cattaneo, 1997) has drawn the world's attention to the male spectacle and Britishness – a subject taken up by Ken MacKinnon in his exploration of the male object within a British context. Petley's work on the murder of James Bulger provides a very British setting for his discussion of the representation of the monstrous child.

In Part I, Identifying Risks, the perilous pleasures that the filmic texts portray are obfuscated, displaced or deferred. In the staging of these desires on screen, the spectator is embroiled in and welcomes strategies that both deny and confirm these very pleasures or, rather, that precisely permit these perilous pleasures through denying them. Thus, the common theme of the chapters in this section is the concept of disavowal, the requisite covering-up of the obvious and its implications. This section is about locating these risky pleasures but it is also about how what is suppressed, hidden or masked impacts on the films' representation of identity and, subsequently, on the spectator's identification with the characters. Of course, disavowal, that marker of inappropriate desire and sexual difference, contains an acknowledgement of 'marked'

5

risks, yet here it is crucial that they are disguised. The primary, but disavowed, perilous pleasure in this section is homosexuality or homoeroticism. Homosexuality, interestingly, haunts this collection. It is not expressed as a represented perilous pleasure itself yet it is undoubtedly present as an extra-textual dangerous desire.

Kenneth MacKinnon's chapter deals precisely with the disavowal of the male erotic object as a processing and perpetuation of the dangerous desire that is male objectification. Man's reluctance 'to gaze at his exhibitionist like' is played off against the enduring phenomenon of male exhibitionism. MacKinnon looks specifically at students' reactions to this phenomenon, and society's – specifically the British public's – long-standing indulgence in the taboo surrounding recognition of the eroticised male.

The films of David Cronenberg are full of male spectacles, yet the masculinity that they express is 'uneasy'. According to Linda Ruth Williams, the graphic body horror and/or sexual scenes – the visceral pleasures – of Cronenberg's work not only challenge notions of a sovereign or narcissistic masculinity but rely upon a disavowed homoeroticism to ensure the heterosexual identity of the male protagonist. The feminised abjection of the male interior as the breaking of the boundary between male and female is shown, by Williams, to be part of a steady dissolution of divisions which includes the borders between fantasy and reality and inside and outside. These borders are shown to be especially charged with erotic risk in Williams's discussion of the highly controversial film *Crash*.

The blurring of boundaries, or 'crisis of categories', is central to Helen Hanson's chapter, which focuses on the portrayal of the male to female transvestite in *The Crying Game*. In exploring the play upon sexual and political identity in the film, she finds that the transvestite figure, rather than being the questionable figure, is the questioning one. S/he calls the identity of all the other characters and also of the viewer into question, precipitating not only a crisis of categories – such as male:female and heterosexual:homosexual – but a host of perilous pleasures from cross-dressing to homosexuality. The act of passing (as a man) is an implicating but invisible perilous pleasure: a perilous pleasure, in its own right, in that it is fraught with the fears of discovery but, through its 'deceptive' or 'questioning' potential, it depends upon and triggers the dangerous desires of others. While most cross-dressed figures in mainstream cinema are central to the return to heterocentric norms, Hanson finds that *The Crying Game* refuses a recovery of temporary transgressions.

In the spate of films about lesbian couples who kill, in 1994–5, there is no recovery of heterosexual stability. Yet, while the films broke with tradition in offering the 'consummation' of gay partnerships, they were, at the same time, familiarly framed by the linking of homosexuality and murder and by cinema's disavowal of lesbian relationships. In my own chapter, I examine how the blatant perilous pleasures, embodied by the passionate yet murderous females, implicate the spectator within them. What is more, the appearance of this new genre is shown to respond to the cultural desire for the female sexual killer and thereby reflects more general or pervasive dangerous pleasures.

Part II, Untold Risks, addresses perilous pleasures represented within film and fiction and their relationship to the culture that determines them. In the texts that are explored, the figure of the child, the vampire, the cyborg and, always, the woman as monster provide lucrative cultural products that depend on the developing markets for them. The chapters acknowledge the cultural desire for these forms but expose how, within their popularity, other more perilous pleasures are at play. The dangerous delights that are represented in the texts are shown to give way to the more pervasive ills of society or ideology. The risks are 'untold' not only because those on screen or page belie societal fears or desires but also because there is a conspiratorial silence surrounding them, for example, in terms of children (Petley) or patriarchy (Mason).

Julian Petley traces the historical representation of the child as an ambivalent figure, the way in which children have been portrayed as either innocent or threatening, absolute good or absolute evil. Transposed to the screen, children thus become naturals for horror or melodrama, yet images are haunted by this ambivalent potential that combines the two sides: the dangerous and the adorable. Yet there is, as Petley argues, a strong and enduring connection between these representations and deep-seated social anxieties. The recent and increasing demonisation of children is exemplified by the media's portrayal of the boys who killed James Bulger in 1993. This portrayal epitomises the relationship between cultural representation and social sentiment recalling, for Petley, the emergence of the devil-child in films like *The Exorcist* and *The Omen*.

In Fran Mason's reading of Richard Calder's *Dead* trilogy, it is the figure of the demonic female who is ripe for demystifying the novels' dangerous desires. The novels are replete with perilously pleasured 'cyber' characters, driven by necrophiliac, vampiric and, in *Dead Boys*, fascistic desires. Yet, according to Mason, this vision of a 'death-driven culture of negativity' is far from unfettered by the weight of conventional paradigms. Instead, Mason teases out the ways that these highly transgressive activities reveal 'the fears, paranoias and desires about women that have underpinned male domination of European history'.

While Mason sees Calder's cyborgs as a metaphor for the 'deathly' history of male Western culture, Barbara Kennedy's reading of the cyborg in contemporary film noir rejoices in the cyborg's liberatory power, 'her' ability to articulate female desire. Kennedy's exploration of *Romeo is Bleeding*, through French Feminist perspectives of *jouissance* and current cyberdiscourses, promotes a reconsideration of the erotogenics of the filmic experience. The female spectator is freed from the constraints of more traditional film theory as well as the constraints of the films' (traditional) risks. The dangerous desires of the 1990s noir world of *Romeo* – of sex, drugs and violence – are supplemented by the 'monstrous feminine'. Rather than confirming 'old' anxieties, Kennedy identifies the pleasures afforded by her new subjectivity.

The monstrous feminine is again celebrated in Anna Powell's chapter on the vampire fiction of Poppy Z. Brite and Freda Warrington. These writers' female vampires are not ideologically inscribed, legitimating male fears and male control, as in Mason's readings, but rather offer new and forbidden pleasures of transgression within a previously 'male' genre. Having underlined the parallels drawn between vampire bites and intravenous drugs in the novels, Powell connects these to the very process of reading: the absorption or penetration of the words through the eye, of the act itself, but also the 'fantasy-state' that the reader enters. As Powell writes: '[f]antasy fictions . . . seem to offer a relatively safe form of narcotic effect'. The perilous pleasures afforded by drug and blood addiction in the novels are strongly aligned with those of the compelled reader and the growing number of fans of Gothic film and literature. Yet while the texts maintain a steady transgressive spark, Powell scrutinises society's investment in such tales of the abandonment to risk. She offers a persuasive discussion of the psychic lure of textual perilous pleasures, arguing that the texts reassure the psyche, reaffirming the Pleasure Principle for the reader. This argument could be equally applied to the other texts discussed in the collection, but this sense of the representation of the body's perilous pleasures as reassuring the public becomes especially important in Part III.

In Part III Marked Risks, the 'pleasuring bodies' are already marked by their dangerous desires: by tattooing or piercing, by explicit sex acts or by AIDS. While the risk for the particular body is known, the cultural interest or investment in their expression is not. The chapters in this section question this interest or investment, determining whether these marked risks ultimately subvert or reiterate social norms, whether they are 'conservative' in motivation and thereby placate cultural anxieties.

Both Paul Sweetman and Tanya Krzywinska weigh up the transgressiveness of their respective, seemingly subversive, fields. Sweetman's chapter addresses the accelerated trend of tattooing and body piercing. Although they are supposed symptoms of fashion, these 'body projects' are far from conventional. Instead, Sweetman distinguishes them in terms of their perilous pleasures, by their permanence and the pain with which they are acquired. In addition to the sadomasochistic implications explored in this chapter, these body projects challenge conventional boundaries; for example, their merging of ink or metal with flesh dissolves the border between the organic and the technological and inside and out.

Krzywinska's focus upon the explicit sex film, *Cicciolina in Italy*, reveals a genre that is so laden with repressed and 'abjected' desires as to deem its 'explicitness' or, indeed, its transgressiveness, deceptive. Through an exploration of the social and psychological significance of transgression, Krzywinska finds that the explicit sex film affords critical insight into sexuality and its representation. While, ultimately, the film is shown to depend upon conventional models of desire, *Cicciolina* offers a range of 'risky' pleasures, made all the more perilous through the mythic significations that construct them.

Monica B. Pearl's work exists within the growing field of inquiry surrounding AIDS representation. She examines how the meaninglessness of the virus associated with AIDS becomes inscribed with meaning within cultural products. Looking at two mainstream film genres – what she calls reincarnation films and sex thrillers – that make no explicit reference to AIDS, she demonstrates how they articulate and placate cultural anxieties about the disease.

The idea that the representation of the body's pleasures can appear quite unrelated to the cultural fears and desires to which they speak provides a poignant closing point. This collection argues that the body's perilous pleasures underlie our engagement with culture in late twentieth-century Western society. Yet, as mechanisms for expressing them develop and these pleasures appear more overt or pronounced, they will, at the same time, become all the more displaced, showing up or acting out in the unlikeliest of places. And while new technologies allow old horrors to be recharged and reconstituted in the search for greater thrills, AIDS provides a crucial paradigm for understanding the evolution of dangerous desire in contemporary culture. This is not only because of its pandemic proportions but also because it merges sexual expression with potential death, a combination that seems always to leak out of society's unconscious into its perilous, if ostensibly innocent representations.

April 1998

NOTES

1. See Elizabeth Grosz and Elspeth Probyn (eds), *Sexy Bodies: The Strange Carnalities of Feminism* (London and New York: Routledge, 1995).
2. See Jane Caputi, *The Age of Sex Crime* (London: The Women's Press, 1988).
3. Judith Squires, editorial, *New Formations: Perversity*, 19, Spring 1993, p. v.
4. Carole S. Vance (ed.), *Pleasure and Danger: Exploring Female Sexuality*, 1984 (London: Pandora Press, 1992), p. xvi.

PART I

Identifying Risks

1

After Mulvey:
Male Erotic Objectification

KENNETH MACKINNON

The reference in this chapter's title is to Laura Mulvey's most celebrated work, her 'Visual Pleasure and Narrative Cinema' article for *Screen*.[1] This was written in 1973 and published in 1975. For over twenty years since its publication, it would appear to have acquired the distinction of having become the most cited work in the history of Film Studies, but to have also had its uses in impassioned debate well beyond Film or Media Studies. The intellectual basis for most feminist antipornography argument, for example, seems to be in Mulvey's article, whether or not its theses were conceived with that application in mind.

The article's principal, and well-known, thesis is that in 'dominant' narrative cinema woman is constituted as image – the looked-at (spectacle) – while man is the bearer of the look (spectator). For Mulvey, it appears untenable to believe that a male can be in the position of erotic spectacle, the to-be-looked-at or relatively powerless object of the gaze. She expends little time on exploring this possibility, instead placing most faith in her observation that: '[A]ccording to the principles of the ruling ideology and the psychical structures that back it up, the male figure cannot bear the burden of sexual objectification. Man is reluctant to gaze at his exhibitionist like.'[2] The observation is cogent. The conclusion (that, because male sexual objectification is burdensome, because maleto-male gazing occasions reluctance on the part of the spectator, it therefore does not happen) is much less so.

What of the female spectator, one might ask, whose erotic gazing

13

could allow the eroticised male object to avoid dominant cinema's taboo[3] of homoeroticisation? This, though, might be a less promising direction than it might at first appear, at least within Mulvey's terms, since her 'Afterthoughts' paper[4] undermines faith in the credibility of a (recognisably) female spectator. Instead, it argues that, in order to qualify for the pleasurable position of spectating subject, the biologically female spectator must undergo 'masculinisation', must identify as a man to enjoy a fantasy of subjectivity. By this argument, then, whether or not the biological sex of the spectator is male or female, it follows that it would have to be for the pleasure of a male or 'masculinised' subject that the eroticising of the male would occur. Any such eroticisation must, therefore, be homoerotic and, according to Mulvey's thinking, must be likely to produce a reluctance to gaze on the part of the spectator.

In the two decades since Mulvey's doubts about the tenability of a male erotic object were published, there has been dissent. That dissent is largely couched in terms which approach the question in ways that do, however, accept her observation of spectatorial nervousness about the gazing transaction when the object is male. The key word is 'disavowal'. This term indicates the means by which the reluctance of the male or 'masculinised' gazer to confront his (or 'his') gaze and its object is recognised but yet dealt with. Thus, it is argued, the spectator may enjoy male spectacle, provided that 'true' specular relations are constantly masked and rationalised in quite other terms, terms which would, for instance, deny that the gazing has any erotic component to it.

Richard Dyer, for example, draws attention to the male object's refusal to recognise his object status in male pin-ups. This refusal is effected by a refusal, in turn, to recognise a subject: the turning away of the object's eyes upwards, sideways or elsewhere; or else a hard, 'castrating' stare into the camera which thus seems to pose a threat to the viewing subject. (The threatening stare recognises the subject, as it were, but not in terms of subject power nor in terms of the pin-up's own subjection.[5]) Steve Neale, following Paul Willemen's lead in relation to Anthony Mann westerns, notices how, within narrative film contexts, potential erotic looking at the male is disguised and effectively disavowed by certain narrative devices. These may, for example, 'explain' the visual focus on the male body with the rationale that it has been traumatised or temporarily threatened with malfunction. The hero's body is, then, a site of concern within a narrative which demands his final triumph over his enemies rather than his acquiescence as an object of erotic contemplation (although, secretly, it may be that too).[6]

The present chapter's observations are 'after Mulvey'. They are so in the obvious sense that they are made in the wake of not only her questioning of the feasibility of an eroticised male object, but also with the benefit of illumination of disavowal as a principal tactic by which this object may exist, just beyond the limits of recognisability, in the half light of denied sexualities and delimited erotics. They are also, though, 'after Mulvey' in that they attempt to follow her line of reasoning. So, for example, the notion is accepted, for the purposes of the debate, of a human subject's deployment of the gaze, and hence the notion of gendered looking. It could be objected that the Gaze, understood in its full Lacanian sense, is transcendental, that it does not 'belong' to any human subject of either gender. Not only could it be objected but it has been – by, for example, Kaja Silverman who uses *The Night Porter* (Liliana Cavani, 1973) to make the point that the male subject claims the gaze as his own only by imposture.[7]

A great deal of Film Studies, after the publication of Mulvey's 'Visual Pleasure' article, ought surely to be provocative. After all, it challenges 'common sense' when it claims that beneath what would appear to be apolitical narrative demands lies a relay of looks which both aligns with and promotes power differentials based on gender. It ought to provoke, but usually does not, at least within Higher Education, perhaps because students are immersed in the patriarchal in their daily lives or because the rendering visible of the patriarchal invisible is such a routine procedure within their studies. Whatever the reason, arguments about female objectification are absorbed and deployed without palpable shock or even much in the way of doubt or resistance.

On the other hand, students' easily observed shock at, and dogged if often subtle resistance to, arguments about male eroticisation are both disturbing and curiously exhilarating. One of the more apparently rational student reactions to mere suggestions of a male object is to insist on multiple possibilities of active reading, so that any apparently preferred reading in terms of male objectification may be unseated with appeal to the array of inflections of signification that gender, class, ethnicity and particularly sexuality make possible. A sudden interest in active reading is highly welcome. Yet it is suspicious that this interest becomes so intense in the presence of even a possible male object. Deflection of attention to alternative readings seems to be unwelcome – dismissed as legitimising a reactionary sexual politics – in the context of the female object, for example. Are we experiencing, in the guise of the acute and unusual interest in active reading in this one area particularly, a peculiarly academic form of disavowal?

The results of the shock and resistance may indeed be, as suggested in the preceding paragraph, exhilarating – but only in the long run. At the time, the reaction on this teacher's part has been more akin to a bewilderment and irritation that could threaten to undermine the normally smooth professional relations between staff and students. Yet, in the long run, strong reactions are likely to produce, in normally thoughtful students, not to mention normally thoughtful teachers, energetic arguments and further refinements in thinking on the matter.

Two examples should successfully illustrate this phenomenon. Both of them occurred within a taught unit called 'Questions of Visual Pleasure' but in different academic years. The unit attempts to elucidate, critique and extend the positions of Mulvey's 'Visual Pleasure' essay.

The less pleasant of the two incidents occurred in the context of a student-run seminar on the previous week's screening of *Chariots of Fire* (Hugh Hudson, 1981). At the University of North London, Film Studies students are responsible for the running of their own seminars. At the time of the incident, they gained ten per cent of their unit marks for their conduct of and within seminars, whether organising (as each sub-group is required to do for one of the usually six seminars) or participating in them. The sub-group which had elected to organise the *Chariots of Fire* seminar had decided beforehand to ask the class to examine Steve Neale's article on the film. This article seeks to expose the covert eroticisation of athletes under such disavowing mechanisms as the boys' own narrative.[8]

The rest of the class, one which was usually open to controversial debate and to the disinterested examination of even far unlikelier ideas, behaved from the start of the seminar as if the points which it was being invited to consider were patently ridiculous. It scoffed at the article and at the sub-group which had had the temerity to ask for its sober consideration in relation to a film which, the class wished it to be known, was nothing other than it purported to be – a celebration of sporting victories. Under the gleeful scorn of their colleagues, some members of the sub-group actually joined the majority in the refusal to give time for serious consideration of

Neale's theses. Soon, the bulk of the seminar class was ranged against the only individual from the original sub-group who was still trying to obtain a hearing for the ideas in the article.

Normally, Film Studies teaching staff stay out of the running of the student seminar and enter its deliberations only on student invitation to do so. In this case, I was unable to abide by the usual contract, but broke into the seminar on behalf of both the isolated student and of the ideas which the class seemed to feel so justified in dismissing without a hearing. After ten minutes or so of resentment, both silent and verbalised, from a class which had acted in concert to distance itself from the suggestions in Neale's article, a few of the women students professed willingness to take a more responsible line. One claimed that she did find sportsmen highly erotic and found Leni Riefenstahl's *Olympia* (1938) a feast of voyeuristic pleasure. Her friends smiled in admiration of her candour. The male students largely took refuge in silence or else continued to express grievance both at the unwarranted claims of the article and at my own evident annoyance with this attitude. The most vociferous of these claimed that he went to football each Saturday to see men who were 'younger, fitter and more athletic' than he putting on a fine show. What could possibly be erotic, or even objectificatory, about that?

On the other occasion, I had chosen certain video extracts to illustrate various methods by which male objectification seemed to have been achieved, while the achievement was successfully disavowed. I began with the sequence from *Gentlemen Prefer Blondes* (Howard Hawks, 1953) in which Jane Russell sings 'Ain't There Anyone Here For Love?' to an Olympic team which concentrates on its athletic exercises, ignoring the admiring females who betray pleasure upon beholding them. The sequence was watched without demur. The male spectacle provided by the semi-clad gladiators of *Spartacus* (Stanley Kubrick, 1960) again created no surprise. The movie was known to the class. The ignominy of slave status, in any case, provides a persuasive narrative rationale for male display.

It was when the final extracts were shown that the class's embarrassment and discomfort became obvious. Two video sequences had been chosen which accompanied the Take That songs 'Do What You Like' and 'Pray'. The first has a determinedly playful quality. The then five singers frolic amid what looks like jelly and ice cream, sometimes receiving the confections on their largely bare body parts. At one point, they lie on their bellies naked, and a young woman is seen cleaning them perfunctorily with a mop. To

17

underline the joke element, a large dark oblong bearing the legend 'Censored' obscures their buttocks from view, at least on the first occasion that the mopping sequence is shown. In 'Pray', the various young men of Take That adopt straightfaced narcissistic poses on a beach and appear to enjoy the sensuality of body exposure. The females in the sequence are, as it were, held in place. They are tree-like, markedly less human than the male singers, and too dehumanised to become convincing spectators whose femaleness might hope to alibi the young men's fetishisation.

The class's discomfort was registered by whispers and distancing giggles. However, during the extended break after the projection of the videos, several individuals sought me out to tell me, in comparative privacy, that they had found the Take That songs 'a turn on'. Most interestingly of all, each individual, of whichever gender, of whatever self-identified sexuality, claimed and stressed awareness that the visual pleasure was not 'for' her or him. An older woman thought that it was surely meant for teenage girls; a younger woman was sure that it was meant for gay males; and a remarkably 'out' male who should, by the latter's logic, have recognised his centrality in the audience for these videos claimed with certainty that they were not for 'the likes of' him.

The first instance, the *Chariots of Fire* seminar, demonstrates the very point that Laura Mulvey and Steve Neale attempt to make, which is that the spectator, however constituted in commonsense gender or sexual terms, cannot bear to look at a male frankly exhibited. More than this, the spectator cannot bear that it might be assumed that anybody of 'normal' viewing habits could believe that an exhibited sportsman might be an object of erotic contemplation. The stout resistance, the concerted unwillingness even to consider the arguments for disavowed eroticisation in relation to the Hugh Hudson film, surely suggest this. It is not the film which explains the resistance. Under the viewing conditions normally obtained, it causes no such embarrassment. Rather, it is the exposure in Steve Neale's essay of how the visuals of male sportsmanship cast an erotic spell whose workings must at all costs not be noticed which explains the class's discomfiture. Mulvey's observation about the intolerable burden of male objectification is persuasive only if it refers to the spectator 'caught looking'. As long as the spectator can shelter from imputations of homoeroticism by declaring that he or she is 'only' enjoying sport – or, significantly, sports viewing – there is no problem. It is the awareness that there is even a possibility of other dimensions to the spectatorship which is unbearable.

In the other seminar incident, the strong sense that there may be eroticisation of males but that, where there is, it is 'for' somebody else somehow more legitimately entitled to view is particularly interesting. It suggests a belief that there is a sort of eroticisation which is licit and encouraged, another sort which is, if not illicit, 'against the grain'. The group to which the spectator may feel that he or she belongs is not accorded legitimacy in desiring terms by that spectator. At the same time, some other group is believed to be endowed with that legitimacy. It is as if belief has moved on from initial resistance to a suggestion of the mere possible existence of male erotic objects in such contexts as track and field to another: that there may be erotic objectification of the male, but that the subjects created for this objectification are of some other kind and of some other group.

The second class cited did not claim that there was a public admission of deviancy on the part of any person capable of seeing objects of the admiring fan's gaze in an erotic light. There seemed to be awareness that the males in question were definitely erotic spectacles in context, but that another sort of spectator was demanded. This spectator was apparently a more credible version than the particular individual declaring erotic interest. The individual had, as it were, gatecrashed into the audience of what was intended to be an exclusive show, and ran the risk of being cast out, as not really belonging to the audience addressed.

One obvious means of disavowal is, as with Neale, to suggest that there are cogent narrative reasons for a hero to take off his shirt (in a western, to check on a bullet wound, in a melodrama such as Douglas Sirk's *Magnificent Obsession* (1954), for a surgeon to scrub up that bit more thoroughly before an operation). By extension of this logic, a sportsman wears high, insubstantial shorts because this attire, it must be believed, helps him to achieve appropriately stellar levels of athletic performance. Anybody who gazes at the sportsman admires his performance and what contributes to it. What is erotic about that gazing? The person who looks with desire at the man in his skimpy attire must be so deviant that he or she misses the commonsense point.

It is perhaps at this juncture that a connection is worth considering between the group which would deny eroticisation *even as a possibility for some quite different sort of spectator* and the group which felt that it could detect erotic male spectacle even if it felt uninvited to do so. Perhaps there should be added, prominently, to the range of ways by which male erotic spectacle can be disavowed and so naturalised within a heterosexist society, deployment of the notion that there is a 'correct' sort of spectatorship. Less acceptable forms may shelter under it, provided that such erotic viewing be kept under wraps or denied altogether. ('They might have looked in that way – I expect that they did, in fact – but I didn't. I couldn't.')

This is surely analogous with the way that the female spectator, whose existence Laura Mulvey questions, is constantly invoked in mainstream forms of male objectification. Sports photographs in the broadsheets tend to present themselves as just that – photographic records of moments of sporting achievement. On the other hand, tabloids betray a great fondness for presenting the male athlete in comparative or total undress – alternatively, evincing in the verbal text a fascination with athletes' body parts. This is effected, however, only under the pretext that a desiring female is imagined to be receiving pleasure from the information. Photographs of beefcake pin-ups are there as 'something for the ladies'. If noticed at all, the same body parts must, it appears, provoke ribald, mocking laughter in the male reader. The credibility of pleasure-seeking females who care nothing for sport other than as a chance to ogle pectorals or curvaceous male rears is in doubt. Even more in doubt is that of the female who leafs through tabloids' sports pages in the hope of finding something 'for' her – but definitely not for the male reader who appears otherwise to be envisaged as the sole consumer of tabloids' sports sections. Better, however, to risk a threadbare pretext, in female pleasure, than to leave the male reader to cope with a near-naked male object, even with the help of the heavy and unfunny puns by which the male body's erotic zones are wilfully disavowed by means of laddish humour.

Perhaps the pretext is not as threadbare as all that. There must be such myriad readers who need reassurance that the sporting star pin-up of the tabloid is not 'for' them that they find that they devoutly believe in the actively desiring female. Their psychological need to believe becomes the basis for the rock-solid nature of that belief.

This is not, of course, to suggest that there cannot be such a female spectator in social actuality. Rather, it is to highlight the weight of the responsibility which she is called on to bear: responsibility for the appearance of all objectificatory visuals in a context which would otherwise threaten the peace of mind of males proudly identifying as heterosexual. Her imagined demands ward off the spectre of homoeroticism – at least if Laura Mulvey's 'Afterthoughts' argument about female spectators' masculinisation is circumvented simply by being ignored.

On the other hand, where an erotic entertainment has been conceived with the female spectator in mind, it is hedged about with uncertainties and compromises. An American sociological study of the phenomenon of the male strip show uncovers a variety of tactics by which the otherwise highly unnatural-seeming offering of male objects for female subjects to gaze at is rendered natural, unthreatening, to those unwonted subjects. The early part of the strip show evening becomes a form of induction into the entertainment's requirements. Thus, female solidarity is promoted through a girls'-night-out ethos and an ideology of sexual liberation grafted on. This ideology functions to distance wives from husbands and their domestic control, as well as to encourage willingness to ape 'male' habits of turning desirable members of the opposite sex into erotic objects. Painlessly, the study suggests, the female audience for male striptease imbibes instruction as to what constitutes, for this particular context, 'proper' female behaviour. Without the induction and a relatively subtle, if swift, schooling in the meaning of male display, the show might be an intimidating and awkward experience for the women witnessing it.[9]

Perhaps the most helpful information as to the constructed female spectator's presumed 'demands' is to be seen in the British magazine, *For Women*. The title declares the magazine as 'for' one gender and sexuality (it can be assumed here that 'women' is not intended normally to include self-identifying lesbian women). Yet, this does not mean that it is read solely by the group which is ostensibly targeted by it, any more than *Playgirl* is. All the same, the female reader who is alone acknowledged by the magazine's title seems to be a relatively uncertain and even decorous *voyeuse* to judge by the contents, the items marked as visual erotica. Throughout most of 1995, for example, there seemed to be an embargo on frontal nudity and a restriction of eroticised male body parts to the breasts and, occasionally, bare buttocks. (There does seem to have been an abandonment of this 'policy' at the start of 1996, again owing to alleged female demand. Since the modesty of male exposure up to this point was also in the name of female demand, the female reader constructed by the magazine occupies an uncertain position *vis-à-vis* viewing, at least of the male.)

21

What is attributed to women's opinion may, of course, be a rationalisation of other tendencies, such as the magazine's wish not to incur penalties for infractions of the always unclear legal limits of representational freedom in published material on display in British shops. Still, it is evident that, for the attribution to be credible, there must be an assumption of greater tentativeness and more potential embarrassment in the spectatorial position for women as an undifferentiated category than fits with tabloids' claims concerning women's demands in relation to photographed sportsmen.

Where the claims for the existence of female spectatorship (in, for example, magazines ostensibly created 'for' women) are credible, it is as if there is recognition of women's uncertain status as subjects of the gaze. Where, however, female spectatorship is a mere possibility, not by any means guaranteed, it is as if such avid objectifiers have been created for (by?) the male imagination that these objectifiers will not brook denial when they make demands to pry and peek on sports pages. These female spectators are supposed, in these cases, to behave like their male heterosexual counterparts. Seeing is all. The 'right' to gaze at the male in the way that the male has traditionally gazed at the female object is, as it were, incapable of being refused. In the name of a particular conception of equal opportunities, the posture of tabloids, fanzines and of much 'male action genre' cinema[10] is that, in this regard, the objectifying erotic gaze, women are simply men in reverse.

Yet, in many areas of popular culture, the female erotic objectifier is a joke figure. This gives a clue to another great means of disavowing the male object – the use of the joke to mask actuality. If the woman who demands the male object is ultimately not to be taken seriously, so it can be managed that the object itself is rendered unserious. The unseriousness therefore defuses the potential threat posed by it. By means of the posture of joking, male eroticisation can be tolerated. It was thus with saucy holiday postcards. (One thinks here of naughtily joking sub-McGill postcards of the 1950s, Highland variety. 'Come on, Maggie. The higher you climb, the better the view', a kilted mountaineer yells back to the woman who pauses to admire the view above her. 'Oh, I see you have ginger nuts', a woman customer informs the red-haired kilted grocer who is halfway up a ladder to find her choice of purchase among the biscuits.) Thus again with the *Carry On* jokes at the expense of male body parts. ('What a lot of fuss over such a little thing', a nurse scolds Kenneth Connor in *Carry On*

Nurse (Gerald Thomas, 1959) when she has whipped off his pyjama trousers in spite of his protests.) Again and again, the tabloids point cameras at cricketers changing their whites or rugby players ripping their shorts. ('What a bum deal!' is the level of the wit shown by the caption writers, although it is obviously enough for the purpose.) The certainty seems to be that, if their interest in male anatomy is to give the readers 'a laugh', they are evading charges of homoeroticism. And just in case any of these charges should somehow stick, they claim any erotics to be for those empty-headed 'ladies' who know nothing of the rules but who fancy seeing a man in as little clothing as possible.

In the celebrated jeans commercial of the mid-1980s, Nick Kamen's stripping to his boxer shorts in the launderette provoked looks of curiosity, censure and delight among the other customers. Since that time, commercials appear to have declared that the male erotic object has now shed its disguise, and is out of its wraps. Certainly, the tone within such commercials may be less apologetic or facetious, although the suspicion that all the male flesh on display is for the benefit of some female with purchasing power lingers on as a form of disavowal.

What is surprising is that the male object could seem to be of such recent invention. He has been there throughout the history of Classical sculpture, of fine art. How can a male be an object if he is so clearly a subject?, it could be counterposed. This is essentially what Laura Mulvey asks rhetorically about the male on the cinema screen. He has the power to initiate action, to create the narrative on which dominant cinema depends. He is clearly, unequivocally, a subject. In diegetic terms, yes, but every character on screen is also an object of the cinema spectator's gaze. Mulvey bypasses the evident truth of this by claiming that the spectator fantasises *with* the active male on screen, shares through fantasy in his power, which is the power to be active, to subjugate the villain, to demand the female's passivity as a complement to his heterosexual activity. Yet, in less cerebral terms, the cinema spectator, male, female or 'masculinised', looks *at* the powerful male on screen.

The admiring gaze, on which male action cinema depends as obviously as fine art, can easily be converted into, or become one with, the desiring gaze. Knowledge of this facility helps to explain the pin-up qualities of certain celebrated Tarzans – Johnny Weissmuller, obviously; Lex Barker less overtly; Miles O'Keeffe when Jane is forced to recognise that he is prettier than she is. The seeming paedophile who asks the youngster in *Airplane!* (Jim Abrams, 1980) if he likes gladiator movies has a real point. At one level, the peplum, for instance, offers a plot of trial and triumph which bears some distant relation to Greco-Roman myth. At another, it provides an excuse for the display of male muscularity both within and outside struggle.

For the purposes of the present argument, the important element in high art or in the most downmarket of the popular products is to insist on another purpose to male spectacle. Equally important, it would seem, is the insistence that that spectacle is merely for fun, a joke, not to be over-examined. Most important of all in the present decade may be the putative demands of the ravenous female spectator who cannot view sport without fragmenting and fetishising players' body parts. The energy with which she is created and the steadfastness with which she is believed in seem to tell a different story. Or, rather, not to tell it. What may be proved through this fetishistic belief is less what it purports to insist on – that, in specular relations, women are just heterosexual men in reverse. Rather, all this industriousness may have a quite different function: to render male exhibitionism beyond detection by giving such a high profile to imagined female voyeurism. After all, in Freud, despite Mulvey's refusal to consider this aspect even for female objects, exhibitionism is a sexual pleasure. The point may be, though, that, while it is a pleasure that society widely believes to be proper to the female, it is viewed as a pathology when it is evidenced in men. Alternatively, it is viewed as a signal that these are not 'real men' at all. Mulvey argues that the spectating subject shares through fantasy the active power of the male subject on screen. Why may this subject in the audience not also share the erotic male object status in fantasy? Is it possible that, if this were the case, we have not so much a question of female spectators being masculinised as male spectators being feminised?

Perhaps the greatest disavowal of all is that, where there is a male erotic object, there is a heterosexually complementary female subject. This form of disavowal performs an important function – it ensures that male pleasure in exhibitionism remains the cultural secret that it has been for centuries.

An equally important function is, however, that the energy invested in the creation, and then alleged satisfaction, of an insistently demanding female spectator diverts attention from what would otherwise be unavoidably raised for consideration: the relation of the male spectator to the male object, and whether, even if the objecthood of the male should be conceded, that the relation is to an object that is recognisably erotic in culturally male terms.

The question of male erotic gazing at the objectified male is more easily answered. Homoeroticism, an apparently terrifying spectre which is only with difficulty banished by heavy and near exclusive emphasis on the female gazer, can be admitted in the area where that eroticism self-evidently seems to belong – the area of homosexuality. That the self-identifying gay male is expected to respond enthusiastically to erotic representations of the male, or even to eroticise the 'innocent' photograph of the sportsman in activity, is easily conceded – by implication. If attention is not permitted to focus on the gay male within popular culture it is not because there is puzzlement at that level about the likely relation of this particular category of viewer to the male pin-up. It is, rather, because male homosexuality itself is not permitted equal space with either male or female heterosexuality in, for example, journalistic coverage of the eroticised male. The tabloids ostensibly cater for the 'real man' and, with more condescension and more self-limitation, to the 'little woman' who might be expected to become the 'real' male's partner. The model of erotic behaviour is significantly dependent on, in turn, the model of what is imagined to be that of the 'real man'. Because of that, women are assumed to want to look at men in exactly the way that men are 'known' to want to look at women. With male erotic behaviour implicitly established as the norm, there is no difficulty in presuming that gay men look at male objects in the way that 'real' (that is, heterosexual) men look at female objects. That sort of looking is not allowed extended, unembarrassed discussion, but the presumption appears to be that it is easily accomplished. It is not acknowledged in, for example, the captions for candid shots of players with ripped shorts or caught changing their clothes. These images are intended as 'for' the ladies. Yet there is, presumably, no difficulty in imagining them being consumed as pleasurable viewing fare by certain men, such men being beyond discussion in that context. (How could a tabloid imagine itself to be catering to the masturbatory tastes of the homosexual male? Their hunk pin-ups are for women and nobody else, as far as the caption writers are concerned.)

Those magazines – usually simply termed 'gay magazines' – which self-advertisingly cater for the male seeking out objectifiable nude models, for example, make no secret of that aspect of their appeal. If the photographs themselves were not obvious testament to the basis for their appeal to a particular section of the market, the captions, and particularly the appreciative readers' letters, leave no possible doubt. Such British magazines as *Vulcan* (for the admirer of more youthful male beauty) and *Zipper* (featuring more muscular, more mature 'hunk' types) and such American publications as *Honcho, Inches, Advocate Men, Playguy*, each with their particular 'specialisms', share an unembarrassed, upfront frankness about the sort of visual pleasure on offer within them. All that Mulvey argues to be present in the viewing relations of popular entertainment, in terms of 'classic' narrative cinema, is almost self-evidently discoverable here, albeit in same-sex terms: above all, patterns of eroticised domination/submission, both within and beyond the customarily accepted subject/object relations between viewer and to-be-looked-at.

Yet, while these publications are on open sale, at least in certain – usually urban – outlets, they are far from being mainstream. However glossy and brochure-like the pages, however upmarket their publishing style, they are dependent on the broad cultural understanding of homosexuality, about which the most obviously popular news-type publications, the tabloids, profess either ignorance or a curious mixture of amusement and revulsion. While the male erotic object makes appearance after appearance in magazines marketed 'for' gay men, that is precisely the problem. How can a male object which is so flaunted, above all in gay video pornography, be detached from a public posture of homoeroticism, since homoeroticism is not comfortably accepted or acceptable within broad popular culture?

Awareness of the difficulty and deviousness by which the object may be detected and then made available to constituencies relatively unaddressed within popular culture surfaces within critical debates (and, most significantly, informs Steve Neale's study of disavowal as a crucial mechanism). Thus, for example, there is a dispute between Suzanne Moore and Mark Finch about the viewers addressed by the former American soap *Dynasty*'s 'hunk appeal', with its relatively undisguised invitation to visual pleasure. Each of these writers recognises that a viewing constituency which is often deprived of recognition or legitimation manages to evade being caught looking, as it were, through use of the other group. However, this evasion of detection is achieved, in their accounts, by exploitation of the other group's imagined higher profile in gazing terms. For Moore, it is the female gaze that is permitted in *Dynasty*, by sheltering under gay male looking. For her, 'the codification of men via gay male discourse enables a female erotic gaze'.[11] Is it likely, though, that male privilege in terms of erotic gazing is easily carried to gay male privilege? Mark Finch argues quite the reverse: that a gay erotic gaze is enabled in the soap 'through the relay of the women's look'.[12] Both female and gay male gazing may be lumped together in contradistinction to 'real male' gazing (object choice being a factor that immediately seems to distinguish the former from the latter). Nevertheless, although this may be done, at least female gazing may be 'licensed', as the earlier sections of this essay have attempted to argue, through a logic of heterosexual complementarity. While Moore is surely correct when she recognises that males, regardless of sexuality, have been socialised to believe that they have a right to gaze, her conclusion that female erotic gazing is less permissible culturally than *any* male erotic gazing seems flawed. If male erotic gazing seems at a popular level to be practically definable as 'male' in the first place, in terms of a female object, surely male erotic gazing at the male object cannot be accorded the same level of 'naturalness' as otherwise the male gaze takes to itself. Female erotic gazing at the male object is recuperable in terms of male privilege and especially of heterosexual privilege. For this reason, it appears to be offered some recognition within *Dynasty*. Through the female gaze, according to Finch, a gay male gaze is enabled, albeit conveniently without *Dynasty*'s awareness, as it were. On the available evidence, this account is more persuasive than Moore's.

If the indulgence of male voyeurism of male object is both recognised and yet kept at bay in the ways just described, how on earth can there be male-male gazing involving the 'real man' category of subject at least? If the very understanding of the masculinity embodied by the 'real man' excludes appreciation of, let alone desire for, male erotic appeal, what is one to make of the sportsmen in the tabloids' candid-camera shots, for example? Are they to be taken at face value, as something 'for the ladies' and otherwise appreciable only by means of laddish humour? This, after all, is the tactic suggested by the tabloids themselves, with such captions as 'What a bummer', 'Nuts! Gazza's got it cracked', 'Hair today, Gone tomorrow' (of Andre Agassi's shaved chest bared at Wimbledon). Do Paul Gascoigne, Andre Agassi, Ryan Giggs, David Ginola, or any other young vigorous sportsman, represent strictly a male erotic object for women, strictly another subject for men?

Mulvey's celebrated article comes to the rescue when we are faced with this conundrum. Female objectification is achieved in two ways, or rather two different sorts of objectification are recognised: voyeuristic/scopophilic and fetishistic. As an example of the latter, the female star is 'overvalued', made into a breathtakingly beautiful sight by means of an armoury of effects, such as lighting, gauzes, make-up. The psychological explanation for this is that the female object is thus phallicised. The castration anxiety engendered by the desirous look at the female is lessened by rendering the object apparently more powerful, because *more like* the male subject. Mulvey clarifies the two different forms of objectification, and the reasons for that differentiation, as follows:

> The first [pleasurable structure of looking], scopophilic, arises from pleasure in using another person as an object of sexual stimulation through sight. The second, developed through narcissism and the constitution of the ego, comes from identification with the image seen. Thus, in film terms, one implies a separation of the erotic identity of the subject from the object on the screen (active scopophilia), the other demands identification of the ego with the object on the screen through the spectator's fascination with and recognition of his like. The first is a function of the sexual instincts, the second of ego libido.[13]

Surely, it is all the easier for the subject to identify with the object if that object is so manifestly the subject's like, in terms of sharing a sex. In the same article, we read that man is reluctant to contemplate his exhibitionistic like. Surely, though, the two apparently opposing notions when applied to the male subject confronting the male object can be reconciled – by energetic suppression of the sexual side of the gazing, by almost exclusive stress on the ego satisfaction obtainable through (mis)identification with the 'role model' male, whether that male be Jean-Claude Van Damme, Humphrey Bogart, Burt Lancaster, or Agassi, Gazza at the 1990 World Cup, Pat Cash winning Wimbledon.

If the more evidently sexual potential of even the identificatory, fetishistic gaze threatens to break through, that can be explained in terms of female gazing and its meaning for the 'securely heterosexual' male. Looking at the eroticised male can then be rationalised as a matter of admiration all the way to envy and hostility. 'Great body. Shame he's bloody ugly', as was overheard of Miles O'Keeffe's Tarzan when two male students were leaving the screening of John Derek's 1981 film *Tarzan the Ape Man*. 'Surely girls wouldn't fancy him looking like that.' An unconvincing verdict on the actor, perhaps, but a surprisingly neat encapsulation of the reasoning by which his looks are allowed to be of even momentary conscious interest to 'real male' subjects.

NOTES

1. Laura Mulvey, *Visual and Other Pleasures* (London: Macmillan, 1989), pp. 14–26.
2. Mulvey, *Visual*, p. 20.
3. Above all, within the period of 'classic' Hollywood and of the studio system.
4. Mulvey, *Visual*, pp. 29–38.
5. Richard Dyer, 'Don't Look Now: The Male Pin-Up', in *The Sexual Subject: A Screen Reader in Sexuality* (London and New York: Routledge, 1992).
6. Steve Neale, 'Masculinity as Spectacle: Reflections on Men and Mainstream Cinema', *Screen*, 24 (6) November–December 1983.
7. See Kaja Silverman, 'Masochism and Male Subjectivity', in Constance Penley and Sharon Willis (eds), 'Male Trouble' Special Issue, *Camera Obscura*, 17 May 1988.
8. Steve Neale, '*Chariots of Fire*, Images of Men', *Screen*, 23 (3–4) September–October 1982.
9. For fuller detail, see David M. Peterson and Paula M. Dressel, 'Equal Time for Women: Social Notes on the Male Strip Show', *Urban Life*, 11 (2) July 1982.
10. See Yvonne Tasker, *Spectacular Bodies: Gender, Genre and the Action Cinema*, (London and New York: Routledge, 1993).
11. Suzanne Moore, 'Here's Looking at You, Kid!', in Lorraine Gamman and Margaret Marshment (eds), *The Female Gaze: Women as Viewers of Popular Culture* (London: The Women's Press, 1988), p. 53.
12. Mark Finch quoted in Suzanne Moore, 'Here's Looking at You, Kid!', p. 53.
13. Mulvey, *Visual*, p. 18.

2

The Inside-out of Masculinity: David Cronenberg's Visceral Pleasures

LINDA RUTH WILLIAMS

> Every body is a book of blood;
> Wherever we're opened, we're red.[1]

In her 1992 collection of short stories, *We So Seldom Look on Love*, Canadian writer Barbara Gowdy includes a marvellously bizarre tale of fulfilled female exhibitionism which culminates in a fantasy of the gaze of surgery. In 'Ninety-three Million Miles Away', Ali lives in a condominium apartment, the architectural cousin both of David Cronenberg's anodyne Montreal condo in *Shivers* (1974) and James Stewart's panopticon in Hitchcock's *Rear Window* (1954), vacuously antiseptic yet also constructed around a voyeur's dream, with 'floor to ceiling windows'. She takes up painting; in fact, takes up painting herself nude, standing by the plate glass until she is seen by a man in the next building. Her body responds to his masturbatory gaze, bypassing her agency or shame, as involuntarily:

[She] circl[ed] her nipples with the same sceptical thrill she used to get when she knew it wasn't her moving the ouija board. And then it was her feet that were moving, taking her from behind the drapes into a preternatural brightness.[2]

Her fantasy of his look becomes a bizarre response of organ speaking to organ, of his eyes animating her hands. Individual agency is bypassed when bits of the body get together – this is not simply an identification with his male gaze, but with the image and

30

force of his eyes themselves as fleshly orbs. Gowdy, ever seeking to
push things to the limit, makes this gaze a question of the organic
power of the eye itself – it is not (just) that power is manifest in the
look, but that the eye becomes the graphic fulfilment of that
power and its pleasures. But whose pleasure is this?

[I]t was as if her eyes were in his head, although not replacing his
eyes.[3]

His eyes seemed to enter her head like a drug, and she felt herself
aligned with his perspective.[4]

Her exhibitionistic identification with (her fantasy of) his view of
her thus becomes almost a question of organic transplant. In light
of this, every phrase assumes an awful literality, as each reference
to the visual connects not primarily to a discourse of power
(although it does this too), but back to a sense of the eye as a key
site of body horror. As Gowdy scrutinises the desire of the look,
she also relishes its specific organic site – the eye itself.

It is therefore appropriate that the voyeur opposite is a surgeon,
'a general surgeon . . . a remover of tumours and diseased organs',[5]
allowing the fantasy to grow like a culture in a petri dish:

She imagined him saving people's lives, drawing his scalpel along the
skin in beautifully precise cuts. For something to do she worked on
her painting. She painted fish-like eyes, a hooked nose, a mouth full of
teeth.[6]

From here on in it gets weird. Ali buys the surgeon a pair of binoc-
ulars, all the better to see her with, which she secretly delivers to his
mailbox. Female exhibitionism becomes female narcissism indulged
via the imagined vision of the other. The man's cutting look is
staged entirely for her pleasure – his eyes become the consummate
visual sex toy. Yet still the two – seer and seen, surgeon-voyeur and
painter-exhibit – do not meet, in the time-honoured tradition of
the scopophilic contract in which a distance of disavowal and secrecy is maintained between the looker and the looked-at. She follows this with a dream which sites the surgeon as prime spectator
of voyeuristic culture – the gaze of surgery is where the fantasy
blossoms:

One night she dreamed that Andrew was operating on her. Above the
surgical mask his eyes were expressionless. He had very long arms. She
was also able to see, as if through his eyes, the vertical incision that
went from between her breasts to her navel, and the skin on either
side of this incision folded back like a scroll. Her heart was brilliant

31

red and perfectly heart-shaped. Somebody should take a picture of this, she thought. Andrew's gloved hands hardly appeared to move as they wielded long, silver instruments. There was no blood on his hands. Very carefully, so that she hardly felt it, he prodded her organs and plucked at her veins and tendons, occasionally drawing a tendon out and dropping it in a petri dish. It was as if he were weeding a garden.[7]

For a fantasy of the interior this is remarkably clean – self-contained and perfectly policed. A body has been sliced open, but there is neither pain nor suffering. Gowdy's heroine has become one of Clive Barker's 'books of blood': in the terms of the epigraph to his series of collected short stories, the *Books of Blood* (which I have also included as my epigram), each one of us is an openable, corporeal text. Here hearts *really are* heart-shaped, and the viscera glows with what David Cronenberg's protagonists call 'inner beauty' (more on that later).

'Somebody should take a picture of this', writes Gowdy, and someone has.[8] As one of our most consistent surgeons (or geneticists) of the mutating cinematic body, David Cronenberg has long animated this fantasised move from the visceral to the visual. While critics have not been slow in recognising the acute visual consciousness of Cronenberg's work, particularly how surgical and televisual looks figure in his films of the 1970s and 1980s, I want to raise some issues which have developed through to his most recent film *Crash* (1996). His ongoing concern with 'masculinity in crisis' is frequently dramatised through an impossible vision of male interiority, often of male bodies literally breaking apart at the seams, or developing new, feminine seams which then break open. However, this spectacle is represented as much through a performative or exhibitionistic agenda as through a self-reflexive foregrounding of vision and the camera-eye. Like Gowdy's Ali, showing is the thing, the act of displaying an interior which is there to be seen. Although frequently the narrative point-of-view positions of seer and seen collapse into one body – like Ali, the opened body and the eye which sees are subjectively the same – the act of 'opening up' is far more interesting to Cronenberg than that of viewing it. As his work has progressed, these forms of display have crystallised into a unique cinematic analysis which redefines the crossovers between body horror and theories of gender as performance, culminating in the mainstream epic *M. Butterfly* (1993). In this chapter I will address how Cronenberg stages the exposure of male interiors in *Shivers*, *Videodrome* (1982) and *Dead Ringers* (1988), films which are doubly concerned with the interior of the gendered body and the forms of vision which meet that body on screen. I will then conclude by discussing Cronenberg's stark, sexualised externalisation of those interiors in *Crash*, his most extreme meditation on techno-sex and the limits of performance art.

'THEY CAME FROM WITHIN':
VISUALISING INTERIORS

It is our proximity to the body and its interminable transformations – its decay, its mutation, its potential for possession and inhabitation by other life forms – which grips Cronenberg's work. In his discussion of Renaissance interiority, Jonathan Sawday accounts for our fascination with others' insides as an effect of the impossibility of seeing our own insides (and surviving that sight). Quoting surgeon Richard Selzer, he traces the taboo which is bou[nd] 'inner knowledge':

The sight of our internal organs is denied us. To how many 1 given to look upon their own spleens, their hearts, and live? The hidden geography of the body is a Medusa's head one glimpse of which will render blind the presumptuous eye.[9]

Cronenberg seeks to challenge the Medusa by making his bodies eminently visible, but it is his interior vision of masculinity which is most insistent and precarious, suggesting a very specific form of male 'to-be-looked-at-ness'.

But Cronenberg's body horror is also purposive. That the body has an agenda of its own, quite separate from the conscious concerns of the moral self, makes it more alien than the aliens. As Seth Brundle puts it, as his old narrative of selfhood gives way to a new story of Brundlefly, 'I seem to be stricken by a disease with a purpose'. Cronenbergian identity, and particularly masculine identity, is an uneasy pact between the rational (or becoming-irrational) self and its ever-mutating carcass, a pact which gradually breaks down as Cronenberg's narratives unfold. Even death becomes simply the body's victory over individual agency, as it mutates into a dazzling variety of life forms in decay. The half-man, half-fly which Brundle becomes (Brundlefly) cannot even die, but instead is trapped in a pattern of eternal mutation. And like death, disease has to be read as only another form of natural life, degeneration and change becoming simply a matter of perspective. 'A virus is only doing its job', Cronenberg has said in interview; '[t]o understand it from the disease's point of view, it's just a matter of life . . . I think most diseases would be very shocked to be considered diseases at all'.[10]

This opens up a number of splendid possibilities for visceral spectacle. In making the visceral visual, Cronenberg indulges a desire to slide beneath the skin to a fantasy of the body's exposed interior. Contemporary horror has specialised in making the inside visible, opening it up and bringing it out and pushing the spectacle of interiority to the limit to find out what the limit is. Body horror cinema is obsessed with limits – with the skin as a boundary, with the tolerance of audience expectation and desire, and with the connection between the two, as on-screen visceral violation provokes visceral response (fear, sickness, vomiting) in the auditorium. It might be said that body horror's emphasis is not the bad dreams of the supernatural or the external threats of conventional monstrosity but the disturbance of interiors – a terrorism, as it were, of the blood and the viscera. Even the ostensibly metaphysical-paranormal powers of the freak-heroes of both *Scanners* (1980) and *The Dead Zone* (1983) are rooted in a brain disorder. Yet Cronenberg chooses to look positively from the inside out, asking 'How does the disease perceive us?'

This has an impact on how he visualises the relationship of public to private, inside to outside. The films made up to and including *The Fly* (1986) (with the possible exception of *Fast Company* [1978]) unfold a process through which bodily interiors cease to be private spaces, articulating the breakdown of the distinction between within and without, both by the invasion of external beings which then take up parasitic residence or force a disturbance from the outside-in, or interior aliens who find a life from the inside-out. In *Rabid* (1976), a vampiric projectile penetrates its victims with a virus, but itself emerges from inside the body of a woman. The telepathic power of the scanners allows one mind to penetrate another across a dividing space, constituting a transgression of both the scanner's and his victim's bodily boundaries, as his 'scanning' reaches through the skin and the skull of the other and infamously breaks down that division to the point of heads exploding. 'Scanning'-telepathy expands the physical limits of the brain; those in 'range' of the scanning are effectively living inside the body of the scanner. In *Shivers*, the inhabitants of an anodyne Montreal condominium (actually Cronenberg's own apartment) are turned from the bland bourgeoisie into foaming, wanton desire-machines by a 'plague' of sex-grubs which can be seen writhing like the stigmata of sex beneath the skins of their subjects, provoking a bizarre, hilarious, and distinctly non-utopian, sexual revolution from the *inside*. Like the scene in which 'Help me' appears through the stomach of the possessed child Regan in *The Exorcist*, William Friedkin's horror classic of 1973, *Shivers*'s sex-grubs render explicit, perhaps even parody, the film's playful hysteria.[11] *The Exorcist* foregrounds Regan's putative adolescent hysteria: the body symptomatises what the subject cannot speak, the skin signalling the voice of a dying body as well as a soul crying for help. But *Shivers* does not work according to this surface-depth dynamic, for here the symptom is also the cause; 'a combination of aphrodisiac and venereal disease' (as one character in the film puts it), the sex-grubs display their wares through the skin and drive on the sickness. Coming initially from the *outside* (another body), these grubs are the entities which give the film its alternative American title, *They came from within*.[12] Echoing the apocalyptic titles of Cold War science fiction, 'They came from within' is the exemplary Cronenberg phrase: his monsters are not things which jump out of the closet; instead, the body is the closet from which the monster jumps.

These are uneasy physical thresholds; moments of tension when the skin begins to open, when the inside turns out, when difference is exposed, and when the one slips into the other. However, while feminist critics such as Barbara Creed have emphasised monstrous femininity in Cronenberg's work (the mutant women of *Rabid* (1976), *The Brood* (1979) and *Dead Ringers*), overall, and certainly in his most recent work, Cronenberg has been much more interested in mutating masculinity, focusing on deviant men and their protracted, explosive deaths. The Cronenbergian abject is male, articulated first through exploration of male bodily interiors which may not be male at all, and then, moving away from the *mise-en-scène* of his early visceral body horror, through the psychological gender-play of *Dead Ringers* and *M. Butterfly* (*Naked Lunch* (1992) lies somewhere in between). Even in the relatively low-schlock *Dead Ringers*, the internally abnormal woman is finally normalised by her proximity to the bizarre bodily doubling of the ostensibly perfect Mantle twins – a masculinity so seamlessly certain of itself that it can only be precipitated into a desperate unravelling.[13] However, it is the bizarre bodily challenges to masculinity represented in *Shivers* and *Videodrome* which are most characteristic. Here the grotesque body is more 'naturally' a male one: Cronenberg's unique exploration of interiority is intimately bound up with how he articulates masculinity itself. It is true that the central image of

The Brood also visibly articulates the breakdown between inside and out, as the heroine develops a womb-sac on the outside of her body, the interior exteriorised, from which emerge the mutant children of her rage. Yet that transgression is all the more significant when it is men who incorporate those openings. For the Cronenbergian male subject, there is not only, in Steven Shaviro's words, no 'mental privacy',[14] but no physical privacy either, no individual bodily interior where the boundaries can be successfully policed.

Male pregnancy, and men displaying female reproductive organs, is one form this takes. The kicking and writhing of foetal or unwelcome strangers within has been a common motif in the crossover between body and more supernatural gynaecological horror since the 1960s. *Rosemary's Baby* (Roman Polanski, 1968) as a fantasy of the common body horror of pregnancy was only one mainstream representation of this potential for inhabitation, setting the agenda for a future mode of body horror in which men get pregnant too. John Hurt's incubation of the developing alien in Ridley Scott's *Alien* (1979) rendered his body feminine because of the way in which the alien embryo etched out a space within which was necessarily womb-like. The exploding-stomach scene over the *Nostromo*'s dinner table was also a birth scene, its mess a delivery room, and Hurt's character is feminised as a result; but it is also possible to read the metaphoric relationship between inhabitation and pregnancy as signalling a wider sexual breakdown. Rather than inhabitation feminising the inhabited subject as a consequence of its likeness to pregnancy, the aberrant pregnancies of body horror might be just one way in which inhabitation expresses itself. For Seth Brundle, the 'inner truth' of what the rational scientist is becoming emerges first through the skin (with the growth of fly-hairs), and then through the orifices (with fly discharge and a digestive process which takes place outside of the body and is then re-internalised). There is a direct correlation between how much of his insides come out and how little of his reasonable self is left. Brundlefly itself is the genetic 'child' of Seth and housefly. Although the fly with which he is genetically spliced is never itself gendered (it is always an 'It'), nevertheless a mating has taken place ('and we hadn't even been properly introduced' says Seth wryly). It is this mating which systematically 'unmans' him. Thus, the avant garde 'Brundle museum of natural history', the curious exhibition of organs and body-parts which Brundlefly puts on in his bathroom as they drop off, is a self-display of the inside on the outside – but not just any old organs are here. The ear and the penis are boundary-organs, partly defining the border. In hanging them up as display, Seth fully externalises them and, we presume, they leave behind gaping holes. But as he commentates on the exhibition, he refuses to name the male member which we see. Surely this unnamed part he passes over is simply the most graphic representation of all the lost fragments of masculinity which are cast off as Cronenberg's films systematically tear apart their heroes *as heroes*.[15]

Videodrome is also full of these transgressions, its central thesis being the breakdown of the fundamental division between fantasy and reality, video-hallucination and real experience, interiors and exteriors. A core image presents the hero Max Renn (James Woods) at the point of this transgression, when a pulsating vaginal orifice spontaneously opens up in his stomach. If hitherto Cronenberg has brought the inside *out* through bugs, mutations, vampyric penises emerging from women's armpits, here he gives the gash, which ought to articulate the difference not only between outside and inside but between men and women, to a *man*. The image graphically realises Carol Clover's point, that horror is a genre for which 'gender is less a wall than a permeable membrane',[16] the membrane here constructed out of the man's own flesh. Insides are only interesting for Cronenberg in their uneasy proximity to outsides, for this is a threshold articulating both/and rather than neither/nor – the vagina is both inside and outside, its body is both female and male. Renn prods at his new opening with his gun, penetrates himself with the barrel, then watches as the vagina becomes a mouth and swallows the gun. The lost gun later emerges as a fused appendage bound to Renn's wrist by tissue, not held *by* the hand but emerging *from* it. This might be a supreme image of male hysteria (the malaise made flesh through the surface symptom), except that the surface of the body does not 'speak' for the inside here: it is not a somatic expression which originates beyond the body, itself merely the symptom of a psychological malaise. For Steven Shaviro, this is only one point at which that distinction between inside and outside breaks down, but it is also more and less than a breakdown. It is an activation, an organic realisation of the seam, an interface which joins and distinguishes the two sides.

We might want to say that all these bodily 'changes' are always the mutations of gender, that whatever its sex, the mutant is feminised by aberration. Femininity is central to Cronenberg's masculinity, precisely because of its interiority. Maggie Humm writes that 'Cronenberg traverses interiority thereby encouraging his male characters into intimacy with the feminine'.[17] More radically, mutation signals a more pervasive postmodern 'gender-fuck' at work: women conceive without men (*The Brood*), and men turn themselves into women. In *Dead Ringers*, Bev (one of the gynaecologist brothers at the centre of the film) addresses female abnormality as a way of articulating his own slide into insanity: 'The patients are getting strange'. Becoming strange is often the same here as becoming woman, a position which would align Cronenberg with the postmodernism which challenges the boundary between masculinity and femininity at the same time as it privileges the femininity of alterity (a preference which Patricia Waugh identifies as 'a new space of the sacred').[18] Barbara Creed addresses this in her essay on postmodernism and horror, as does Tania Modleski in her paper on the postmodernism of *Videodrome*. This 'breakdown in distinctions between subject and object' is read as postmodern and, for Creed, means that '[t]he individual is a prey to everything, unable to produce the limits of his own body or being'.[19]

This invasion, transformation and opening of the male also allows forms of non-heterosexual male sexuality to take place on screen. The earlier, more edgy, *Shivers* had shown a man-on-man struggle, in which Tudor (Allan Migicovsky) and Linsky (Joe Silver) fumble from fight to embrace to what looks like rear penetration, before Linsky dispatches Tudor. Nora's parthenogenesis in *The Brood* is at least matched by men's mutant abilities to generate sexual difference, and even female sexual threat, from their own bodies, as the fisting scene later in *Videodrome* demonstrates. Here Renn's vagina-turned-VCR becomes the film's *vagina dentata*. Thrusting his arm into Renn's 'slot' (in order to programme him with a video), Harlan attempts a form of rape, but is undone when the vagina chews off his hand, leaving him waving around a grotesque bloody stump. The sexual ambivalence which pervades Cronenberg's interest in the threshold of inside and out is sharpened in this scene through what we might call a form of heterosexual-homoeroticism. By this I mean that, in this fisting, men can experience men sexually and explicitly if they first disguise themselves as women. To put it another way, in a same-sex situation, one man will become a woman to keep the balance 'rightly' heterosexual. In Cronenberg's early short film, *Crimes of the Future* (1970), women have been wiped out by cosmetics and the only surviving female, a little girl set up to be impregnated by the men, was once herself a man. In *M. Butterfly* a man falls in love with a woman who is a man. The fisting in *Videodrome* can only happen as long as the orifice is a vagina, illicitly displaced and legitimising a form of homosexual penetration on mainstream screens. The consequences, as the image takes pains to remind us, can only here be gruesome and funny, but the basic premise remains that, for Cronenberg, anatomy is anything but destiny.

THE THEATRE OF INNER BEAUTY

If the mutant man who develops a vagina is the focus of *Videodrome*, the beautiful woman with the mutant vagina ought to be the focus of *Dead Ringers*. Claire Niveau, played by Geneviève Bujold, has a triple cervix, but this is finally not the key issue of difference which the film presents, as Claire is progressively eclipsed by the stranger double masculinity of the perfect twins played by Jeremy Irons.[20] The film is a fantasy of surgery and its gazes. In a key moment early on one of the twins submits Claire to an internal examination, 'looking' inside her with his hand. Afterwards he rhapsodises over her bizarre interior landscape: '[s]urely you've heard of inner beauty?' he says. 'I've often thought that there should be beauty contests for the insides of bodies – you know, "Best spleen", "Most perfectly developed kidneys" . . . .' Two things are at stake in this passage. Claire is a television actress, working in a 'showy' profession, but the judgement of her here privileges an interior view through which she is (as Elliot later puts it) 'fabulously rare'. The diagnostic gaze of science here meets a parody of the objectifying gaze of Hugh Heffner and the categories, like the bodies, also begin to turn inside-out. One simple point to make about this is that the organs Elliot chooses for this image of visual scrutiny – kidneys and spleens – are a-gendered. He may be a gynaecologist but he chooses absolutely asexual inner organs as touchstones of judgement. The way in to a view of these organs may well be through a male or female orifice, but the bizarrely egalitarian thrust of this statement is that we are all really siblings-under-the-skin.

Yet, even if there is a sexualised look here, it is not the male doctor's in any straightforward sense. In the film as a whole, it is women who have the problematic role of separators, dividers of the bonded twins, and spectators of men. The work of Claire's eyes is more important than that of her doctor's, as she engages in a protracted battle to find the visual difference between the two versions of Jeremy Irons. Thus, women's sexualised bodies are not foregrounded as spectacle in any conventional sense. Women here function more as seers, with their eyes as the most important organs. If there is a central spectacle here, it moves around and between the double body of Jeremy Irons as both Elliot and Beverly, the male twins named in a way which suggests that sexual difference lies uneasily between them, even though they are ostensibly 'the same'. More peculiar than the women, then, are the men. This is a film about the identical as aberrational, the same as more bizarre than difference. At the centre are two men who are pure duplicates of each other. Cronenberg's women look, often as an effect of the uneasy homoeroticism of Cronenberg's films (which needs them so that male bodies are seen to be visually enjoyed). Claire negotiates the task of finding the difference; but perhaps the real difference lies in the fact that she cannot.

Similarly, *Videodrome* passes up the spectacle of Debbie Harry, instead preferring to foreground the mutant body of Max Renn. Although we first see Nicki Brand (Harry) on television, her character unfolds primarily as voyeur, watching the *Videodrome* tapes. Harry the sex-object becomes Brand the masochistic seer; and even when she features on television as part of the Videodrome transmission, it is still as an interactive image which seems to *look back* at the all-too-feminine male spectacle of the opened-up Renn. Indeed, television itself articulates a breakdown between seer and seen, technology and flesh, passive and active – it sees, responds, pouts, sighs, kisses, and (finally), Renn whips it and has sex with it. Videotapes pulsate, drip, *ooze*. The Videodrome signal which accompanies the images broadcast by Spectacular Optical, the monolithic television and optical corporation at the heart of the film's black fantasy, produces a brain tumour in its recipients, which itself produces hallucinations. Television becomes flesh, or, in the words of Brian O'Blivion, the film's Marshall McLuhan character, 'the video word made flesh': '[t]he visions became flesh, uncontrollable flesh'. The motto of Spectacular Optical, which sends out the Videodrome signal, is 'Keeping an eye on the world'. In a world in which televisions return the gaze, the mutating body becomes the subject of a variety of systems of corporate surveillance worthy of the darkest Foucauldian nightmare.

Indeed, from his early shorts to *Crash*, Cronenberg is fascinated by the way in which corporate bodies on the one hand, and technological bodies on the other, not only police but replicate, begin to become or fuse with organic bodies. His wonderfully paranoid institutions are frequently organised around changing and controlling biological processes – Hal Raglan's Somafree Institute of Psycho-plasmics which encourages patients to give shape to their rage in *The Brood*, Consec in *Scanners* which tries to control the ESP powers of the scanners themselves, the Keloid Clinic in *Rabid* engaging in bizarre new forms of plastic surgery. Spectacular Optical might first produce and might seek to police the tumours, but its mon-ster-creation (in the shape of Renn) becomes too strong, and what instead results is the 'New Flesh' invoked in the film's mantra. Like the hero of Shinya Tsukamoto's *Tetsuo* films (1989, 1992), flesh and technology merge in a bizarre marriage which also echoes the fate of Murphy in Paul Verhoeven's 1987 film *Robocop*. 'Long Live the New Flesh' incants Renn as the film loops final image upon final image, closing the gap between the real and the fantastic, and between distant technological surveillance and interior organic control. As human flesh mutates into the technology of vision, so that technology also becomes more fleshly. Cronenberg's machines echo the organic at every opportunity – think of the Teleportation Pods in *The Fly*, Renn's handgun, the insect-typewriter in *Naked Lunch*, developments of Cronenberg's seductive vision as, in David Thomson's words, the 'juxtaposition of warm flesh and bright steel'.[21]

In *Dead Ringers*, however, warm flesh meets bright steel in the theatre. Elliot and Beverly are both gynaecological surgeons, and in this film they 'perform' at the point of interface. This is not (simply) the next stage in Cronenberg's anxiety about women's reproduc-tive functions, following *The Brood*'s central concern, or the dream in *The Fly* which shows the Geena Davis character giving birth to a large maggot, offspring of herself and Brundlefly. Gynaecology focuses on that most obvious part of the anatomy which is inside and accessible, not entirely inside because of its proximity to the outside. Creed addresses this in her Kristevan reading of *The Brood*:

> Horror films that depict monstrous births play on the inside/outside distinction in order to point to the inherently monstrous nature of the womb as well as the impossibility of ever completely banishing the abject from the human domain. The concept of inside/outside sug-gests two surfaces that fold in on each other; the task of separating inside from outside seems impossible as each surface constitutes the 'other' side of its opposite. The implication is that the abject can never be completely banished; if 'inside' the abject substance forms a lining for the outside; if 'outside', it forms a skin for the inside.[22]

Beverly and Elliot's clinical gynaecology (played out in the mini-institution of the twins' clinic) allows an immediate visual and tac-tile encounter with this uneasy interface of inside and outside,

while in the surgery scenes, the spectacle of this process is emphasised by costume, gothic-camp rituals and pseudo-medieval instruments. In one of these scenes Elliot commentates to a group of
students on Bev's surgical performance, which is being relayed to
them on television monitors as well as being directly visible through
a glass screen. What we and they see is not just the operation *in* its
theatre, but the operation *as* theatre, and theatre adapted for television. All we see of the surgeon and patient are the bare organs
which have roles to play in this scene; everything else is covered,
emphasising the direct meeting of eye and inner abdomen. The
layers of looking pile up the focus on the gaze itself here: the point
of view positions us watching as the diegetic audience watches
both the live spectacle framed by the plate glass and the televisual
spectacle upon which Elli commentates. At the centre of all this,
Bev looks through the keyhole apparatus. It seems almost churlish
to point out that underneath it all there is a woman, but it is the
apparatus of surgery which is the spectacle here, not the covered
woman's body, nor even the cardinal-like presences of Bev or Elliot
(we only know it is a woman's body by the mention of fallopian
tubes, even as those tubes are being 'modified' by adjacent tissue).

This is also a dramatisation of organ speaking to organ. In
Videodrome, Brian O'Blivion calls the television screen 'the retina
of the mind's eye; therefore the television screen is part of the
physical structure of the brain'. In *Scanners*, ESP is presented as
entirely non-metaphysical; scanning is 'the direct linking of two
nervous systems separated by space', and to make that link is to
produce wholly corporeal symptoms or effects in the scanned –
pain, bleeding, exploding heads. I am reminded again of Barbara
Gowdy's woman whose body responds in a way which bypasses her
will with a 'sceptical thrill she used to get when she knew it wasn't
her moving the ouija board'. Body horror articulates a relationship
between organs in different bodies, despite the physical space or
different identities which might separate them. There is a level on
which elements of the body politic speak to each other, missing out
the governing system of the individual. Clive Barker writes of a
similar conspiracy between organs in his short story 'The Body
Politic'. This is partly a reworking of the old horror staple, the
hand with the life of its own (*Mad Love*; *The Hands of Orlac* [Karl
Freund, 1935]). Barker builds on this a massive, witty biological
conspiracy theory. First, organs and limbs begin to sever themselves
from the main body, then they band together and incite other body

parts to do the same. Hands, arms, legs, conspire and take off in a rebellion of body parts overthrowing the corporate dictator or colonial unifier, the whole body. Surveying the spectacle of his severed legs making off into the distance, Charlie is left musing on his role as victim of an organic revolution:

And did his eyes envy their liberty, he wondered, and was his tongue eager to be out of his mouth and away, and was every part of him, in its subtle way, preparing to forsake him? He was an alliance only held together by the most tenuous of truces. Now, with the precedent set, how long before the next uprising? Minutes? Years?
He waited, heart in mouth, for the fall of the Empire.[23]

Gowdy's heroine becomes a group of organs in search of a surgeon. The tumour will generate itself as a response to the stimulus of the Videodrome signal, and the two will conduct their relationship regardless of the will of Max Renn. In *The Brood*, Dr Raglan, as one character puts it, 'encouraged my body to revolt against me. I have a small revolution on my hands, and I'm not putting it down very successfully.' This is at the heart of Cronenberg's antihumanism.

THE MECHANIC-ORGANIC: CRASH'S AUTO-EROTICS

Much of this takes a new form in *Crash*. Despite its impressive lingerie-clad female cast – Oscar-winner Holly Hunter (playing Helen Remington), sex-siren Deborah Unger (Catherine Ballard) and Rosanna Arquette playing what one critic has called 'her usual, stoned, giggly, fuck-me character' (Gabrielle)[24] – female sexuality is not central to the erotic mechanics of *Crash*. This may be because the film succeeds in its attempt to be genuinely polymorphously perverse; as the character-pairings cross and counter-cross in multiple sexual engagements, masculinity and femininity become less defining categories and more performative possibilities. It could be argued that the cumulative sexual encounter of the film is finally that between James Ballard (James Spader) and Vaughan (Elias Koteas),[25] and thus that the heterosexual moments which led up to this become insignificant once the two have fucked. Up to this point the ghost of femininity has still mediated the auto-erotic encounters of men, albeit in a different form. The directional text of the James Dean crash scene in the published screenplay describes Dean's car as 'small and curvaceous . . . being fussed over by several men in overalls'.[26] In keeping with the gender form of popular automythology which feminises the car in order to heterosexualise the partnership of (male) driver and (female) vehicle, Dean's 1955 Porsche is the feminine element which mediates and thus legitimises the bodily collision of men.

However, later Ballard and Vaughan have sex without women, 'interfac[ing] without their female juncture, rear-ending each other in Vaughan's semen-smelling 1963 Lincoln Continental Convertible (JFK's death car)'.[27] By this point, the car, like Max Renn, has changed sex. No longer 'fussed over' and curvaceous, it has become the third male body in a homosexual-mechanical *ménage à trois*. Earlier Vaughan has identified himself spatially by stating, of his photographic studio, 'I live in my car. This is my workshop.'[28] But the organic-mechanic is soon consolidated through the film's developing homoerotic agenda. As *Crash* progresses, and as same-sex relationships begin to be foregrounded (Helen and Gabrielle as well as Ballard and Vaughan; Catherine and her assistant Karen also have a liaison), the identification of male flesh with car anatomy develops. Like his characters, perhaps the eroticism of Cronenberg's cars is finally polymorphous, but it may also be true to say that the film's auto-sexual emphasis shifts from femininity to masculinity as *Crash* proceeds. As male sex is foregrounded through the Ballard–Vaughan liaison, so the film shifts its interest from mainstream culture's banal feminisation of cars as women to *Crash*-culture's masculinisation of cars not as penis substitutes, but as male sexual arenas, not as tokens of virility, but as scarred extensions of damaged male flesh.[29]

This is borne out by a number of scenes. When she is talking dirty to Ballard by involving Vaughan in their sex lives, Catherine refers to Vaughan's Lincoln Continental as 'a bed on wheels'.[30] Later, having had images of car-damage scars tattooed on to their bodies, the men lick each others wounds, perform the first kiss of the film and fuck. Once again, then, the inside-out question is raised by *Crash*'s developing agenda about the car-in-fusion with male flesh. Not only do Ballard and Vaughan have sex in Vaughan's car, the car is seen as part of his body: Ballard has sex *with* Vaughan's body, *in* Vaughan's body. Then, after Vaughan's death, Ballard and Catherine go to claim this car, now wrecked. The scene itself is a kind of fulfilment of Vaughan's wishes: the Pound Officer says 'it's got to be a total write-off. I don't see what you could possibly do with it', but to Ballard it *is* Vaughan. Chris Rodley comments in *Cronenberg on Cronenberg*:

*When Ballard claims the dead Vaughan's car at the end it's as if he's claim-
ing his body. The movie does seem to imply that after a fatal crash, a merging
has taken place.*[31]

In his response, Cronenberg gives this a significant gender gloss:

Yes. I still remember when Marilyn Monroe's body wasn't immediately
claimed. As a kid I thought, 'Well fuck, I'll claim her body. OK, she's
dead, but she's still Marilyn Monroe.' . . . Taking the car in that scene
is exactly like claiming Marilyn Monroe's body.[32]

Women have bodies, men have cars – or rather, women *are*
their bodies, and, in *Crash*, men *become* embodied by fusing with
their cars. Ballard takes the car, inhabits and reanimates it.
Bringing it, as the screenplay puts it, 'back to swaying, bellowing
life' he then moves into it. The directional notes read:

The restoration of the Lincoln is as Vaughan would have wanted it: just
enough to get it running and nothing more, with ugly brown primer
slapped on to the replaced panels, and whatever was cracked, scraped
and crumpled still cracked, scraped and crumpled – a mobile accident
rolling on badly misaligned wheels.[33]

But the car is not the accident, it is the reanimated corpse of the
accident – a three-dimensional version of Vaughan's photographs.
It is also a kind of Frankenstein's monster – Vaughan's scarred
body has been resurrected, displaying the traces of his death and
carrying forth his wounds in metal. And now Ballard lives in it
('The car is full of junk' reads the directional text, 'all suggesting
that [Ballard] has been living in the car for some time').[34] Through
the process of car becoming male flesh, and male flesh becoming
car, Vaughan achieves a curious kind of immortality (an afterlife
rather like Brundlefly's incessant mutation), and Ballard gets to be
right inside of his body.

Thus, the car has become a kind of interzone where the curious
public–private nature of Cronenberg's male bodies is made explicit.
If Vaughan's car is his body, it is a body with an external interior,
an inside in which sex with others can take place. The 'neo-sex
organ' on Gabrielle's thigh, the long, vagina-like scar which Ballard
fucks in preference to the usual orifices, reminds us of Creed's
earlier point, that women have zones of abjection which are both
inside and outside, and that Cronenberg has also given these zones
to men: Gabrielle's scar-gash is, of course, the direct descendent of
the pulsating vagina-gash which opens up in Max Renn's stomach,
and Creed's comments on the abject impossibility of separating

45

the inside from the outside of a woman's sex applies equally to Max's and Gabrielle's wounds. Gabrielle's body is also a development of the multiple mutancy of Claire Niveau in *Dead Ringers*, except that Gabrielle relishes rather than regrets the fact that she has more 'ways in' than normal (she also has a gash on her hip which, in the screenplay at least, she invites Ballard to fuck).

However, Vaughan's car takes this inside-outside issue in a different direction, reminding us, perhaps, of the curious public-privacy in which we watch *Crash* in the first place. Like the cinema, the car gives us what Cronenberg calls a 'weird privacy in public'.[35] The logical conclusion of the car read as (in Catherine's terms) a mobile bedroom is Cronenberg's bizarre notion that this might account for people's antipathy to public transport: '[i]f they had little isolated sleepers in the subways', he says, 'maybe it would work better'. To match the car sexually, public transport would have to provide a private interior as part of its publicness. The car encloses this private arena, enabling sexuality to be expressed in public. Like the man's mutant body, the car-made-flesh allows the inside to be taken out, when the outside is given a moving interior. It seems that Cronenberg's most peculiarly realistic film, focusing his most fetishised organic-mechanic fusion, is simply a realisation of the weird potential, the strange boundary, of our most banal object of desire.

NOTES

1. Clive Barker, epigram to each volume of Barker's series of short stories, *The Books of Blood*, vols 1–6, 1988 (London: Warner, 1991).
2. Barbara Gowdy, 'Ninety-three Million Miles Away', *We So Seldom Look on Love* (London: Flamingo/HarperCollins, 1993), p. 84.
3. Gowdy, 'Ninety-three', p. 88.
4. Gowdy, 'Ninety-three', p. 90.
5. Gowdy, 'Ninety-three', p. 93.
6. Gowdy, 'Ninety-three', p. 93.
7. Gowdy, 'Ninety-three', p. 95.
8. Gowdy, 'Ninety-three', p. 84.
9. Jonathan Sawday, *The Body Emblazoned: Dissection and the Human Body in Renaissance Culture* (London and New York: Routledge, 1995), p. 8.
10. Interview with David Cronenberg in Chris Rodley (ed.), *Cronenberg on Cronenberg* (London: Faber, 1993), p. 82.
11. Chris Rodley suggests that the film might bear witness to 'the end of the unconscious', Rodley, *Cronenberg*, p. 40.

12. It was originally called 'Orgy of the Blood Parasites' and was released in Canada as *The Parasite Murders*.
13. The twins are an exercise in externalisation. As the film unfolds, what becomes clearer is that whatever should be inside Beverly and Elliot Mantle lies on the surface of their skins and between them in their absolute sameness.
14. Steven Shaviro, *The Cinematic Body* (Minneapolis: University of Minnesota Press,1993), p. 130.
15. Shaviro points out that the museum is one more sign of the process of endless mutation (not death) which Cronenberg's subjects face: 'Brundle's past existence is not entirely effaced; it remains in the form of discontinuous fragments. He has not been translated from one state of being into another so much as he has been uprooted from the fixity of human identity, and submitted instead to a process of continual flux. It is at the point of greatest intimacy, in his own home and in his own body, that he has become a stranger'. (Shaviro, *Cinematic*, p. 147)
16. Carol J. Clover, *Men, Women and Chainsaws* (London: BFI, 1992), p. 46.
17. Maggie Humm, 'Cronenberg's Films and Feminist Theories of Mothering', *Feminism and Film* (Edinburgh: Edinburgh University Press, 1997), p. 65.
18. Patricia Waugh, 'Stalemates?: Feminists, Postmodernists and Unfinished Issues in Modern Aesthetics', in Philip Rice and Patricia Waugh (eds), *Modern Literary Theory: A Reader* (London: Edward Arnold, 1993), p. 351.
19. Barbara Creed, 'Gynesis, Postmodernism and the Science Fiction Horror Film', in Annette Kuhn (ed.), *Alien Zone: Cultural Theory and Contemporary Science Fiction Cinema* (London: Verso, 1990), p. 217.
20. Cronenberg often plays visual games in his casting. The heroine of *Rabid*, whose role as sexual threat is figured through the vampiric penis which projects from her armpit, is played by porn star Marilyn Chambers. In *Videodrome*, rock star and punk icon Debbie Harry plays sadomasochist Nicki Brand, a role which dances uneasily between the exhibitionism expected of someone with a star history, and moments of voyeurism which reinforce her role at the subject of vision, but fails to designate her a fixed position as either seer or seen.
21. David Thomson, *A Biographical Dictionary of Film* (London: André Deutsch, 1994), p. 159.
22. Barbara Creed, *The Monstrous-Feminine: Film, Feminism, Psychoanalysis* (London and New York: Routledge, 1993), p. 49.
23. Clive Barker, 'The Body Politic', *The Books of Blood* vol. IV, p. 47.
24. Tim Lucas, 'Crash', in *Video Watchdog*, 42: p. 55.
25. The novel *Crash* upon which Cronenberg's film is based is by J. G. Ballard. Ballard chose to name his protagonist after himself, but my

discussion here refers only to 'James Ballard', the film character played by James Spader.

26. David Cronenberg, *Crash* (London: Faber, 1997), p. 25.
27. Lucas, 'Crash', p. 50.
28. Cronenberg, *Crash*, p. 34.
29. The film does show this as a possibility for its women too, particularly in two scenes involving Gabrielle – first, when she goes to a car showroom and her callipers become caught in the upholstery of a Mercedes, and secondly, when she and Ballard have sex in her invalid car.
30. Cronenberg, *Crash*, p. 37.
31. Rodley, *Cronenberg*, original emphases.
32. Cronenberg, *Crash*, p. xvii.
33. Cronenberg, *Crash*, p. 62.
34. Cronenberg, *Crash*, p. 63.
35. Cronenberg, *Crash*, p. xvi.

3

The Figure in Question: The Transvestite Character as a Narrative Strategy in The Crying Game

HELEN HANSON

'*Transvestism is a space of possibility structuring and confounding culture*: the disruptive element that intervenes, not just a category crisis of male and female, but the crisis of category itself.'[1]

The figure or body of the male to female transvestite character has been the site of much discussion in gender theories and film criticisms of the 1990s. Cross-dressing has become a mainstream cultural trope through the popularity of films like *Mrs Doubtfire* (Chris Columbus, 1993) and *The Adventures of Priscilla Queen of the Desert* (Stephan Elliot, 1994), and the visibility of drag performers such as RuPaul in the USA and Lily Savage in Britain.[2] Primarily in this chapter I want to distinguish between the cultural effects of this drag trope, with its built-in comic safety valve, and the cross-dressed characters who 'pass' and who precipitate 'dangerous desires' in the film I am discussing, *The Crying Game* (Neil Jordan, 1992).[3] In the context of gender ambiguity, 'passing' is a term with particular importance. To pass as the opposite sex, through cross-dressing and gender performance, means that one is 'taken for' the opposite sex, 'read' as being that sex. Elaine Ginsberg defines passing as a strategy which questions cultural assumptions about identity formation:

The first of [these assumptions] . . . is that some identity categories are inherent and unalterable essences: presumably one cannot pass for

something that one is *not* unless there is some other, prepassing, identity that one *is*. Further, passing forces reconsideration of the cultural
logic that the physical body is the site of identic intelligibility.[4]

What I want to reiterate is the way that passing involves not only
the person who passes, but those who 'read' them as their assumed
identity. This makes clear the way that the process of passing itself
can be invisible; it is only in the exposure of an act of passing that
its subversion of identity categories is made plain. I will be discussing
the person who 'takes' the passer as their assumed identity in this
article, exploring how the character of Fergus in *The Crying Game*
takes Dil as a woman, and the alliance between his reading of Dil
and the audience's reading of her/him. Thus, Dil might be passing
to the audience through passing to Fergus.

Cross-dressing film comedies, such as *Tootsie* (Sidney Pollock,
1982) and *Mrs Doubtfire*, contrast strongly to *The Crying Game* in
that the reasons why the character is cross-dressing are made clear
to the audience from the outset, and the fact that the transgression
will be a temporary solution is usually implied. The danger of gender transgression is made safe for a 'straight' audience through
their knowledge of the overt performance of masquerade, and it is
only the 'abnormal', the not-properly-male characters who misread
the fiction for the reality. In their exaggerated gender masquerade
the men-in-drag cannot, and are not intended to, pass as women to
the audience. My analysis of *The Crying Game* in this chapter will
focus on the difference between this comedic masquerade, where
the gender identity of the characters in drag is never in question,
and the sustained gender masquerade of Dil in *The Crying Game*. I
will argue that, although Fergus and the film audience see Dil's
body, her/his gender identity remains in question; and I will
explore the way that the film narrative itself assumes elements of
ambiguity and masquerade.

In her discussion of comedic drag, Sarah E. Chinn shows the way
in which the political potential of gender parody is often dispersed.
Retaining its edge depends on its practice and on its audience:

A mainstream reading of the stereotype of the swaggering butch or
effeminate queen does not expose gender as much as it restates the
lines between identity and behaviour: men and women aren't supposed to act that way. Similarly, comedic half-baked drag by 'obvious'
men . . . tells us 'real men can't help but be masculine, even in
women's clothes' . . . Drag self-consciously denaturalises gender only if
it *is* self-conscious and its agenda, or the agenda of its audience, is
antiessentialist.[5]

In presenting drag figures whose unquestionable maleness is always visible *through* their masquerade, the mainstream transvestite film text operates a strategy of 'recuperation'. Thus, any gender transgression is recuperated, regained to support, not destabilise, the identic *status quo*, as Chinn suggests.[6] This strategy of recuperation, which restates conservative cultural norms, is at odds with the popularity of the transvestite character in contemporary gender theories. These theories perceive the cross-dressed figure as a genuinely transgressive and political one. Much of the political weight that drag has come to bear in contemporary theories of gender stems from, and refers to, the work of Judith Butler.

The performance of drag forms a central critical 'scenario' in Butler's *Gender Trouble* in which she extends a sustained interrogation of 'compulsive heterosexuality' and the 'naturalness' of gender identity: *'[i]n imitating gender, drag implicitly reveals the imitative structure of gender itself – as well as its contingency'*.[7] What is central to Butler's political argument is the necessity of separating and identifying as dissonant anatomical (bodily) sex, gender identity and gendered performance. Butler sees this dissension as allowing a distancing of gender identity from the body, breaking the hegemonic maxim 'anatomy is destiny'. Her critique is complex and she situates her notion of gender as performative within a specific theoretical nexus. Her theory of gender performativity develops the work of J. L. Austin on speech acts, through the Althusserian concept of the interpellation of the subject and Foucauldian analyses of the relationship of subjectivity to discourses of power.[8] Situating her theory of performativity in the network of these specific debates was strategic for Butler in that they provide a background to her thesis that 'there is no gender identity behind the expression of gender; that identity is performatively constituted by the very "expressions" that are said to be its results'.[9] In her later work, *Bodies That Matter*, she clarifies 'performativity' as follows: 'performativity must be understood not as a singular or deliberate "act", but, rather, as the reiterative and citational practice by which discourse produces the effects that it names'.[10]

Thus she denies the ideal of a subject that chooses its gender performance, and her continuing project in *Bodies That Matter* is to examine the 'reiterative and citational practice' of discourses which sex as well as gender the body:

What I hope will become clear . . . is that the regulatory norms of 'sex' work in a performative fashion to constitute the materiality of bodies and, more specifically, to materialize the body's sex, to materialize sexual differences in the service of the consolidation of the hetero-sexual imperative.[11]

However, *Gender Trouble* was taken by some critics as a formulation which epitomised a parodic postmodern subject.[12] Drag was figured as a metaphor for performative identities *per se*, rather than being specifically situated within a complex network of medical, legal and social discourses. A critical drive in many subsequent discussions of the drag figure attends what is 'below' the performance, the body of the performer beneath the actions and costume of the performance. This drive, which is exemplified in the mainstream strategy of recuperation discussed above, figures the body as the 'real' to the 'imitation', 'fact' to the 'fictional' other and has reconstituted 'anatomy is destiny' as 'anatomy is origin'. This is clearly different to Butler's analysis of discourses materialising a sexed body, referred to above. Butler strongly resists the idea of the material body as a refuge of original or 'true' identity. She suggests that it is always already constituted by discourses which interpellate it.

Marjorie Garber notes the recuperative drive as suggestive of 'vested interests' that critics display in an encounter with a cross-dressed figure. She writes:

[T]he tendency on the part of many critics has been to look *through* rather than *at* the cross-dresser, to turn away from a close encounter with the transvestite, and to want instead to subsume that figure within one of the two traditional genders. To elide and erase – or to *appropriate* the transvestite for particular political and critical aims.[13]

This elision and erasure of the transvestite figure works in a similar way to the overt and exaggerated masquerade of mainstream drag which asserts that there is an original body in view through its performance. While much has been made of the possibilities drag can offer to question gender identity, I want to suggest that it is the *recovery* of temporary transgressions in the return to heterocentric norms that marks most encounters with cross-dressed figures in mainstream filmic narratives. In my analysis of *The Crying Game* my specific focus will be the way that this film refuses such a recovery.

The recovery of gender transgression in mainstream comedic drag is often achieved through the exposure of a divested transvestite figure. The term 'divestiture' suggests stripping away not only clothing, but also the subject's property, authority and vested rights, and thus emphasises the cultural weight that gender identity assumes. Scenes in which the cross-dresser is undressed take on significance as they focus questions on an identity rendered questionable and in need of investigation. *The Crying Game* is a film which dramatises this scenario through the shock revelation of the body of a gay male transvestite to a male protagonist who has taken her/him to be female. This scenario is the result of a narrative progression, a series of encounters between the transvestite and the film's male protagonist. A central question that the narrative circles around is how the transvestite character, Dil (Jaye Davidson), is seen and desired by the protagonist, Fergus (Stephen Rea). Initially the operation of the cinematic narrative suggests Dil as a questionable figure but, as it progresses, propelled by Fergus's desire for her/him, s/he shifts from being a *questionable* figure to a *questioning* one. I will be considering how this film narrative problematises not only the gender of the transvestite character, but also her/his body. This, in turn, challenges theories of cinematic spectatorship based on sexual difference. In this film the protagonist is assumed to be oblivious to the gender ambiguity of the transvestite character; that is, Dil passes, and for the purposes of my argument I will take it that s/he passes to the film audience as well; they share the protagonist's perspective. In contrast to the mainstream comedic drag narrative, the gender performance in this film is much more covert, and to Fergus it is invisible until Dil's body is revealed.[14] In fact, the film narrative itself constructs specific strategies which play around with the idea of masquerade and revelation; and through a continual replaying and reinflecting of masquerade the film profoundly questions the idea of fixed gender identity.

By deploying a succession of masquerades, written into the narrative structure, *mise-en-scène* and cinematography, Neil Jordan shows that an interrogation of gender precipitates a questioning and crisis of other categories. This ultimately leads to an examination of social, racial, national and political identities. At the centre of the film's narrative is a relationship between a male to female transvestite and a (as far as we know) straight male. However, as Jordan makes clear in his discussion of the origin of the story, the importance of the relationship between Dil and Fergus is that it is mediated by their connection to Jody (Forest Whitaker). Jody is a black British soldier whom Fergus guards as a hostage for the IRA, and he was Dil's lover before his death. The idea of the story came to Jordan after working on his first film *Angel* (Neil Jordan, 1982) and was inspired by two other texts: a short story called 'Guest Of the Nation' by Frank O'Connor and a Brendan Behan play called *The Hostage*.[15]

The attraction of such a theme for Irish writers, the friendship that develops between two protagonists in a conflict, that grows paradoxically deeper than any of their other allegiances, lies in the broader history of Anglo-Irish relationships: two cultures in need of each other, yet at war with each other . . . Underlying this friendship lay an erotic possibility, a sense of mutual need and identification that could have provided salvation for their protagonists . . . With *The Crying Game*, I brought the erotic thread to the surface. Instead of two, there were now three. A hostage, a captor, and an absent lover. The lover became the focus for the erotic subtext, loved by both men in a way they couldn't love each other.[16]

The Crying Game became infamous for the 'twist in the tale'. It is testament to the power of the transvestite that the fleshly revelation of Dil's penis gained such notoriety that the other important elements of the film came to be seen as peripheral. However, I think that it is impossible to read the film as separately portraying different issues; that is, the IRA members Fergus, Maguire and Jude as 'the Irish question', Jody and Dil as 'the racial question' and Dil alone as 'the gender question'. The leaking of issues across the plot boundaries is one example of the narrative masquerade I referred to above; indeed, *The Crying Game* is a film which defies generic categorisation. It could be argued that it is an alternative love story or a political thriller, depending on the reading of it. Jane Giles describes the film as:

[a]n exceptionally bold and seductive combination of the personal and the political, the film radically *crossed over* from its independent roots to ask conservative mainstream audiences to root for the love affair of an IRA terrorist and a gay transvestite.[17]

The idea of the film crossing genres and, potentially, audience groups is interesting in that it suggests that it is not only a transvestite character *within* the text that suggests a 'crisis of category', but that the presence of the character facilitates the ability of the text itself to 'cross'.

In the shot revealing Dil's nakedness, and the 'secret' it discloses, Jordan makes a point about revelation itself. The present 'fact' of Dil's biological gender (its presence) does not only affect future events, it reinflects the past narrative as well. Jordan shows the impossibility of containing instability, suggesting the transvestite as figuring a 'crisis of category'. When the camera moves slowly down Dil's body, in a lingering point of view shot, to rest on 'his' penis, the viewer, like Fergus, becomes initiated into the complexities of his desire. The moment of Dil's revelation is for Fergus a self-revelation of what he has not previously known, and a realisation of how much he has not known. I want to analyse the moments of sexual encounter in the film as they are staged as disrupted and repetitious scenarios. They echo earlier events or foretell coming ones, the characters displace and repeat actions, occupying different positions. I will begin with the first sexual encounter between Dil and Fergus and, through a process of 'reading backwards' through the cinematic narrative, suggest the way the scenarios both repeat and reinflect earlier events.

The first encounter between Dil and Fergus replays the earlier sexual action between Jody and Jude (Miranda Richardson) at the beginning of the film. In a re/view of the earlier shot at the fair where Jody runs his hand up Jude's leg, Fergus runs his hand up Dil's leg and then is stopped by Dil assuming the sexual initiative. Although the conclusion of this scene in Fergus's sexual satisfaction differs from the earlier scene between Jody and Jude, where Fergus disrupts Jody's pleasure and takes him captive, there are important parallels. The displacement of the characters is particularly resonant; Fergus displaces Jody with Dil, Jody's 'special friend', as Jody earlier took Fergus's place with Jude.[18] The moment of Fergus's climax is disrupted by his thoughts of Jody; the film shows a 'dreamy' image of Jody running up to bowl a cricket ball. Here again is an echo of an earlier scene; at the fair Fergus was present as a voyeur watching over Jody and Jude, 'now' Fergus is haunted by the ghostly memory of Jody, watching over Dil and himself. This connection between the two characters through their lovers suggests that the relationships in the film are not clear one-on-one relations; where there appears to be two, a third person or presence intrudes.

This third presence is suggestive of Garber's formulation of the power of the transvestite figure to disrupt the gender binary male/female:

The 'third' is that which questions binary thinking and introduces crisis – a crisis which is symptomatized by *both* the overestimation *and* underestimation of cross-dressing. But what is crucial here . . . is that the third term is not a term . . . not an instantiated 'blurred' sex . . . The 'third' is a mode of articulation, a way of describing a space of possibility. Three puts into question the idea of one: of identity, self-sufficiency, self-knowledge.[19]

This mirrors Jordan's idea of the connection between the three characters: 'instead of two, there were now three'. The repeated intrusion of a third in Jordan's film not only 'puts into question the idea of one' but also the idea of *two*. It is interesting that in his introduction to the screenplay, Jordan suggests Dil as 'the third', but in the film it is often Jody who functions in this position. The four central characters of the film, Fergus, Jody, Jude and Dil, are linked together in a series of triangular relationships which are constantly changing as the characters displace and replace each other. Dil becomes a focus for the film's crisis of category but this crisis is seemingly already being signalled in the shifting sexual relations of the other characters. I want to look in detail at the ways in which crisis is initially instituted in the realm of gender, but then proves uncontainable and takes in the realms of the sexual, political, social and national. The uncovering of Dil's gender masquerade is at the same moment an uncovering of a narrative masquerade. What has passed as a story about a remorseful IRA soldier who falls in love with the lover of his hostage changes before the eyes of the audience into the soldier's struggle to come to terms with his desire, not only for the lover, but for the dead hostage too.

It is the revelation of Dil's penis that precipitates Fergus's sexual crisis and this is also the moment from which the viewer of the film returns to (re/view) the earlier sexual scenarios. The sight of Dil's penis implies a crisis of seeing in Fergus and in the viewer; Dil's unveiled body is not what it was expected to be. The shots leading up to it are already evoking a return in the narrative; a 'coitus disruptus' occurring as Fergus's gun – in the scene at the fair – and Jody's ghost – in the first sexual encounter between Fergus and Dil – intrude on the sexual action. The development of the sexual action in both scenes, both men's hands sliding up the legs of their partners, has been leading the viewer to expect a revelation of the female body. The disruptions to these scenes prevent any glimpse of the female genitals.[20] The development of these shots leads the viewer to expect a revelation; the camera is involved in a titillation which is then frustrated. In the moments of sexual encounter the narrative leads the audience to expect, and to desire, bodily revelation. They are moments in which the body begins to be undressed, divested of its covering of clothes.

Peter Brooks, citing the work of Roland Barthes, suggests a link between the reader moving through narrative and the desire to have the 'body' of the text revealed and displayed.[21] He suggests that the process of undressing the body in the text paradoxically progresses through moments of delay. Brooks's suggestion of the simultaneous desires to see (and consequently know) the body of the other, and the waylaying of the process of revelation in a fixation on detail, has become a familiar framework in film theories of spectatorship. Laura Mulvey asserted the opposing aspects of the male protagonists' look, as the voyeuristic, reflecting the desire to progress the narrative, and the fetishistic fixating on detail and delaying progression.[22] The work of Brooks and Mulvey is relevant to the progressions and delays of the narrative of *The Crying Game*. Up until the moment that Dil's body is revealed, the look of the cinema spectator has been allied with Fergus's look and the exchange of looks between Fergus and Dil has been along the lines of Mulvey's famous divisions: male – looker, female – looked at. In two different scenes in The Metro bar, Dil comments to the barman Col (Jim Broadbent) about Fergus's 'looks'. The first occasion is when Fergus looks at Dil via the mirror behind the bar; and the second time is after Dil's performance of the song 'The Crying Game' where Dil, resplendent in gold sequins, is coded as spectacle.[23] Looking back to this exchange of looks from the scene of Dil's revelation produces an interesting counterpoint to Mulvey's theory. On a first viewing of the film Fergus is looking at, and desiring, Dil as a woman. His look is alternately fetishistic, as he beholds her/him as spectacle, and voyeuristic as he follows her/him, observes her/his relationship with Dave (Ralph Brown) and stands in the park below Dil's window. However, in the moment that Dil's body is revealed, the male gaze, structured on sexual difference and gaining its power through the symbolic role of the phallus in patriarchy, undergoes a profound disruption.

I want to take this scenario, the disruption in seeing what is expected (desired), and read it back to the moments of coitus disruptus (Fergus's gun threatening death, Jody's ghost as the figure of death) that I referred to earlier. I will read this disruption in relation to two of Freud's essays, 'The Uncanny' (1919) and 'Fetishism' (1927), in order to establish a dialogue between the gendered construction of Freudian psychoanalysis and the 'crisis of category' in gendered identities that the transvestite figure offers in *The Crying Game*.[24] First, I will contextualise the theories. Freud's work on the uncanny posits an aesthetic of the defamiliarisation of the familiar: the known made strange through repression. The strategies of defamiliarisation, and of repetition, seem to me to be particularly relevant to *The Crying Game*. It is a text which paradoxically proceeds through repetitions and reveals through repression. The balance between revelation and repression has much in common with the concept of disavowal which Freud elaborates in 'Fetishism'. These theoretical concepts then, the uncanny return of the repressed and the precarious disavowal of female castration through fetishism, function as articulations of denial. In order to examine these denials, and perhaps to suggest what is being denied, I want to return to the film, and the moments of coitus disruptus, and read them through these theoretical concepts.

The moments of the film in which sexual action is disrupted and delayed are the moments when the viewer expects to see the female body, specifically the genitals, revealed. In Freud's theories of 'The Uncanny' and 'Fetishism' he describes the sight of the female genitals as disturbing, figuring castration and even death to the male looker. This threat of death at the potential sight of the female genitals is also signalled in the film: Fergus pulls a gun on Jody as he runs his hand up and under Jude's skirt, and Jody is a ghostly presence between Fergus and Dil later in the film. These delays suggest a 'looking away' from the female genitals in *The Crying Game*, and they could be interpreted as a return to the Freudian moment of trauma in the boy's childhood which leads in the fetishist to a substitution of the fetish object for the absent (mislaid/displaced) maternal phallus. Freud opines, 'probably no male human being is spared the fright of castration at the sight of a female genital'.[25] This disavowal is, however, a precarious solution, for a belief in the presence of the maternal phallus is maintained *through* its substituted fetish object. Freud writes:

[A] compromise has been reached . . . in his mind the woman *has* got a penis, in spite of everything; but this penis is no longer the same as it was before. Something else has taken its place, has been appointed its substitute, as it were, and now inherits the interest which was formerly directed to its predecessor.[26]

The compromise of disavowal can be read as marking the uncertainty of female castration. This uncertainty is instructive in the return and disavowal of the film. There is an uncanny recurrence of the same scenes in the film narrative, but the uncertainty of the disavowal means that there is not a return *of* the repressed, but a return *to* the act of repression itself.

In the first instance of coitus disruptus (Fergus pulling a gun on Jody as he runs his hand up Jude's thigh) Fergus's gun could be read as the fetish object, 'standing in for' Jude's assumed 'lack'.

This is a classic example of Freudian substitution which restores the maternal phallus to the woman, rendering her body tolerable to the (male) fetishist through the maintenance of disavowal. This fetishistic substitution is symbolically repeated, as throughout the film Jude is often seen in positions traditionally associated with male phallic power. She arrives at the hostage hideout on a motorbike, she is frequently seen in possession of a gun, and when she sees Fergus for the first time in London she holds him at gunpoint and demands 'Fuck me, Fergus'.[27] The fetishistic displacement (replacement) of female lack with male presence institutes the fantasy that the woman still possesses the symbolic maternal phallus. While I acknowledge the Lacanian reading of the phallus as symbolic, and ultimately important for its 'seeming value'[28] as distinct from the material presence/absence of the penis, it is the visualisation of the *material* penis that precipitates the shock at the centre of the film. Indeed, this visualisation, and the shock it produces, seems to blur the distinctions between the material penis and the symbolic phallus, in that the material penis somehow literalises (embodies) the symbolic phallus, not as an equivalence, but as a crisis of category. The importance of Fergus's gun as a fetish object is that it is subject to the sexual attention of Jody. The 'usual' displacement of the penis in fetishistic disavowal becomes reinflected in the later context of the close relationship between Fergus and Jody. When read through the frame of fetishism, Jody's hand moving up Jude's thigh towards Fergus's gun suggests that what becomes dangerous is not Jude's 'lack' of a penis, but Fergus's possession of one.

The second instance of coitus disruptus features Jody as a ghostly presence. At the moment of his climax, as Dil fellates him, Fergus 'sees' Jody dressed in cricket flannels and sweater, running up to bowl a ball. This suggests a return to the last time Fergus saw Jody, when Jody was running away from him, making his escape from his confinement as a hostage. As he runs, Jody shouts to Fergus, reminding him of their conversation about whether cricket or hurling is the 'best game in the world'.[29] As such, Jody's ghost 'stands in for' his material absence, as Fergus is guiltily taking Jody's place as Dil's lover. Jody's ghost could be seen to symbolise further a kind of uncanny fetish object. Fergus's vision is a kind of denial of Jody's death, this denial (disavowal) being founded on the fantasy of Jody's ghostly presence. In a sense, Fergus's sexual closeness with Dil 'stands in for' the closeness that had begun to develop between himself and Jody; indeed, later in the film Dil, with her/his hair cut short and dressed in Jody's cricket clothes, is an embodied re/presentation of the dead Jody. Fergus's vision of Jody's ghost replaces a visualisation of Dil's genitals, suggesting this vision itself as a fetish object 'standing in for' Dil's assumed 'lack'.

The third instance of coitus disruptus occurs at the revelation of Dil's penis. Earlier I suggested that the film figured the female genitals as uncanny, the camera's gaze diverted from showing them, and fetish objects in the narrative disavowing them; thus the shots leading up to the sight of Dil's penis are full of suspense and anxiety. The sight of Dil's penis could suggest a return to the Freudian scene when the male child sees, and immediately disavows, female castration. However, this return complicates rather than explicates the fantasy of disavowal. In terms of the frame of psychoanalytic theories, Dil could be seen as a symbol of what the child originally hoped to see – the 'woman' in possession of the maternal phallus; the penis is there 'after all' and has been all along. If we read the scenario in terms of the formation of fetishism, when the camera moves down Dil's body we might expect, in light of the previous substitutions for the female genitals, that we will find something 'standing in for' Dil's expected 'lack'. What is seen is not a phallic fetish object, but somehow Dil's penis is 'standing in for' itself. Dil's naked body – the divested transvestite – is not categorisable within what Garber calls 'the two traditional genders'. The tension that Fergus's desire for Dil creates is not dispersed by the revelation of Dil's penis; and Dil cannot be recuperated to figure 'masculine' even when s/he is seen naked. The directions in Jordan's screenplay do not concretely define Dil either: '[t]he kimono falls gently to the floor with a whisper. The camera travels with it, and we see, in a close-up, that *she is a man*'.[30]

This, and subsequent crises in the film, are instituted at the appearance of the penis. This crisis between seeing and believing suggests the dissonance that Butler sees between gender performance and anatomical sex; a 'crisis of category' between the symbolic phallus and the material penis. If Dil's gender was a previously undecided 'fact' that was fixed at the revelation of her/his penis there would be no debate about the ability of the penis to signal anatomical sex as continuous with gender identity; and no debate about the ability of the phallus to signify sovereign masculinity. At the moment that Dil's penis substitutes for (displaces) itself, what it might be possible for the phallus to signify is called into question. To read Freud against the grain: 'this penis is no longer the same as it was before. Something else has taken its place, has been appointed its substitute, as it were, and now inherits the interest which was formerly directed to its predecessor'.[31]

The revelation of Dil's penis is an uncanny moment in that it replays the earlier moments of near exposure of the female genitals, but it is also the moment marking the return of the repressed, and a moment which itself becomes repressed. In his etymological examination of the *unheimlich*, Freud notes the ease with which the terms *heimlich* and *unheimlich* cross over into the other's realm of meaning: '*heimlich* is a word the meaning of which develops in the direction of ambivalence, until it finally coincides with its opposite, *unheimlich*'.[32] Freud finds that the uncanny seems to be founded on ambiguity, and the point at which there is a slippage between *heimlich* and *unheimlich* is through the use of the term *heimlich* to describe knowledge and concealment. Tensions between knowledge and concealment are constantly evoked in *The Crying Game*, the concealment of knowledge from oneself being strongly played out in the disavowal of the characters, and in the narrative itself. The crossing over of Freud's term between the two categories is strongly suggestive of what Garber refers to as a 'transvestite effect'.[33] It illustrates the crisis between seeing and knowing that categorises Fergus's experience of the sight of his lover's naked body. In his analysis of Hoffman's 'The Sand-Man', which he takes to be typical of an uncanny narrative, Freud finds a crisis in perception marked by 'a doubling, dividing and interchanging of the self . . . the constant recurrence of the same thing – the repetition of the same features or character-traits or vicissitudes'.[34] This doubled, divided self is suggestive of Garber's 'third', calling into question 'the idea of one: of identity, self-sufficiency, self-knowledge'. The constant recurrence of character displacement in *The Crying Game*, the narrative structure and the recurrent displacements of the penis are all uncanny effects. They stem from the physical revelation of Dil's penis and its uncanny interchange with itself. This calls into question Fergus's 'self-knowledge' and, through his position as the representative 'eyes' of the cinematic spectator within the fiction, the ability to 'read' the film narrative accurately.[35]

Fergus himself undertakes a process of reading back from the moment of revelation, wryly remarking to Dil that '(he) should have known'. He is also concerned to know what Jody knew. Fergus asks Dil 'your soldier knew didn't he?', Dil replying 'absolutely'.[36]

Fergus now has to face a return of what was repressed in his inter-changes with Jody, as well as a continued repression of his desire for Dil, despite his knowledge of her/his 'secret'.

The return to re-examine what was repressed in Fergus's conversations with Jody also inevitably involves a traumatic return to the circumstances of Jody's death, which Fergus failed to prevent. It is significant that, as the plot moves forward in London, the narrative doubles back on itself. Jody's ghostly presence haunts the cinematic frame more and more insistently; Fergus works on a building site adjoining a cricket pitch, photographs of Jody are littered around Dil's flat and, most potently, Dil disguised in Jody's cricket clothes strongly figures a return for Fergus to the moment of Jody's death. This time Fergus determines to save 'him'. Dil 'stands in for' the dead Jody, as the presence of her/his penis 'stands in for' the presence of Jody's disavowed penis in the earlier scenes between Jody and Fergus.

The final reading back I want to undertake is of the moment of Jody's unmasking by Fergus. Fergus has to argue with Maguire (Adrian Dunbar) to be allowed to remove the hood from Jody. It is this moment that initiates the revelation of personal information between Jody and Fergus. I want to suggest these revelations as further displacements of the penis, which come to figure sexual desire. Male bonding of the characters takes place through the discussion of their girlfriends and sport. On one level, these topics are markers of a traditional masculinity, a strategy for marking their (hetero)sexuality. The discussion of sporting prowess is related to strength and to their sociability – they bond as part of a team of men. When read back, however, a further level of signification becomes clear. Jody shows Fergus a photo of Dil and reacts angrily to his admiration of her/him: '[d]on't you think of it fucker', then adds 'anyway she wouldn't suit you'.[37] This appears to be a throwaway comment at the time, but comes to be deeply significant as Fergus discovers what Jody already knew. Jody is revealing that his sexual preference is different to Fergus's; he has already said that Jude 'isn't (his) type', a comment that could be read as a racial preference.[38] Jordan keeps the dialogue ambiguous, there is always a veiled meaning waiting to be revealed; there is always more than one type of difference.

The discussion of sport is also reinflected on reading back the discussion of cricket and hurling; two sports centring on the use of bat and ball can be seen as yet another displacement of the male genitals. Jody's remark to Fergus that if he has to kill him he will 'be getting rid of a shit hot bowler' is particularly resonant and is replayed later as Fergus's orgasmic vision.[39] This marks the complex relationships between death and sexual pleasure, desire and disavowal that are played out in the film. It is not just Jody as the absent/displaced lover that returns to haunt Fergus, but his own disavowed pleasure and his own loss of Jody.

I now want to suggest a parallel between the undressing (divesting) of Dil and the unmasking of Jody. Garber provides a reading of the displacements of the penis 'upward or downward' through Freud's essay 'Medusa's Head' so that '"face" and "penis" become symbolic alternatives for one another'.[40] Garber's reading illuminates the anxieties caused by an unmasking of Jody's face in *The Crying Game*. A displacement of the penis upwards to the face accounts for the dramatic tension in the scene between Jody and Fergus, and is echoed in the conversation that follows it. In a sense it is a 'double' unmasking, Fergus revealing his face to Jody's look as well as Jody being seen by Fergus. The strategy of displacing the penis, so central to the symbolism of the film, also thematically reiterates an uncanny disavowal. The displaced penis is inescapably related to the fear of castration; indeed, it could be seen as a signifier of castration itself. Freud notes the uncanny affect of mobile body parts often found in fairytales, and that the 'language of dreams . . . is fond of representing castration by a doubling or a multiplication of a genital symbol'.[41] These displacements of the penis, with their allusion to the fear and fascination of castration and death, 'put into question the idea of one', the idea of the phallus as a single, canny term. The possibility that the presence of the displaced penis might figure castration, a paradoxical presence of the penis figuring its potential absence, is clear in the following extract from Freud's 'Medusa's Head':

[T]he Medusa's head, can be traced back to the same *motif* of fright at castration (the phallic mother) . . . The sight of Medusa's head makes the spectator stiff with terror, turns him to stone. Observe that we have here once again the same origin from the castration complex and the same transformation of affect! For becoming stiff means an erection. Thus in the original situation it offers consolation to the spectator: he is still in possession of a penis, and the stiffening reassures him of the fact.[42]

Here Freud articulates the twin poles of fear and desire experienced in a face-to-face encounter with the Medusa (a mythological figuration of the phallic mother – a figure crossing gender boundaries).

Fergus's 'face-to-face' encounter with Dil's body divested of her/his mask of clothes could, as I suggested earlier, be read as a theoretical return to the moment instituting disavowal. It is also a return to the unmasking of Jody, with Jody's face and Dil's penis displacing each other in the return of the repressed. The 'unmasking' of the male to female transvestite figure in *The Crying Game* suggests that the *presence* of the penis has the potential to institute crisis rather than to stand for the socio-symbolic order. The presence of the penis thus brings into question the concept of 'a defining term' between the sexes, and brings into question the relative gender positions of masculine or feminine within the symbolic.

Thus, in *The Crying Game*, what becomes divested of its masquerade, stripped of its robes and veils of authority, is not the transvestite figure but the phallus. Dil retains her/his sexual and gender ambiguity, and it is the phallus as a signifying figure that is called into question.

NOTES

1. Marjorie Garber, *Vested Interests: Cross-dressing and Cultural Anxiety* (London: Penguin, 1992), p. 17, original emphases.
2. As well as the visibility of these films and *To Wong Foo, Thanks for Everything! Julie Newmar* (Beeban Kidron, 1995) and *The Birdcage* (Mike Nichols, 1996), there was the critical success of *Farewell My Concubine* (Chen Kaige, 1993) which shared the 1993 Palme d'Or with *The Piano* (Jane Campion, 1993).
3. *M. Butterfly* (David Cronenberg, 1993) and *Mascara* (Patrick Conrad, 1987) are two more examples of other films which would be relevant to this discussion if there were space to develop it further.
4. Elaine K. Ginsberg (ed.), *Passing and the Fictions of Identity* (Durham, NC and London: Duke University Press, 1996), pp. 3–4, original emphases.
5. Sarah E. Chinn, 'Gender Performativity', in Andy Medhurst and Sally R. Munt (eds), *Lesbian and Gay Studies: A Critical Introduction* (London: Routledge, 1997), p. 301.
6. It is pertinent that the term 'recuperate' is primarily used to describe a recovery of health or strength. A return to 'healthy' masculinity renders gendered and sexual ambiguity as 'abnormal' or 'invalid'.
7. Judith Butler, *Gender Trouble: Feminism and the Subversion of Identity* (New York: Routledge, 1990), p. 138, original emphases.
8. See J. L. Austin, *How to Do Things With Words: The William James*

Lectures Delivered at Harvard University in 1955 (Cambridge: Harvard University Press, 1962); Louis Althusser, 'Ideology and Ideological State Apparatuses', *Lenin and Philosophy and Other Essays*, Ben Brewster (trans.), (London: New Left Books, 1977); Michel Foucault, *The History of Sexuality: An Introduction*, Alan Hurley (trans.) (New York: Vintage, 1977).

9. Butler, *Gender Trouble*, p. 25.
10. Judith Butler, *Bodies That Matter: On the Discursive Limits of 'Sex'* (New York: Routledge, 1993), p. 2.
11. Butler, *Bodies That Matter*, p. 2.
12. 'The construal of gender-as-drag . . . appears to be the effect of a number of circumstances. One of them I brought on myself by citing drag as an example of performativity, a move that was taken then, by some, to be *exemplary* of performativity. If drag is performative, that does not mean that all performativity is to be understood as drag'. (Butler, *Bodies That Matter*, pp. 230–1, original emphases).
13. Garber, *Vested*, p. 9, original emphases.
14. This line of argument is therefore assuming a male heterosexual spectator; through the progression of this argument I demonstrate the precariousness of this position rather than to take it as a 'norm'.
15. Frank O'Connor, 'Guest Of the Nation', *Collected Stories: Volume I* (London: Pan Books, 1990); Brendan Behan, *The Hostage* (London: Methuen, 1959).
16. Neil Jordan, *The Crying Game* (London: Vintage, 1992), p. viii.
17. Jane Giles, *The Crying Game* (London: BFI, 1997), p. 9, my emphases.
18. Jordan, *Crying*, p. 17.
19. Garber, *Vested*, p. 11.
20. At this point in the film Dil's masked body is still being read as female by Fergus.
21. Peter Brooks, *Body Work – Objects of Desire in Modern Narrative* (Cambridge: Harvard University Press, 1993), p. 18.
22. Laura Mulvey, 'Visual Pleasure and Narrative Cinema', in *The Sexual Subject: A Screen Reader in Sexuality* (London and New York: Routledge, 1992), p. 29.
23. 'Dil: "See that, Col?" Col: "See what, Dil?" Dil: "He gave me a look"; Dil (at the bar after s/he has finished miming): "He's still looking, Col"'. (Jordan, *Crying*, p. 27, p. 31.)
24. Sigmund Freud, 'Fetishism', in *Penguin Freud Library Volume 7: On Sexuality*, James Strachey and Angela Richards (eds and trans.), 1927 (London: Penguin, 1991), pp. 345–58; 'The Uncanny' in *Penguin Freud Library Volume 14: Art and Literature*, James Strachey and Angela Richards (eds and trans.), 1919 (London: Penguin, 1990), pp. 335–76.
25. Freud, 'Fetishism', p. 354.
26. Freud, 'Fetishism', p. 353.

27. Jordan, *Crying*, p. 49.
28. Jacqueline Rose, *Sexuality in the Field of Vision* (London: Verso, 1986), p. 66.
29. Jordan, *Crying*, p. 12.
30. Jordan, *Crying*, p. 41, my emphases.
31. Freud, 'Fetishism', p. 353.
32. Freud, 'The Uncanny', p. 347, original emphases.
33. Garber, *Vested*, p. 17.
34. Freud, 'The Uncanny', p. 356. Freud relates much of the uncanny effect of 'The Sand-Man' story to the parallels it draws between blindness and castration, which in turns reverses the link between seeing and knowing, vision and 'the rational' and the mastery that it allows the male subject.
35. Jordan further confirms the idea of seeing through the eyes of the narrative protagonist in his comments on his choice of Stephen Rea for the part of Fergus: '[h]e's got a face that you can project every thought into . . . *He's like a lens for the whole story*'. *The Orange County Register*, 24 November 1992, my emphases; in Giles, *Crying*, p. 32.
36. Jordan, *Crying*, p. 47.
37. Jordan, *Crying*, p. 11.
38. Jordan, *Crying*, p. 11.
39. Jordan, *Crying*, p. 12.
40. Garber, *Vested*, p. 247.
41. Freud, 'The Uncanny', p. 356.
42. Sigmund Freud, 'Medusa's Head', *Standard Edition, Volume 18*, James Strachey (ed. and trans.), 1922 (London: Hogarth Press, 1940), p. 273.

4

'Til Death Us Do Part:
Cinema's Queer Couples Who Kill

MICHELE AARON

The shift from Alfred Hitchcock's *Rope* (1948) to Tom Kalin's *Swoon* (1992) represents the two areas that I want to examine in this chapter in relation to contemporary cinema: the homoeroticisation of murderous intent and the representation of passionate commitments of lesbian and gay relationships. Informed by New Queer Cinema, this chapter will consider the cultural and cinematic contexts necessary for an understanding of the surge of mainstream movies in 1994–5 of same-sex couples who kill. This surge consisted of four films: *Heavenly Creatures* (Peter Jackson, 1994), *Fun* (Rafael Zelinsky, 1994), *Sister my Sister* (Nancy Meckler, 1994) and *Butterfly Kiss* (Michael Winterbottom, 1995). In these films, the murderous couples are women, and their relationships, while not always explicitly sexual, are undoubtedly queer. The films must certainly be positioned in terms of their queer heritage but also, and more importantly perhaps, in terms of the cinematic construction of the female sexual killer and an exploitation of lesbian sexuality that is integral to 1990s lesbian chic. In considering the four films' temporal coincidence as well as their many similarities, I am, ultimately, questioning whether these films offer a new possibility for an empowering representation of lesbian and gay lives or simply repeat cinema's homophobic manipulation of the 'murderous gays'.[1]

Kalin's *Swoon* provides an updated and decidedly queer rendition of the Leopold and Loeb murder case: the true story of two men killing a young boy in 1920s Chicago, upon which Hitchcock's *Rope* was based. Whereas Hitchcock omits the murderers' homosexual relationship, Kalin positively revels in it. In *Swoon*, their sexual dynamic is the essence of the stylised provocation, the dizzying erotic and aesthetic charge to the piece; in *Rope*, the subtextual sexual relationship is the deadly potential of the film's claustro-phobic atmosphere, hanging over it, yet absent. Together with Gregg Araki's *The Living End* (1992), *Swoon* heralded the birth of New Queer Cinema and a flurry of articles welcoming it. Here at last were moving and powerfully seductive images of gay men and the aesthetic representation of passionate gay relationships. The films were uncompromising or, as J. Hoberman put it, 'proudly assertive' in their characters' sexual desirability and murderous motivations.[2] However, while 1992 was claimed by B. Ruby Rich, as the 'watershed year for independent lesbian and gay filmmakers', it was the men, on both sides of the camera, who were enjoying the limelight.[3] Acknowledging the familiarity of this male-dominated terrain, Amy Taubin pointed out that:

in fact, this queer cinema has much more in common with the current crop of male violence films (with Quentin Tarantino's *Reservoir Dogs* or Nick Gomez's *Laws of Gravity*, for example) than it does with any feminist cinema. Like Tarantino and Gomez, Araki and Kalin are also the sons of Scorsese, whose films define and critique masculinity through violence but also make Robert de Niro a homoerotic object of desire.[4]

New Queer Cinema, however, offered the primacy of homo-erotic tension. Intoxicated by the beauty and the rarity of the image of *Swoon*'s lovers, one almost forgives, or rather forgets, their crime. As Richard Dyer has commented, the couple are so attractive that the spectator has to remind 'him'self of their dread-ful deed.[5] Publicity for the film declared that it '[p]uts the homo back into homicide' but I believe it does more than this: it puts it back but it also draws it away.[6] The film not only reinstates the homosexual content, filling in the holes in Hollywood's history, but it also separates homosexuality from murder.[7] Homosexuality and murder are not mutually implicated but rather coexist within a world determined to so implicate them. It is this world that is to be revealed as corrupt. Kalin unrepentantly works with the homo-phobic stereotype rather than against it and in so doing undoes its authority. Rich writes that Kalin 'demonstrates how easily mainstream society of the 20s could unite discrete communities of outsiders (Jews, queers, blacks, murderers) into a commonality of perversion' and *Swoon* reveals the two men as victims of not only their internalised homophobia but also of anti-Semitism.[8] Thus, New Queer Cinema's couples who kill operate within both a corrective and a progressive project and '[t]he queer present negotiates with the past, knowing full well that the future is at stake'.[9]

In addressing this more recent crop of films, I am concerned similarly with their sense of correction and progress, and with the primacy of a homoerotic tension in the pleasures that they offer. I have opened with this introduction to New Queer Cinema not only in order to connect the four films to their queer antecedents and a 1990s pattern of innovation but also to suggest the inadequacies of such a context for explaining them. The representation of a lethal lesbian sexuality has its own strong history grounded in the imag(in)ings of male fantasy so readily conjured in the femme fatale. The four films I mentioned of lesbian couples who kill are, in the main, targeted at a mainstream audience for whom the assignment of a queer reading seems hopelessly generous.[10] *Sister my Sister* stands out here, as it will continue to do, as an exception, for it was screened as part of the 1995 New York Lesbian and Gay Film Festival. While it most closely qualifies as a queer film, it has much in common with the others. Thus, while the genre would seem to offer familiar mainstream pleasures, the thrill and threat, or thrilling threat, of the lesbian's dangerous sexuality has been doubled. It is this 'innovation' that reinflects both the traditional, albeit perilous, pleasures of the representation of dangerous female sexuality and the films' queer heritage.

Made three years after *Swoon*, *Heavenly Creatures*, *Fun*, *Sister my Sister* and *Butterfly Kiss* have been seen as constituting a new genre of lesbian couples who kill, or as Michael Musto dubbed them in July 1995, those 'oh-if-only-those-whacky-incestuous-lezzies-would-stop-murdering-people flicks'.[11] It is not only their coinciding but the cumulative impact of their 'splatter' scenes that left this spectator at least alarmed by their similarities. In interrogating their genre status and, indeed, its 'newness', I will look at both the commonalities and the differences among the films.

Heavenly Creatures is based upon the true story of the intense friendship of two schoolgirls, Pauline and Juliet, who, when they are threatened with separation, kill Pauline's mother. *Sister my Sister*, the only female-directed film of the group, is based on the true story of the Papin sisters, Christine and Léa. In 1933, also faced with separation, they murdered the mistress of the house in which they worked as maids, and her daughter. *Fun*, the only American film, was apparently inspired by a 1982 California murder case. It tells of two teenage girls, Hilary and Bonnie, who meet, bond and go out and kill 'for the fun of it'. *Butterfly Kiss* is the only one of the group neither inspired by nor founded upon true events. It tells of the relationship between Eunice and Miriam and their murderous travels along the British motorways. It ends with Miriam drowning Eunice, in accordance with her lover's wishes.

The films are strikingly similar in narrative structure, as Rich writes of *Fun* and *Heavenly Creatures*:

> Take a couple of adolescent girls, utterly captivated by each other but unable to name that intensity. They create their own world of shared secrets and fantasies. Establish the sense of an unnatural tie between the women, complete with an eerie intensity beyond the grasp of mere mortals. Place them in families that don't understand them, or actively abuse them, then add a social or institutional setting of repressive authority. Let the energy build and build, searching for a way out ... They flirt and they may even lust, but ultimately their courtship takes the form of bloodshed. Homosocial even there, it's women they kill.[12]

Taken together the four films are slim variations on this one theme. While they are all independent films, they range in period, budget and, of course, place of production. *Butterfly Kiss* and *Sister my Sister* are British, *Fun* is American and *Heavenly Creatures* was made in New Zealand, yet their settings all display a cultural and geographic specificity. Each recreates a very fixed *mise-en-scène*: *Sister my Sister* of 1930s France, *Heavenly Creatures* of 1940s Christchurch, and the two others providing the contemporary landscapes of California and England. Each film employs a historicising aesthetic, not only in the temporal location but in the harkening to authenticity through documentary effect. In their connection to real events they appeal to a sense of historical record as well as to the potential politics of documentary. They employ this style to assert the sense of authenticity and authority; the evocation of fear and sympathy and lust is highly charged through their biographical aspirations. Two of the films are based on true cases, the others, *Fun* and *Butterfly Kiss*, operate as flashbacks from prison interviews. The emphasis upon the pinning down of information is created not only through the interviewing technique but through, for example, the diary keeping in *Heavenly Creatures*.

The *cinéma vérité* style invests the narrative with greater danger through its implied status as real. This sense of the re-creation of events might suggest an interactive or reflective politic, a negotiation with the past and its omissions, which I suggested earlier was queer.

While each film might 'positively' represent the lesbian couple – allowing the protagonists their own voice and conjuring a considerable degree of sympathy in establishing their oppressive personal situations – only *Sister my Sister* truly intervenes in the past in a manner similar to *Swoon*. Distinguished from the group again, it revisits an already mythic narrative rather than the actual raw events.[13] *Sister my Sister* makes a deliberate intervention into the business of storytelling and, especially, a tradition of men telling women's stories. The case of the Papin twins provides the material for the only female director in the group, and the first female reworking of the true story. It also offers the only exclusively female world. A photographer is the sole male figure in the film, existing purely as a voice. Yet how telling or strategic it is that he should be the one behind the camera, ultimately controlling the 'image'. Nicole Ward Jouve, in reference to *The Maids*, suggested that:

the sisters have not finished generating representations. There have been films, other plays . . . there is a strange dynamic at work here that continues to vex interpreters. What emerges strikingly . . . is the refusal of the act, the denial of the 'eye', the 'I' of the sisters by all commentators identifying with a 'male' position.[14]

Written prior to the film, this excerpt introduces *Sister my Sister* as precisely a return to and a filling in of past omissions. It also foregrounds my discussion on the disavowal of lesbianism.

The films' flirtation with 'authenticity' heightens their pleasures by investing them with possibility. The threat of the lesbian is not only doubled but legitimated. These filmic lesbians with their deadly potential yet passionate desires – their frenzied, almost joyful, acts of murder – embody the simplest perilous pleasures that the films have on offer. Yet it is not only the characters who own such pleasures, for identification with the women or spectatorial enjoyment of the diegesis immediately implicates the spectator within these dangerous desires. The cultural desire for these representations, evidenced in their coming so closely together and in their popularity as well as their cultural context, speaks of more pervasive, more general risky or *risqué* delights being indulged by these films. The question lingers as to whether the films are doing anything new: are they repeating old patterns of popular fantasy or are they offering and depending upon dangerous pleasures not previously encountered? The connection between homosexuality and murder has an ugly homophobic past (and more insidious

71

present), and the connection between female sexuality and dangerousness is similarly charged, yet these films marked the definite arrival of the lesbian protagonist to the cinema and, what is more, she had found love. I want now to consider this double bind of these representations, the linking of queer sexuality with deadliness, and the portrayal of passionate relationships.

THE HOMOEROTICISATION OF MURDEROUS INTENT

The linking of homosexual potential with danger is not new. It has existed throughout the history of Hollywood film either as the absent yet deadly potential of an often subtextual homosexuality or as the overt exploitation of its deadliness in numerous films from *Cruising* (William Freidkin, 1980) to *Silence of the Lambs* (Jonathan Demme, 1991) to *Basic Instinct* (Paul Verhoeven, 1992). The different forms reflect the changing shape of censorship laws but, more importantly, they testify to the endurance of homophobic assumptions. Vito Russo's book *The Celluloid Closet* provides a concise history of homosexuality in the movies and in so doing exposes the partnership between murder and lesbian and gay characters. A glance at his necrology, in which he charts the fatal outcomes of Hollywood's lesbian and gay characters, provides a startling and sobering confirmation of this marriage.[15] Within the development of cinema, the queerness or the implied lesbian or gay potential of a character ran concurrent with their murderous motives and with the predictable form of narrative closure: all were killed either by themselves, by others or by 'accident'. Andrea Weiss, in *Vampires and Violets*, follows on from Russo, in her attention to the history of lesbians in film. In exposing the litany of ill-fated lesbian characters, she reveals the prototypical deadly lesbian pair: the lesbian vampires. Although I do not want to pursue this here, these figures serve to introduce us to the centrality of male heterosexual fantasy within the cinematic representation of lesbianism.[16] Several film theorists, including Barbara Creed and Carol Clover, have addressed the conflation of female sexuality with danger and violence,[18] while others have addressed the relationship between violent women and lesbianism within contemporary cinema. Lynda Hart, for example, explores the 'series of phobic displacements of criminality onto lesbianism'.[18] In placing these films of lesbian couples who kill within their cinematic context I will briefly examine the place of lesbianism within the female buddy movie and the erotic thriller.

These are, I believe, the new genre's mainstream cinematic antecedents to which it can be seen to respond.

Through her discussion of the female buddy film, using *Thelma and Louise* (Ridley Scott, 1991) and *Mortal Thoughts* (Alan Rudolph, 1991) as her examples, Hart demonstrates how: 'the female protagonists of these films make "shameless liaisons," which expose the dominant culture's underwriting of lesbianism when the violence of women enters representation'.[19] What marks the genre of the female buddy movie (as has been argued elsewhere with regard to their male pairings) is the attempt to deny the sexual involvement of the central pair.[20] For Hart, the heroines' male interest is the superfluous yet unavoidable heterosexual footnoting to the films. She writes:

[T]he expectation for lesbianism between women who violate the law is so strong that the film works overtime to disavow it. If the lesbian has been constructed as the manifest figure of women's 'latent' criminality, we can expect that representations of violent women will be haunted by her absent presence.[21]

The female buddy film disavows lesbianism: it demands its denial while at the same time depends upon it for its appeal. The disavowed lesbianism is essential to the creation of danger and also to the erotic charge that this danger elicits. Hart quite rightly identifies the exploitation of lesbian-effect, the implicit lesbian codings, for the purpose of male fantasy within the representation of violent women. She writes that: 'the spectacle of a woman assaulting or killing a man makes an unconscious appeal to lesbianism and thus perpetuates the ways in which the presence of lesbians has been used to facilitate the heterosexual pleasure of male spectators'.[22] What Hart fails to identify, however, is that the straight male's pleasure in this fantasy is, undoubtedly, masochistic in that his pleasure originates in the murder of males. This will become more important as I contrast this scenario to that of the films of the lethal lesbian couples. So, rather than the simple denial of lesbianism, the female buddy film promulgates its disavowal: the necessary rejection of lesbianism to maintain the heterosexual economy combined with its tacit presence to allow male masochistic pleasure.[23] Of course, spectatorial pleasure is not the sole domain of straight men and it is important to acknowledge the female and feminist delight in the representation of strong women in, for example, *Thelma and Louise*. The gender of the spectator will become increasingly important as we consider the decidedly female worlds of these lethal lesbian couples films. From the requisite but super-ficial rejection of lesbianism in the female buddy film we move on to the flaunted lesbian erotics of the erotic thriller.

The female sexual killer of contemporary erotic thrillers offers a particular scenario that speaks to these murderous lesbian films: the merging of death and sex whereby the murder of the man runs concurrent with orgasm. Films such as *Basic Instinct*, *Sea of Love* (Harold Becker, 1989) and *Body of Evidence* (Uli Edel, 1992) are pre-occupied with asserting the dangerous sexuality of woman within an elaborate enactment of male masochistic fantasy. They allow the heroine an unusual amount of power, assigning her erotic domi-nance. While they pursue a female sexual autonomy and lesbian potential, the male remains pivotal and the films often conclude with a return to order, to the family and to a secure reinstatement of a heterosexual economy. Lesbianism signifies the danger or threat that needed to be contained, cured or punished. At the same time it is integral to the erotic charge of the films. In this way lesbianism, while not disavowed, is still used to reinforce hetero-sexuality (and to titillate male fantasy). Any independent female sexuality, whether lesbianism, as in *Basic Instinct*, or masturbation, as in *Body of Evidence*, is used to enhance not only the female sexual killer's dangerousness but also male fantasy directly. Both films use such scenes to provoke the male protagonists' desire and involve-ment. In *Body of Evidence*, for example, masturbation is constructed as an invitation to the male's participation.[24] The equation of sex with potential death in these films, as well as in the many others where the protagonist lusts after the suspected murderer, is exac-erbated by the frequent presence of sadomasochistic practices and pleasures such as those in *Basic Instinct* and *Body of Evidence* but also in *Sensation* (Brian Grant, 1994) and *Bodily Harm* (James Lemmo, 1995).

So strong is the connection between woman's deviant or inde-pendent sexuality (and in film these are often reduced to the same thing) and her deadliness, that it haunts all representations of strong women or of strong relationships between women. This reflects as much upon the homophobic and sexist mix of hegemonic society as its determination of male fantasy. Lesbianism is certainly contained by the films in that the pairs are finally separated, their relation-ships prohibited; but it is punished only in terms of the pair's separation rather than by death, which is often conferred as pun-ishment in film. Only Eunice in *Butterfly Kiss* is 'punished' by death, yet it is at the hands of her loved one and at her request rather than

74

being imposed upon her. What is more, the film has already established her sadomasochism, her need for and pleasure in 'punishment', which she both gives and takes, and the film provides several opportunities for the display of the metal chains that bind her bruised body.

The crucial difference of these films of lesbian couples who kill is that their victims, except in *Butterfly Kiss*, are not male. They establish an alternative economy, removed, it seems, from both heterosexuality and masochism. *Butterfly Kiss*'s distinction from the rest of the group, and its similarity to the erotic thrillers, is confirmed by the presence of sadomasochism. Even so, the figure of Eunice is highly unconventional in her sadistic and masochistic practices: '[Eunice] is a walking symbol of the masochistic suffering which she also takes pleasure in and which she also dispenses'.[25] Yet these films seem deliberately to avoid or evade the erotic implications of the female sexual killer by making the characters too young, too stupid, too strange or too committed and thereby distanced from *Swoon* and *Basic Instinct* alike. The danger or threat is doubled yet divided or dispersed in their 'deviance', in their weaknesses as youths, as mad and as unstable. The question that lingers is: for whom is the sexualisation of death? That the couples kill only women – save *Butterfly Kiss* – denies the male fantasy of masochistic identification with their victim (although the pleasure of the dangerous lesbian endures no doubt). Here, as ever, the queer spectator of mainstream cinema is ambivalently positioned, jostling between reading gratuitously against the grain and the brick wall of homophobia. A lesbian spectator might be either masochistically or sadistically delighted in the pairs' activities, which leaves her a neither very positive nor an unfettered position.

This new genre of films, these queer couples who kill, can be seen as responding to the combined elements of the buddy film and the erotic thriller, that I have just outlined; namely, the disavowal of the lesbianism of the female pair and the merging of sex and death and its reflection of the male agenda, male pivotal position and heterosexual economy. Yet, these films set their own agenda in their diversions from the buddy film and erotic thriller with their blatant imagery yet internal confusion.

PASSIONATE RELATIONSHIPS A/VOWED

Heavenly Creatures, *Butterfly Kiss*, *Sister my Sister* and *Fun* emphasise the intensity – both physical and emotional – of the relationship between the central female protagonists. It is only in *Fun* that the central pair are not shown making love, yet Bonnie admits that 'Hilary is my drug'. I would suggest that each of the pairs' relationships are lesbian, a conclusion that I will show to be both suspect and undeniably queer. The films counter the historical disavowal by representing the passionate involvements without recourse to (diegetic) heterosexuality. The extent of the sexual nature of their involvements varies, or rather, the extent to which they are shown (or exploited) varies, especially with regard to the teenagers of *Heavenly Creatures* and *Fun*. In these two films a heterosexual potential is expressed in the form of the girls' male interest, albeit off-screen. *Heavenly Creatures* performs a familiar displacement with regard to lesbianism. When the girls are making love, as part of one of their fantasies of their make-believe world of Borovnia, the shot shows the Borovnian Count – the rubber figure come to life – enfolding Juliet in 'his' embrace. This cinematic trope of transforming the same-sexed lover into the opposite sex provides a familiar disclaiming of queerness that can be seen in other films, such as *Ghost* (Jerry Zucker, 1990), and corresponds to Linda Ruth Williams's assertion of the 'heterosexualising homosexuality' in Cronenberg's films.[26] In the lethal lesbian couple films, heterosexuality does not footnote their dynamic to render it harmless, but rather reiterates the girls' flights of fancy or waywardness.

While these are neither the well-groomed, perfectly spoken 'heroes' of *Swoon* nor the rawly physical attractive 'heroes' of *The Living End*, there is a sense in which the pairs are groomed for the screen. In a way lesbianism is being heterosexualised by the play upon the pairs' visual and enduring differences. While the girls have very much found their soul mates in each film, the films insist upon a visual contrasting of them. One of the pair might be darker or taller, or they might also come from different classes as in *Heavenly Creatures*. Somehow they are pitted against each other; *Butterfly Kiss*, for example, makes this polarisation most obvious in abbreviating the women's names from Eunice and Miriam to Eu and Mi. The notable exception is *Sister my Sister*, which revels in the sameness, with not only a visual similarity between the pairs but also familial connections. This happy and intentional equating of the two women can also be applied to the other females in the house, and I will say more on this later.

While the films focus on the women's connection there is an inability to name it or affix it. The relationships are certainly passionate and suggestively sexual, yet also displaced and doubted

76

both within the film and in response to it. This inability (or resistance) to affix meaning ranges from the films' representations of lesbianism, to their genre, from within the films to without.

It has been written of Pauline and Juliet in *Heavenly Creatures* that: '[t]heir bond falls into unclassifiable territory, being neither an innocent, misconstrued friendship, nor an acknowledged lesbian relationship. This ambiguity is deftly shown in a scene where they make love, imagining each other as their Borovnian idols.'[27] The film might encourage the uncertainty of the girls' relationship, but it is not as indistinct as it seems or as has been suggested. 'After Pauline and Juliet sleep together, the diary entry refers to "the joy of that thing called sin" . . . The whole film is a breathtaking blend of the particular and the opaque, a deft juggling act with the two undefinable notions of joy and sin.'[28] While, here, Stella Bruzzi rightly identifies the contrary forces at work and play within the film, the diary entry itself denies an ignorance of the meanings of joy or sin. It is not the girls who find their meanings confusing, but their observers inside and outside of the film. It would seem that the protagonists can speak a language which the film and its viewers struggle to hear. What critics fail to notice, or perhaps to mention, is that the film makes its homosexual content immediately, if cunningly, clear. Within *Heavenly Creatures*'s opening, in which a British newsreel introduces the story's location, Christchurch, the town is described as New Zealand's 'City of the Plains', that well-known allusion to Sodom.

A question that has drifted through my discussion so far has concerned the generic relationships of the 'queer couples who kill' films. I have suggested this new genre's relationship to, or amalgamation of, existing representations of women. Buddy movie, erotic thriller and lesbian love story are invested with the potential politics of documentary. This multi-genre mix is epitomised by *Butterfly Kiss* which has been seen as '[a]n often breathtakingly original meld of road movie, lesbian love story, psychodrama and black comedy . . . realistic fairy tale of murder and romantic obsession as they travel the U.K.'s highways'.[29] This melange of genres, together with the groups' contextualised existence, has a distinctly 1990s, if not postmodern, feel to it. Rich has already made this connection in terms of New Queer Cinema and I believe her observations can also be connected to these lesbian-queer couples who kill with their traces of 'appropriation and pastiche, irony, as well as a reworking of history with social constructionism very much minimalist and excessive'.[30]

Deborah Cameron and Elizabeth Frazer, in their book *The Lust to Kill*, have pinpointed what I believe to be at the heart of this new genre, its form and its significance: the lack of a language in which to represent authentically the female sexual killer. Discussing the Moors murderers, Myra Hindley and Ian Brady, they suggest the inadequacy of existing discourse to represent Hindley properly:

Writings about Hindley make it very clear indeed that her actions did not have the same meaning as Brady's; they were differentiated by the factor of gender, and by the fact that no language existed for speaking of a woman's lust to kill – indeed one still does not exist.[31]

I would suggest that this is what the films are doing, forging a language to convey this lust. This is akin to countering the disavowal of lesbianism (or indeed, of homosexuality) in that, like *Swoon*, these films revel in and centralise the queer dynamic between the murderers. Murder comes to express their position as lesbians, to express themselves.

In articulating women's lust to kill, these films use murder as a metaphor for lesbian lust, for the consummation of the relationships. For the female sexual killer of mainstream cinema, orgasm runs concurrent with murder, eroticism is aligned with potential death, yet this is all contained within a sexual pairing, the dynamic exists between murderer and victim. In these lethal lesbians films the women own the act – it is based solely on their agenda and (definitely) not their victims', and their motivations are generally made clear if not understood. Here, murder is substituted for the disallowed, rather than disavowed, lesbian satisfaction: murder is once more a 'function of the criminalization of their sexuality', of society's antagonism towards them.[32] Thus the films symbolise the impossibility and inevitable destructiveness of lesbian desire.

Murder accordingly operates as a metaphor for release in a 'genre of drives and impulses, repression and volcanic release'.[33] One critic writes of 'the near manic intensity' of Pauline and Juliet's behaviour and of their 'psychic fever, an intoxication of the spirit, which gains release in wild storms of ideas, words and actions'.[34] This language, and indeed these films, are as much about excess as about release: '[b]ut their commitments are too obsessive, their imaginations too extravagant and their emotions too untrammelled'.[35] It is interesting that in *Sister my Sister* it is not only the two protagonists who are associated with release. In a move that confirms its distinction from the rest of the group but also its investment in complicity – of broadening the sphere of implication – the victims, those common positionings for the spectator, are also charged with excess and release. The mounting, and metaphoric, pace is perfectly demonstrated in a humorous and suspenseful scene in *Sister my Sister* in which the sisters' sexual fervour, as they make love in the kitchen, is cross-cut with the building speed of the card game of the other female 'couple': Madame and Mademoiselle. The film revels in the sexual echoes and tension in the house. To what extent is this film a step ahead of the others? Can the cinematic language be excessive in itself? Replete with the sisters' passionate encounters, this film deliberately suggests a pervasive sexualised tension. Whose orgasm is displaced in the murder? Are not all four women implicated in the explosive release of sexual frustration? Indeed, are not Madame and Mademoiselle the most frustrated pair?

In heralding 'the arrival of a trend that may well be the cinematic follow-up to lesbian chic: the murderous maybe-lesbian couples who bond their affections with blood',[36] Rich emphasised the new genre's relationship to contemporary culture, and it is this that has been my primary concern. Rather than providing close readings of the films, I have been interested in questioning their coinciding, their significance as reflecting their cultural and cinematic contexts. If the murder is metaphoric of lesbian union, these films can be seen as 'unholy marriages',[37] as commitment ceremonies of a sort.

Rich asserts that the films not only present the women's passionate relationships but also offer its sanctification, albeit symbolically. They enact the couples' commitment, that bonding of affections often known as marriage. It is therefore interesting that this filmic trend arose at a time when courts throughout Europe and the USA were (and indeed still are) debating, and occasionally passing laws on, the legal rights and recognition of same-sex couples' relationships.[38] At no other time has the lesbian and gay community been so mobilised around, or the liberal population so familiar with, issues of the legal status of lesbian and gay relationships, rather than just individual rights, as with the debates on the age of consent, domestic partnership and immigration policy. The title of this chapter certainly reflects my wish to draw out this connection, or rather the irony of these rare presentations of committed same-sex relationships, so that ''til death us do part' not only affirms their quasi-marital status, but is prophetic of their fateful separation, brought about by the death of another.

If I am suggesting a growing awareness of lesbian and gay lives in mainstream society, or willingness to engage with it, I mean partly to attribute it to the lesbian and gay rights movement, but perhaps, more strikingly, to the AIDS crisis. While I will not be developing this issue here, its impact on the association of homosexuality with disease and death, but also upon the deadliness of homophobia, provides an obvious and lucrative trajectory for the homoerotisation of murderousness. In the light of this 'awareness' one might place the debate on 'outing' and subsequent confessions of the sexuality of individuals from all walks of public life, for example, the comings out of Melissa Etheridge, Greg Louganis, Michael Barrymore and Ellen Degeneres and the star status of Martina Navratilova and kd lang. These exist within or alongside the cultural context or mainstream acknowledgement and fashionable exploitation of 'lesbian chic'.

Rich positions the genre within the current cultural phenomena of 'lesbian chic' and suggests that it is either the filmic reflection of lesbian chic or a reaction to it. While as a term it has been bandied around, 'queer' receives all the critical attention. It becomes necessary to offer some understanding, or rather hazard a definition, of lesbian chic within its similarly slippery usage, in which to place this trend. In many ways it is the gap between lesbian chic and 'queer', the presentability of one and the critical import of the other, that holds the double bind of these films. Lesbian chic refers to the appropriation and exploitation of lesbian culture or lesbian identity by the mainstream and/or heterosexuals for the purpose of cultural cachet or in response to fashion. It might seem to finally untie sexuality from orientation, allowing multiple sexual identities in a sexually unfixed project that feels queer. Of course, if you take the most androgynous of supermodels and give her a short but stylish haircut she would not approach queerdom without a substantial change of attitude. Thus lesbian chic, in pitting the fantasy of the female homosexual against the ultimate taboo of the male homosexual, can be seen to reflect a cultural appropriation of innocuous lesbianism, while maintaining firm restrictions on sexual politics: the gay community's reclaiming of 'queer' might have taken the deadly inevitability out of it, to allow the creation of lesbian chic, yet, lesbian chic is the poor relation of queer, mustering all of its incumbent problems but even more at risk from the temporariness and commercialism of fashion.

While 1990s cinema's queer couples who kill undoubtedly speak to a commercialism of gay culture, what epitomised the cultural currency of this new genre and its timeliness, for me, is its location within the ongoing development of the sex-crime industry generated from the Western world's fascination with serial killers. Within this industry the female serial killer was generally seen as non-existent. The few women who killed did so out of self-defence or killed an intimate. In other words, they did not fulfil the criteria for serial killer status, which involved the random, repetitive and sexual nature of the murders. Of course, where they did exist was on screen and, consequently, within the analyses of these filmic female sexual killers. In these lesbian killer-couple films, while the murders are not always random or repetitive, they are certainly sexual, in their joint 'release' but also in their female victims, or in the case of *Butterfly Kiss*, the sexualised nature of the crimes. *Butterfly Kiss* and *Fun* are fictional and, as such, involve the randomness and repetitiveness of murder that marks the male, not the female, killer.

Myra Hindley had been seen as the closest qualifier for the role of female serial killer, but she 'worked' with her male lover, Ian Brady, and was seen by many as manipulated by him. In the 1990s, it was Aileen Wournos, charged with killing seven men in Florida, who was hailed as the first female serial killer and as the original 'lesbian who kills', prefiguring these movies. As Rich says: '[i]n a post-Aileen Wournos universe, the lesbian killer may be a natural for genre discovery'.[39] However, it was Rosemary West's trial in 1994 that condensed this sense of the female serial killer, combining her lesbian associations with an idea of everydayness, that reflected and reflects this particular and current historical moment and its cinematic expression.

Hindley, with her dyed blond hair at her trial, epitomised the figure of feminine evil, with 'nothing natural, "ordinary", about her appearance . . . The spectacle of the treacherous, sexually active blond has become a popular cliché since the Second World War'.[40] This cliché translated so smoothly to the screen, from femme fatale of 1940s film noirs to her contemporary counterpart. Rosemary West is the antithesis of both Hindley and Wournos in that she looks so incredibly normal, she is the woman who could live in any street in Britain. How interesting then that the release of this new genre coincided with the imprisonment of Rosemary West who compounds and confounds all narratives: part of a murderous couple, had lesbian relationships, finally left to stand trial alone, she murdered her children and strangers.

Lesbianism certainly featured within the lives of Hindley, Wournos and West. Wournos was a lesbian and while West had a lesbian relationship, only she and Hindley were involved in the sexual murders of females as well as males. Thus, their lesbianism was also actualised by murder. Brady and Hindley, and Rosemary and Fred West hardly qualify as queer couples. The cultural interest in, or desire for, the murderous lesbian couple that this new genre of films depends upon and reflects was so finely exemplified by the relish of the media reports of Hindley's and West's friendship, the tabloid images of them holding hands: the archetypal female queer couple who kill. It is important to note the other side of this 'pathology' of lesbianism, evidenced in the major disproportion of lesbians on death row in the USA: not because of any disproportion of crimes but because of the inequality of sentencing.[41] The doubling of the dangerous woman can also be seen as a response to what Hart has noted as 'the profound ambivalence today's spectators feel toward both homicide and homosexuality'.[42] It is worthwhile considering how these queer couples who kill sit within the ever-decreasing parameters of the 'sensational' – doubling the dose of sexual threat.

In conclusion, I seem to have exposed a genre that combines the deadly sexuality of the woman with that of the homosexual, or the fantasy of the lesbian with the horror of the gay man. Yet it can perform a powerful statement on a new cultural climate, surpassing the characterisation of lesbian and gay men as individuals to allow their union in meaningful and committed relationships. However, in the absence of the representation of powerful figures of lesbians and gays, in their familiar association with death, can these really be offering an optimistic review of our times or the same old story? Are they envisaging marriage, allowing committed relationships, or offering frightening portrayals of the only kind of passion that we are capable of – deadly? Do these films offer a new version of the attractiveness of the female sexual killer, or positive images of women in love, because they are sensitively portrayed? Ultimately, are they homophobic or not – for the homosexuality does not exist as an adage of the sexual threat to the heterosexual economy of the film but now exists in a lesbian (post-Wournos) world.

A few years on, we continue to be served lavish fantasies of lesbian lives such as *Diabolique* (Jeremiah Chechik, 1996), yet *Bound* (The Wachowski Brothers, 1996) would seem to offer something different in its sane sexy stars and happy ending. For domestic bloodless bliss it seems we will have to turn to the safe small screen of sitcom and *Friends* and *Ellen*. Having said that, a residual pessimism and far too many questions have been left; no apologies are necessary, for such is the legacy of the history of lesbian and gay lives and anything less would be entertainment.

NOTES

1. See Robin Wood, 'The Murderous Gaze: Hitchcock's Homophobia', in Corey K. Creekmur and Alexander Doty (eds), *Out in Culture: Gay, Lesbian, and Queer Essays on Popular Culture* (Durham, NC and London: Duke University Press, 1995), pp. 197–215.
2. J. Hoberman, 'Out and Inner Mongolia', *Premiere*, October 1992: p. 31.
3. B. Ruby Rich, 'New Queer Cinema', *Sight & Sound*, September 1992: p. 31. It is important to add that Jennie Livingstone's *Paris is Burning* (1990) was among the first 'new queer' films, but, as she herself acknowledges, it is often overlooked in the historicising of New Queer Cinema. Amy Taubin has noted that Livingstone's film has a gay male content, albeit that it features black and Hispanic transvestites.
4. Amy Taubin, 'Beyond the Sons of Scorsese', *Sight & Sound*, September 1992: p. 37.
5. Richard Dyer speaking at Queer Bodies conference, Warwick University, 13 May 1995.
6. Publicity quoted in Rich, 'New Queer Cinema', p. 34.
7. Examples include *Fried Green Tomatoes* (Jon Avnet, 1991) and *Carrington* (Christopher Hampton, 1994).
8. Rich, 'New Queer Cinema', p. 34.
9. Rich, 'New Queer Cinema', p. 34.
10. This queer reading would involve the ability to read against the grain of negative representations, to enjoy the positive portrayal of gay sexuality.
11. Michael Musto, *The Village Voice*, 4 July 1995: p. 10.
12. B. Ruby Rich, 'Lethal Lesbians', *The Village Voice*, 25 April 1995: p. 60.
13. The sisters' story has spawned several representations, most famous perhaps is Jean Genet's play *The Maids*, and many interpretations. Meckler's film is based upon a play by Wendy Kesserman.
14. Nicole Ward Jouve, 'An Eye for an Eye: The case of the Papin sisters', in Helen Birch (ed.), *Moving Targets: Women, Murder and Representation* (London: Virago, 1993), p. 29.
15. See Vito Russo, *The Celluloid Closet* (New York and London: Harper & Row, 1981).
16. See Andrea Weiss, 'The Vampire Lovers', *Violets and Vampires: Lesbians in Film* (New York: Penguin, 1993), pp. 84–109.
17. See Barbara Creed, *The Monstrous Feminine* (New York and London: Routledge, 1993) and Carol Clover, *Men, Women and Chainsaws* (Princeton, NJ: Princeton University Press, 1992).

18. Lynda Hart, *Fatal Women: Lesbian Sexuality and the Mark of Aggression* (Princeton, NJ: Princeton University Press, 1994), p. 28.

19. Hart, *Fatal Women*, p. 67.

20. For a discussion of the male buddy film see Robin Wood, *Hollywood from Vietnam to Reagan* (New York: Columbia University Press, 1986).

21. Hart, *Fatal Women*, p. 75.

22. Hart, *Fatal Women*, p. 76.

23. For further discussion of the deadly or phallic woman as source for the masochistic gaze, see Gaylyn Studlar, 'Masochism and the Perverse Pleasure of Cinema', in Bill Nichols (ed.), *Movies and Methods II* (California: California University Press, 1985).

24. For further discussion of the conservative transgressions of these films, see Michele Aaron, 'The Exploits of The Female Sexual Killer: Taking the Knife to the *Body of Evidence*' in Deborah Cartmell, I. Q. Hunter, Heidi Kaye and Imelda Whelehan (eds), *Sisterhoods: Across the Literature/Media Divide* (London and Sterling, VA: Pluto Press, 1998).

25. Lizzie Franke, review of *Butterfly Kiss* in *Sight & Sound*, August 1995: p. 42.

26. See Weiss, *Violets*, p. 51 and Linda Ruth Williams's chapter in this collection.

27. David Rooney, review of *Heavenly Creatures* in *Variety*, 12 September 1994: p. 44.

28. Stella Bruzzi, review of *Heavenly Creatures* in *Sight & Sound*, 2 February 1995: p. 46.

29. Derek Elley, 'High-Octane Mayhem Elevates "Butterfly"' *Variety*, 20 February 1995: p. 73.

30. Rich, 'New Queer Cinema', p. 32.

31. Deborah Cameron and Elizabeth Frazer, *The Lust to Kill* (New York: NYU Press, 1987), p. 145.

32. Hoberman, 'Out and Inner Mongolia', p. 31.

33. Rich, 'Lethal Lesbians', p. 60.

34. John C. Murray, '*Heavenly Creatures*: an appreciation', *Metro*, 102, 1995: pp. 15, 16.

35. Murray, *Heavenly Creatures*, p. 17.

36. Rich, 'Lethal Lesbians', p. 60.

37. Rich, 'Lethal Lesbians', p. 60.

38. The newly elected Labour government of 1997 changed Britain's Immigration policy to acknowledge (some) same-sex relationships. The legal battle for gay marriage in Hawaii precipitated a backlash of other American states hastily passing 'defense of marriage' acts to counter the possibility of its success.

39. Rich, 'Lethal Lesbians', p. 60.

40. Helen Birch, 'If Looks Could Kill' in Birch, *Moving Targets*, p. 52.

41. See television documentary *Perverted Justice* (Donna Clark, 1996).

42. Hart, *Fatal Women*, p. 14.

PART II

Untold Risks

5

The Monstrous Child

JULIAN PETLEY

But when they find the frowning Babe
Terror strikes thro the region wide
They cry the Babe the Babe is Born
And flee away on Every side

For who dare touch the frowning form
His arm is witherd to its root
Lions Boars Wolves all howling flee
And every Tree does shed its fruit
    William Blake, 'The Mental Traveller'[1]

It's inhuman not to forgive damaged children, and despairing not to try to save them. As if kids who kill come from another planet, and don't deserve the chance to be human, to atone, to repair. The future won't forgive us for this – won't forgive us for our lack of forgiveness. The future will think us childish for how we thought about children.
    Blake Morrison, *As If* [2]

In an issue of *Index on Censorship* on the subject of children, Marian Allsopp stated: 'never before have children and images of childhood had such symbolic force in adult debate. Their pictures are like banners carried into war in a struggle over how best to order our social and economic relations'.[3] Indeed, it is one of the paradoxes of modern life that as real children have become increasingly invisible, being denied access to the streets by night-time curfews and stopped from walking to school by parents fearful of dangerous drivers and paedophiles, images of children have proliferated.

    The meanings of the images that constitute this deluge are varied.

However, as Diana Gittins notes, 'there are certain recurring and central themes: dependency, victimisation/helplessness, loss, nostalgia, innocence, danger, nature'.[4] Of these, 'innocence' is the most pervasive and, in a sense, embraces all the others – even 'danger'. Thus a child might be seen as being in danger because its innocence is taken to mean unworldliness. Or perhaps the child itself is a danger because of its 'innocence of' morality unless or until this is provided by education and general upbringing. As Rousseau wrote in *Emile*:

[R]eason alone teaches us to know good and evil. Therefore conscience, which makes us love the one and hate the other, though it is independent of reason, cannot develop without it. Before the age of reason we do good or ill without knowing it, and there is no morality in our actions . . . A child wants to overturn everything he sees. He breaks and smashes everything he can reach; he seizes a bird as he seizes a stone, and strangles it without knowing what he is about.[5]

Alternatively the child may be seen as infected by 'original sin', a concept which still thrives in our supposedly secular culture. According to this doctrine human beings are born corrupt (thanks to the 'Fall') but are capable of being redeemed by Christianity. This found its most extreme expression in the various forms of Puritanism which swept through northern Europe and colonial America in the seventeenth century, where childhood became a battleground in which the harshest forms of treatment were justified as a means of saving children's souls from the flames of Hell.

In our society, then, apparently contradictory images of children exist side by side. On the one hand childhood is represented as idyllic, carefree, close to Nature, prelapsarian. This is especially true today when, as Marina Warner has argued, 'the nagging, yearning desire to work back to a positive state of goodness, an Eden of lost innocence, has focused on children'.[6] On the other hand, we have an increasing number of representations of children as demons and monsters; to quote Warner again: 'the Child has never been seen as such a menacing enemy as today. Never before have children been so saturated with all the power of projected monstrousness to excite repulsion – and even terror'.[7]

Philippe Ariès locates the birth of the modern conception of the child in the century of the Enlightenment and of *Emile*, that is, the eighteenth century.[8] It is also at this point that the child begins to emerge as an increasingly important figure in art and literature. As Sabine Büssing writes:

[U]p to the last decades of the 18th century, the theme of childhood was generally neglected in literature. To be sure, the child obviously belonged to the human race and was thus allowed to figure occasionally in poetry and drama, in works from Homer through Shakespeare, just as adult men and women appeared. The child as such, however, did not have the qualities that authors (Greeks and Elizabethan alike) considered important – cognitive faculties, rational conduct, adult passions . . . It rarely had qualities appropriate to the child's real nature, and it was never rendered as an individual personality.[9]

In the eighteenth century the situation began to change. In the poetry of William Cowper and Thomas Gray amongst others, one encounters a nostalgic longing for a lost childhood which prefigures Wordsworth's evocations of childhood innocence in *The Prelude*, *Lines Written above Tintern Abbey* and the Ode on *Intimations of Mortality*. Meanwhile in William Blake, particularly in his *Songs of Innocence and Experience*, one finds a powerful attack on the forces that threaten, abuse and exploit childhood innocence: poverty, narrow rationalism, oppressive religiosity, urban life, industrialisation – in short, the full panoply of unfettered capitalism. This theme was to reach its nineteenth century apogee in Dickens but it occurs in many other nineteenth century writers (Samuel Butler and Charles Kingsley, for example) and was not unique to Britain (thus Victor Hugo and Mark Twain). And so, within the course of a few decades, the child emerged from relative obscurity to the literary forefront. The more society appeared harsh, alienated and bewildering the more childhood seemed like a haven, closer to Nature than the adult state, and an echo of happier, simpler times. Indeed, Peter Coveney suggests that since many writers and artists disliked industrialisation:

[I]t is not difficult to see the attraction of the child as a literary theme. The child could serve as a symbol of the artist's dissatisfaction with the society which was in process of such harsh development about him. In a world given increasingly to utilitarian values and the Machine, the child could become the symbol of Imagination and Sensibility, a symbol of Nature set against the forces abroad in society actively de-naturing humanity.[10]

The nineteenth century did, however, contain intimations of a different kind of child, the distant ancestor of the twentieth century child monster. For example, in Heinrich Hoffman's cautionary tales in *Struwwelpeter* (first published in German in 1845) we encounter, amongst other horrors, 'Cruel Frederick':

Here is cruel Frederick, see!
A horrid wicked boy was he;
He caught the flies, poor little things,
And then tore off their tiny wings.
He kill'd the birds, and broke the chairs,
And threw the kitten down the stairs;
And Oh! Far worse than all beside
He whipp'd his Mary, till she cried.[11]

A few years later, in 1850, *The Scarlet Letter* by Nathaniel Hawthorne, a writer who was later to exert a strong influence on the development of the Hollywood horror movie, was published.[12] Set in seventeenth-century New England, it is the story of Hester Prynne, her secret lover Arthur Dimmesdale and their love child Pearl. On one level a denunciation of the Puritanism which had branded Hester a 'fallen woman' and caused her daughter to be regarded as a witch, the novel itself is, nonetheless, distinctly ambivalent about Pearl. As Reinhard Kuhn notes: 'the girl is certainly an enigmatic figure, a living hieroglyph endowed with a tinge of remoteness and intangibility. But whether the nature of this enigma is good or evil is a question left in suspense'.[13] Although clearly not condoning the Puritans who see Pearl as a 'demon offspring', Hawthorne's own narration paints a decidedly ambiguous portrait of the child, who thus comes across as a particularly fascinating mixture of elements in which one can glimpse some of the ambiguities about 'possessed' children which we will explore later. Take, for example, this passage in which Hester meditates upon her child's 'peculiar look':

It was a look so intelligent, yet inexplicable, so perverse, sometimes so malicious, but generally accompanied by a wild flow of spirits, that Hester could not help questioning, at such moments, whether Pearl was a human child. She seemed rather an airy sprite, which after playing its fantastic sports for a little while upon the cottage floor, would flit away with a mocking smile. Whenever that look appeared in her wild, bright, deeply black eyes, it invested her with a strange remoteness and intangibility; it was as if she were hovering in the air and might vanish, like a glimmering light that comes we know not whence, and goes we know not whither.[14]

Hawthorne's attitude to Pearl may be ambiguous, but ambiguity about child characters lies at the very heart of Henry James's *The Turn of the Screw* (1898), the story of two children, Miles and Flora, narrated by their governess, who gradually concludes that their souls have been corrupted, even from beyond the grave, by two former servants who died in mysterious circumstances. There has been much debate over the governess's status as a reliable narrator with suggestions that she is a hysteric who is simply projecting her own neuroses on to her unfortunate charges. However, this is too simplistic and singularly fails to do justice to the story as one of the finest works of the fantastic, a genre whose very essence, as Tzvetan Todorov argues, is ambiguity and uncertainty.[15] The ambiguity over Miles and Flora cannot be resolved because it is the motor force of the story and the source of its tension; furthermore, it is this ambiguity which causes the reader to reflect on the very nature of children. As Gittins argues, James attempts no answers to the questions about children which the book provokes 'but merely provides reflection. The book therefore encapsulates much of what still remains core questions relating to issues of innocence and childhood.'[16]

By the end of the nineteenth century the child protagonist had become quite commonplace, especially in books written for children themselves where they were represented in largely positive terms (for example, Louisa May Alcott's *Little Women* (1868), Robert Louis Stevenson's *Treasure Island* (1883), Frances Hodgson Burnett's *Little Lord Fauntleroy* (1886) and Rudyard Kipling's *The Jungle Book* (1894) and *Stalky and Co* [1899]). And, of course, in the twentieth century children in literature have become as numerous, and as good, bad and indifferent, as adults. While it is true that in children's literature there has been a shift away from the Peter Pan/Christopher Robin image towards the William Brown/Adrian Mole one, and certainly adult novels as various as Richard Hughes's *A High Wind in Jamaica* (1929), J. D. Salinger's *The Catcher in the Rye* (1951), William Golding's *Lord of the Flies* (1954), Vladimir Nabokov's *Lolita* (1955), J. G. Ballard's *Empire of the Sun* (1984) and Doris Lessing's *The Fifth Child* (1988) present a less sentimental, idealised view of children and childhood than do many nineteenth-century works, it would be as difficult to generalise about fictional children as it would be about fictional adults. Thus, let us therefore turn to the emergence of the image of the monstrous child in the cinema.

Since virtually every modern cinematic development can be traced back to the early years of the medium, and since the horror and fantasy genres are as old as the cinema itself, it is perhaps unsurprising to discover that the monstrous child has a long cinematic lineage. In particular, early fantasy film-makers could not resist the temptation, like Lewis Carroll and John Tenniel in *Alice's Adventures in Wonderland* (1865), to distort the child's body in films such as *An Over-Incubated Baby* (1901), *The Bogey Woman* (1909), *Father's Baby Boy* (1909), *What It Will Be* (1910), *The Freak of Ferndale Forest* (1910), *The Key of Life* (1910), *The Baby Incubator* (1910), *Dr Growemquick's Feeding Powder* (1911) and *A Scientific Mother* (1915), to name but a few. Meanwhile, in Cecil Hepworth's *The Gunpowder Plot* (1900), a boy puts fireworks under his father's chair and blows him to smithereens, and in *Father's Hat; or Guy Fawkes Day* (1904) a father poses as a guy only to be set alight by his children. In the early feature *My Friend the Devil* (Harry Millarde, 1922), based on Georges Ohnet's novel *Le Docteur Rameau*, a boy tries to make supernatural forces kill his stepfather; instead his mother is struck by lightning.

The first significant cinematic child monster is, however, Rhoda in *The Bad Seed* (Mervyn LeRoy, 1956), based on the novel of the same name by William March and adapted for the stage by Maxwell Anderson. It was remade as a television movie in 1985 and has been listed by Stephen King as one of the top twenty scariest films ever.[17]

While her husband is away, Christine Penmark begins to fear that her daughter Rhoda, whom she had hitherto considered a perfect all-American child, is a multiple murderer. Investigating her own background she discovers that her criminologist father, Richard Bravo, is her adopted father – and that her real mother was a murderer. Fearing that a 'criminal gene' is being passed down the female line, Christine shoots herself and poisons Rhoda. However, the latter survives, but only in the novel and the play. In the film, thanks to the demands of the Production Code, Christine botches her suicide and Rhoda, in an absolutely literal *deus ex machina*, is killed by lightning.

On one level, at least, *The Bad Seed* reads like a misogynist, eugenic tract and, although contemporary critics did not take the eugenic theme seriously, it is worth stressing that the film takes an explicitly anti-psychoanalytic stance by representing a character who has been psychoanalysed as a ludicrous caricature and also by showing Richard Bravo to be wrong in favouring nurture over nature as an explanation for criminal behaviour. On another level, the film can be seen as a satire on post-War consumerism (a familiar target then) as Rhoda's killings are motivated largely by greed. The film could also be read as reflecting adult fears of the growing phenomena of the teenager and juvenile delinquency, also popular topics for debate at the time. For example, in the *New York Times*, the critic Wolcott Gibb noted that, 'even for a public familiar with the mounting record of juvenile violence, as reported in the press, these horrors may appear a little excessive'.[18] Similarly, the film could be seen as an expression of another contemporary notion, namely that modern American children are growing up too fast. As William Paul puts it in the course of a detailed and richly suggestive study of the film:

[Rhoda] threatens because she seems an adult in a child's body. Not only is she independent and self-sufficient, with defences so strong she seems to lack any emotional vulnerability; not only does she lack traits we would normally regard as inevitable components of childhood, but she treats her parents with an indulgent and sophisticated talent for manipulation derived from an awareness of how adults expect a child to behave.[19]

From our point of view, however, what makes the film so interesting is the ways in which it anticipates the 'family horror' films of the 1970s, and especially their articulation of the theme of 'demonic possession'. In this context the 'supernatural' climax of the film becomes significant, as does the fact that a number of critics referred to Rhoda as a 'Gorgon' or 'baby Gorgon' and that an MGM executive described her as a 'monster'. It is this aspect of the film which pushes what is essentially a domestic melodrama towards the horror genre, or rather, in the direction which that genre would take in the 1970s. Up until then horror movies had tended to represent the monstrous as something distant, past, exotic and foreign. However, as Paul notes:

[W]ith *The Bad Seed* the distance of the foreign disappeared and with it a good deal of the security and comfort familiar surroundings offered as a counter. *The Bad Seed* effectively brought horror home, domesticating it by locating what is most horrible *within* the family.[20]

More specifically, the theme of the absent father here prefigures *The Exorcist* (William Friedkin, 1973) and *The Other* (Robert Mulligan, 1972), while the idea that female reproduction is a source of terror and loathing anticipates *Rosemary's Baby* (Roman Polanski, 1968). However, there is another parallel with that film (and also with Larry Cohen's mutant baby films) in that Christine, like Rosemary, cannot help but love her offspring, no matter how monstrous. The director himself thus described *The Bad Seed* as 'a great love story – the greatest I ever made . . . It's the love of a mother for a daughter she knows is a sadistic killer'.[21]

In the same year that the novel and play of *The Bad Seed* appeared, 1954, William Golding wrote *Lord of the Flies*, which was filmed by Peter Brook in 1963. A decidedly anti-Rousseauesque fable, it is the story of how a planeload of public schoolboys fleeing an unspecified nuclear catastrophe and crashing on a desert island revert to a state of Hobbesian savagery. In 1957 John Wyndham wrote his famous novel of alien children, *The Midwich Cuckoos*, which was made into the film *Village of the Damned* by Wolf Rilla in 1960. Here the children are malevolent and are destroyed, but in the sequel, *Children of the Damned* (Anton M. Leader, 1964), they are benevolent, sent from the future to warn the world of impending nuclear catastrophe. However, they too are killed, albeit by human error. There are clearly Cold War themes at work in both films and, on one level at least, the cold, distant children of *Village* invoke the familiar, propagandist image of the Communist enemy as brainwashed automata. On the other hand, the would-be saviours of the world in *Children* are almost equally cold; thus, like Rhoda, they could be seen as reflecting an anxiety about children growing up as overly adult in the modern world. Whatever the case, Raymond Durgnat aptly terms these two films 'dream-paraphrases of the battle of the generations in perplexingly rapid cultural change'.[22]

Even more interesting, however, is Joseph Losey's 1961 film *The Damned*, based on H. L. Lawrence's novel *The Children of Light*. In this, children are raised in a secret, government-run, scientific establishment hidden deep within cliffs. These children will be the only survivors of the nuclear holocaust which is feared to be inevitable but they themselves are so radioactive that they cannot live outside the underground establishment in which they are entombed and will infect anyone who comes near them without protective clothing. The children are thus both lethal and pitiable at the same time and *The Damned* remains a truly remarkable condemnation of both the Cold War mentality and of ruthless, institutionalised violence in general, and towards children in particular.

It has been argued convincingly that the metamorphosis of the child into monster is the defining feature of horror films of the 1970s. This metamorphosis, moreover, took place in a cinematic context in which the previously discrete genres of horror, science fiction and family melodrama were becoming increasingly intertwined:

[P]reviously distinct narrative sites become contiguous or congruent. The exotic, decadent European world of the traditional horror film, the wondrous, alien outer space of the science fiction film, and the familiar, domestic, and traditionally American space of the family melodrama become closely associated. Exotic, decadent, and alien space geographically conflates with familiar and familial space. The displaced 'There' has been replaced 'Here', and 'Then' and 'When' have been condensed as 'Now'. Thus, the time and place of horror and anxiety, wonder and hope, have been brought back into the American home.[23]

According to Vivian Sobchack, this 'domestication' of horror and the concurrent process of generic convergence are responses to a crisis within family relations themselves, in particular the weakening of patriarchal authority by the young and by feminism and the growing realisation of the huge gap between the mythology of family relations and their actual social practice. This thesis is not, of course, unique to Sobchack, and can be found in (amongst others) Wood and Lippe (1979), Jackson (1986), Wood (1986), Paul (1994) and Williams (1996). However, Sobchack's is its most succinct statement and that is why I have singled it out here.

For Sobchack, 1970s horror cinema's representation of children as monstrous and murderous was part and parcel of bourgeois society's negative response to the youth movements of the 1960s; rebellious young people were narratively transmuted into alien forces that threatened both their immediate families and the wider authority of adult society. The focus here is on children run amok:

[T]heir resentment, anger, destructiveness, aberrance, and evil were seen as unwarranted and irrational eruptions – extrafamilial and pre-civilised in origin. The bodies and souls of such children as appear in *The Other* (1972), *The Exorcist*, *The Omen* (1976) and *Audrey Rose* (1977) are 'possessed' by demonic, supernatural, and ahistoric forces that play out apocalypse in the middle-class home – most often graphically represented by 'special effects' that rage in huge and destructive temper tantrums across the screen. Thus, while these children are verbally articulated as 'possessed' and 'victims', they are visually articulated as in possession of and victimising their households. Family resemblance notwithstanding, these kids are not their fathers' natural children. They are figured as uncivilised, hostile, and powerful Others who – like their extracinematic counterparts – refuse parental love and authority and mock the established values of dominant institutions. They are 'changelings' – the horrifically familiar embodiment of difference. Fascinating the culture that also found them abhorrent, these children collapsed the boundaries that marked off identity from difference and exercised a powerful deconstructive force dangerous to patriarchal bourgeois culture. Their figural presence and work on the screen and in the home restructured and redefined the semantic field of the generation gap – articulating it in vertiginous imagery, as *mise en abîme*.[24]

If the emergence of the monstrous child is one of the hallmarks of 1970s horror movies, the nature of its monstrousness is nevertheless represented in a number of significantly different ways which I now wish to examine.

Taking *The Bad Seed* as a harbinger, it is usual to date the actual birth of the cinematic child monster to Polanski's *Rosemary's Baby*, closely based on Ira Levin's 1967 novel of the same name. However, being born only at the end of the narrative, the infant Satan is almost incidental to it and acts more like one of Hitchcock's 'MacGuffins', enabling Levin/Polanski to weave a superb tale of urban paranoia in the form of an inverted version of the Nativity story. From our point of view, however, *Rosemary's Baby* is interesting not simply as a pre-echo of later 'body horror' movies but rather, as Lucy Fischer has argued in an extremely insightful approach to the film, as 'a skewed "documentary" of the societal and personal turmoil that has regularly attended female reproduction'.[25]

The more convincing cinematic birthplace of the monstrous child is, in fact, George Romero's *Night of the Living Dead* (1968), specifically the still-shocking scene in which the zombiefied child, Karen, murders and then starts to devour her father before hacking her mother to death with a trowel. However, Karen is not represented simply as 'evil' and it is important to understand how her monstrousness is constructed. Firstly, as Robin Wood has intriguingly noted, the scene is like a playing out of the sub-text of that strange, dark, disruptive moment in Vincente Minnelli's *Meet Me in St Louis* (1944) when Tootie violently destroys with a shovel the snow-people she has erected.[26] These are not only obvious parent-figures but, in the context of the narrative, it is perfectly clear that Tootie is expressing her rage at her father, who wants to move the family to New York against their will. Secondly, and relatedly, Karen is emblematic of the tensions that exist within the small group of people defending themselves against the zombies. Thirdly, Karen, like the other zombies, is the victim of nuclear fallout and thus, by extension, of the American government's authoritarian and uncaring attitude to its citizens (compare this explanation for patricide and matricide to that of the seventeenth-century New England Puritan minister Samuel Willard who claimed of one child who came under his 'care' that it was Satan who 'urged upon her constant temptations to murder her parents, her neighbours, or children . . . or even make away with herself'.[27]

In this view of things the zombies, although repulsive, terrifying and murderous are also pitiable and wretched; indeed, as the film progresses a moral equivalence is established between the zombies and the trigger-happy rednecks who gun them down as if on a turkey shoot. The final zombie hunt, filmed from a helicopter and accompanied by an anonymous commentary, both looks and sounds disturbingly like the kind of televised 'search and destroy' mission with which viewers became all too familiar during the Vietnam war. Seen in this light the zombies seem increasingly like the crazily exaggerated, monstrous doubles of 'normal' Americans, a theme which Romero would develop considerably in *Dawn of the Dead* (1979) and *Day of the Dead* (1985), while the Vietnam allegory becomes perfectly explicit in *The Crazies* (1973).

Meanwhile, the neglected *The Other* (Robert Mulligan 1972), based on the 1971 novel of the same name by Thomas Tryon, is a fascinating playing out of the 'evil twin' theme. Set in a small, rural community in the 1930s, the film tells the story of twin brothers Niles and Holland Perry. Holland kills his father to gain possession of a ring which he believes has magical qualities. He himself then dies but lives on in the imagination of Niles who, at his brother's prompting, carries out further killings. Described thus the film sounds simplistic, but the actual narrative only very gradually, obliquely and with the utmost subtlety reveals the deaths of Holland and the father, and that 'Holland' is actually a fantasy projection of Niles, a means whereby he acts out his own unacknowledged, destructive impulses. Although the film carefully eschews conventional cinematic signifiers of 'subjectivity', its lush, lyrical, moody style gives it a distinctly 'interior' quality. As befits its title the film actually demands a psychoanalytic interpretation. To reinforce the point, however, note that Holland cuts off his father's finger in order to obtain the ring, and both boys keep the severed finger, as well as the ring, as a kind of talisman. As Paul suggests, what the film dramatises is a 'bizarre and troubling realisation of an Oedipal fantasy'.[28]

Far better known is *The Exorcist* (William Friedkin, 1973), based on the 1972 novel of the same name by William Peter Blatty. For most people this is the only monstrous child film they have ever seen, and this reinforces the crucial point that *The Exorcist* was not a hole-in-the-corner, low-budget exploitation quickie but, on the contrary, an expensive, prestigious, Academy Award-winning, 'serious', Warner Brothers film starring not only Ellen Burstyn and Jason Miller but also Max von Sydow, with all his connotations of Swedish (and particularly Bergmanian) 'art cinema'. In other words, the monstrous child had come of cinematic age.

What I would like to suggest here is that the film's huge commercial success, the way in which it 'served as a lightning rod for the entire culture, attracting commentary from virtually every possible source',[29] was not due solely to public interest in demonic possession and the finer points of Catholic doctrine on exorcism (although it certainly gave rise to a vast literature on the subject and thus helped to fuel a growing 'Satanic panic' in the USA), nor can it be explained only in terms of audiences flocking to see the spectacle, at once fascinating and shocking, of Linda Blair's body undergoing the most graphically grotesque transformations. Additionally, I would argue, the film was popular because it was seen as having something to say about the current state of children and young people, and also about adult attitudes towards them. There is contemporary evidence in the form of articles in the press to back up such a hypothesis,[30] and Stephen King claims, admittedly with the benefit of hindsight, that substantively:

[*The Exorcist*] is a film about explosive social change, a finely honed focusing point for that entire youth explosion that took place in the late sixties and early seventies. It was a movie for all those parents who felt, in a kind of agony and terror, that they were losing their children and could not understand why or how it was happening.[31]

As the extract above clearly suggests, *The Exorcist* is actually a deeply conservative film. Although it is certainly the case, as Williams has noted, that 'the families in *The Exorcist* live in a deteriorating America that no longer offers any coherent solutions to individual family dilemmas. Despite the prologue's desperate attempt to externalise evil, dissonant forces are definitely within the family',[32] the fact stubbornly remains that the film clearly offers 'demonic possession' as the explanation for Regan's behaviour, and exorcism as the only cure for it. Indeed, *The Exorcist* represents the girl in a way that seems to have stepped straight out of the writings of Cotton Mather, the Puritan minister who played such a key role in the witch trials of seventeenth- and eighteenth-century New England. For example, of the four allegedly 'possessed' children of John Goodwin about whom Mather wrote in *Memorable Providences* (1689) he noted that 'their heads would be twisted almost round',[33] and of the eldest girl that 'she would be carried hither and thither, though not long from the ground, yet so long as to exceed the ordinary power of nature in our opinion of it'.[34] Another 'possessed' child, Mercy Short, spoke in 'big , low, thick' demonic voices, while yet another, Margaret Rule, experienced exactly the same kind of levitation as Regan.[35] Thus, according to Mather, 'her tormentors pulled her up to the ceiling of the chamber and held her there before a very numerous company of spectators, who found it as much as they could all do to pull her down again'.[36] Now, in the case Regan herself, it is certainly true that one can also point to non-demonic disturbances in the girl's life – she misses her father and resents her mother's relationship with film director Burke Dennings – but these can scarcely explain her monstrous 'possession' and, what is more, they carry all sorts of value-laden connotations about single-parent families and working mothers.

It has also been suggested that the sheer physical scale of Regan's 'possession', its completely over-the-top gross-out qualities, carry some kind of anarchic, subversive charge. Now clearly, as mentioned above, one of the key attractions of *The Exorcist* is sheer physical spectacle: a pre-pubescent girl's body undergoing the most gruesome, bizarre yet thrilling metamorphoses (and in this respect it is significant that the real-life victim on whom the story is based was, in fact, a twelve year old boy). In her 'possession' Regan is certainly a fascinatingly liminal character, crossing gender boundaries, challenging conventional sexual roles and, in general, suggesting the full polymorphous perversity of childhood: 'both attractive in its sense of liberation but repulsive in its refusal to recognise boundaries that are set by the time we reach adulthood'.[37] In this respect Regan can be seen as an 'abject' male and female entity embodying oppositional elements repressed by conventional family structures:

[Her attack] is not only an anally excremental assault against Western civilisation's supreme symbol of motherhood but also a subversive return of socially repressed 'phallic' qualities traditionally denied to women. During her demonic possession, Regan embodies aggressive qualities in her assaults upon the forces of law, medicine, religion and motherhood – patriarchal institutions that depend on the family to maintain female subordination.[38]

This may be so, but, as Williams himself admits, the film represents the monstrous in overwhelmingly negative terms as evil, alien and irredeemably other. Indeed, as the film progresses it pushes the spectator into wanting to see, and to take pleasure in watching, Regan being physically assaulted, climaxing in the scene in which Father Karras literally beats her up – a point at which some audiences have been heard to cheer. As Paul notes, in this respect 'the film makes a powerful case for the value of child abuse'.[39] On the other hand, however, there are elements of the *mise-en-scène* which occasionally work against the main thrust of the narrative:

[T]he dominant tone of the film is punitive, derived from its overpowering sense of disgust at the body, but there are moments, however fleeting, in which we are allied with precisely those elements that give rise to this sense of disgust . . . For all its failings as a coherent work, *The Exorcist* established this push-pull aspect of disgust as mass entertainment for a large audience.[40]

The Exorcist also established monstrous children as regular fixtures in horror movies, both American and European (especially Italian), and little is to be gained from analysing their every appearance, since so many follow the basic *Exorcist* pattern. For example, in the equally prestigious *The Omen* (Richard Donner 1976), Katherine, the wife of an American diplomat, loses her child at birth, although she is too ill to realise what has happened. Before she fully recovers, her husband Robert secures the newborn baby of a woman who has just died and presents it to his wife as their own. Unfortunately the child turns out to be the Antichrist. Far more functional, low-key and naturalistic than *The Exorcist*, *The Omen* actually plays with the idea that Damien is not the devil but, rather, the victim of parental paranoia and insecurity. In this respect the film could almost be seen as an extension of the pregnancy traumas of *Rosemary's Baby*, with Katherine feeling that Damien is in some way not her own baby and unable to reconcile her desire for a 'perfectly perfect family' with the flesh-and-blood reality of a disruptive and demanding young child. In other words, *The Omen* could be read as a fantasy on the theme of how real-life parents sometimes regard their children as not simply intrusive but almost as alien invaders within their hitherto private domestic space. Inevitably, however, the film utilises these domestic elements as little more than red herrings to sow the occasional, tension-sustaining, temporary doubt about the supernatural causes of Damien's actions. In the end, he really is Satan's child. Once again we seem not to have moved very far beyond the days of Cotton Mather.

Monstrous child movies do not have to be like this, however, although most are. The most interesting exceptions are Larry Cohen's truly remarkable trilogy *It's Alive!* (1974), *It Lives Again* (1978) and *It's Alive III: Island of the Alive* (1986) and David Cronenberg's *The Brood* (1979).

In *The Brood* we encounter Dr Hal Raglan who, at his Somafree Institute of Psychoplasmics, has developed a bizarre form of treatment in which patients are enabled to transform repressed negative feelings into actual physical manifestations. One of his patients is Nola Carveth, whose deep-seated anger causes her to give birth, via an external womb, to a 'family' of miniature, murderous monsters. One of the prime examples of 'body horror' (and not without its problematic, misogynistic elements), the film is of particular interest here as it makes it abundantly clear that Nola's subconscious hatred is directed fairly and squarely at her family members – her mother, father and daughter Candice. At the end of the film, Candice, who has been terrorised by her monstrous 'siblings', also begins to develop grotesque 'psychoplasmic' symptoms – and so the consequences of familial dysfunction look set to continue. Cronenberg himself has called *The Brood* his *Kramer vs Kramer*[41] (Robert Benton, 1979) but a better parallel with this truly Atrean depiction of the damage caused to children by families might be Ken Loach's *Family Life* (1971).

In many ways the *It's Alive!* trilogy is like a massive prolongation of the final scene of *Rosemary's Baby*, in which Rosemary moves from rejection to acceptance of her infant, however monstrous. The films concern the birth of a number of mutant babies, and their parents' and the authorities' reactions to them. Cohen rejects the demonic mumbo-jumbo of *The Exorcist*, *The Omen* et al. and suggests (but no more than that) that the causes of these mutations lie deep within our society: tensions within the nuclear family, pollution and inadequately tested, irresponsibly marketed medications. As Robin Wood states:

The areas of disturbance exposed in the first few minutes of *It's Alive!* – disturbance about heterosexual relations, male/female gender roles, the contemporary development of capitalism, its abuse of technology, its indifference to the pollution of the environment, its crass materialism, callousness and greed – encompass the entire structure of our civilisation, from the corporation to the individual, and the film sees that structure as producing nothing but a monstrosity.[42]

101

However, as *It's Alive!* progresses, it becomes clear that the monstrous baby has feelings, and the parents, Frank and Lenore, become increasingly protective of the offspring which they initially regarded with horror and rejected. In the sequel, Frank helps another couple, Eugene and Jody, who have conceived a mutant child, to smuggle it to a secret base run by Dr Perry, who believes that the babies may represent 'the beginning of a new race of humanity which is going to eclipse our own, the way the human race is going to survive the pollution of the planet'. In both films the babies are threatened by the forces of law and order who, it is clear, are in the pockets of the drug companies which may have caused the mutations in the first place and now want their inadvertent 'products' dead and buried. The babies may be dangerous, but it is also clear that their violence is, to some extent, a protective reaction to the violence directed against them. Fascinatingly, and in complete contradistinction to most horror movies, the films actually take the side of the monster against society and encourage the audience to want to see it protected from the forces of 'normality'. Like the end of *Night of the Living Dead*, Larry Cohen's trilogy asks, implicitly at least, who are the real monsters? As the aptly named Frank himself puts it, remembering how as a child he thought that 'Frankenstein' was the name of the monster and not of its creator, 'somehow the identities get all mixed up, don't they?'

Robin Wood has persuasively argued that: 'Cohen's films never repress the possibility of imagining that the world might be changed; indeed, they positively encourage it',[43] and his films are unusual in that they thus lead the spectator towards a recognition and qualified acceptance of 'otherness' and the monstrous. This is nowhere truer than in Cohen's *It's Alive!* trilogy, in which love and humanity assert themselves against both physical and mental deformity, and the full might of the military-industrial complex. Wood is indeed correct when he argues that *It Lives Again* is among the most humane and progressive of all horror films.

Such representations of the monstrous child were, however, rare. Much more typical is John Carpenter's *Halloween* (1978) which, at the end of its virtuoso, four-minute, Stedicam opening shot, reveals the hitherto unseen murderer to be the six-year-old brother of the victim, Judy, whom he is apparently punishing for having just had sex. Enter a seemingly endless line of similarly traumatised children as instruments of Puritan repression and vengeance. In the 1980s and 1990s, however, the monstrous child is increasingly frequently joined in the cinema by the figure of the child as victim – usually of adults; thus the *Stepfather*, *Poltergeist* and *Elm Street* cycles, *Halloween III: Season of the Witch* (John Carpenter, 1982), *Flowers in the Attic* (Jeffrey Bloom, 1987), *Parents* (Bob Balaban, 1989) and *Psycho IV: the Beginning* (Joseph Stefano, 1991) to name but a few of a myriad possible examples. At the same time, however, films dealing with children and families, monstrous or otherwise, appear in greater numbers outside the horror genre – in, for example, the comedy or the family melodrama – so that themes are tackled in a much more direct, head-on and less displaced fashion: hence, from a long potential list, the *Home Alone*, *Problem Child* and *Look Who's Talking* cycles, *Baby Boom* (Charles Shyer 1987), *The Good Mother* (Leonard Nimoy, 1988), *The Good Son* (Joseph Ruben, 1993) and so on.

Does this therefore mean that our culture is now finally able to deal sensibly with children as real, complex, flesh-and-blood human beings, as opposed to abstractions of 'innocence' or 'evil'? That we are now at last aware of the sad fact that children are far less likely to be monsters than the victims of monstrous poverty, homelessness, neglect, sexual abuse and other forms of violence? Sadly, the answer has to be a resounding no, at least as far as Britain is concerned.

As Phil Scraton rightly observes: 'the killing of James Bulger unleashed a level of adult vindictiveness unprecedented in recent times'.[44] This vindictiveness was expressed, in the first instance, against the boys who killed him, Robert Thompson and Jon Venables, but soon spread to encompass children as a whole. However, this was merely the culmination of a process of child-demonisation that had been gathering force since the beginning of the 1990s. Indignant newspapers, politicians and assorted pundits fulminated against juvenile 'joyriders', 'bail bandits' and 'ram raiders', and a tiny minority of 'persistent young offenders' was made to seem emblematic of the 'lawless' state of young people as a whole. Journalists repeatedly scoured the country for 'the most evil child in Britain'. A homeless boy was found living in the central heating ducts of a housing development in Newcastle and was immediately dubbed 'rat boy'. As John Pitts has parodically put it, it seemed as if the entire country had been overrun by the 'persistent pre-pubescent predators from purgatory'.[45]

With the murder of James Bulger and the capture and trial of the boys responsible, however, the steady trickle of such sentiments turned into a raging torrent. And here, bizarrely and disturbingly, we start to re-encounter all sorts of images and ideas discussed, in a very different context, earlier in this chapter. Thus, with tedious regularity, *Lord of the Flies* was repeatedly invoked; for example in *The Guardian*, 16 February 1993, where Melanie Phillips and Martin Kettle argued that 'it begins to seem that William Golding's fictional universe of juvenile savagery in *Lord of the Flies* lies all around us in our housing estates and shopping malls', while a *Mail* editorial of 25 November 1993 cites the novel as proof of its 'thesis' that 'any ordinary group of children . . . can turn into pre-pubescent savages capable of killing one of their number'. Golding's novel was also cited by the same day's *Independent* and by *The Sunday Times* on 28 November 1993.

Most probably encouraged by the trial judge's irresponsible description of the killing as 'an act of unparalleled evil and barbarity', a *Times* editorial of 25 November thundered:

[C]hildren should not be presumed to be innately good. In the lexicon of crime there is metaphysical evil, the imperfection of all mankind; there is physical evil, the suffering that humans cause each other; and there is moral evil, the choice of vice over virtue. Children are separated by necessity of age from none of these.

Quite clearly, then, a version of 'original sin' is being offered in all seriousness as an explanation of the crime. Thus, Walter Ellis in *The Sunday Times*, 28 November 1993, put forward the notion that some children have a 'Satan Bug' inside them and confessed that he no longer believed that 'evil is not innate, but [that] nurture, temptation and the ills of society call it into being'. Inevitably *Lord of the Flies* was dragged into the fray yet again although, in fact, Ellis's thoughts are more reminiscent of *The Bad Seed*'s 'explanation' for Rhoda's crimes.

Indeed, in spite of a vast mass of evidence pointing to many and varied other reasons why Thompson and Venables killed another child, Britain's press, tabloid and broadsheet alike, overwhelmingly favoured 'evil' pure and simple. Thus, *Today*, 25 November 1993, referred to the friendship between the two boys as a 'chemistry of evil' and described them as 'an evil team', with Venables singled out as a 'demon' and Thompson as 'plain wicked'. The *Mail*, 25 November 1993, headed its sixteen-page supplement on the crime 'The Evil and The Innocent' and referred to Thompson and Venables as the 'boy brutes'. Meanwhile, the same day's *Star* inveighed that 'when we look at Robert Thompson and Jon Venables we are staring pure evil in the face. Wickedness has existed since the dawn of man. Do-gooders tell us there is no such thing. They are blind, dangerous fools', while the *Express* suggested that 'this horrendous crime is another demonstration that within the human heart and soul reside dark forces'.

Most extraordinary of all (and also, incidentally, what prompted the idea for this chapter) was the fact that certain newspapers, in their eagerness to suggest a 'demonic' dimension to Thompson's alleged 'evil', actually dragged in references to the kinds of horror films discussed earlier. Thus the *Telegraph*, 25 November 1993, alleged that Thompson's nickname was Damien and, furthermore, that he was born on Friday the 13th (enter Jason . . .). Meanwhile the *Mirror*, 25 November 1993, reported that 'Amityville', a reference to a cycle of horror films about murders in a haunted house, had been scrawled across the Thompsons' boarded-up home.[46]

In the 1990s, particularly in the aftermath of the Bulger case, children have, in the words of Barry Goldson, been pilloried in the most base and vulgar sense and their childhood has been systematically constructed so that those who offend are identified primarily as offenders rather than as children. Children in trouble have been defined as 'different', 'alien', 'other', 'evil' and 'wicked'; they are children 'possessed', little 'demons' from lawless planets – the planet 'inner city' and the planet 'outer housing estate'.[47] Unfortunately there is much evidence to suggest that these punitive and bitterly reactionary attitudes to children are not simply the property of Conservative politicians and Britain's notoriously Rightwing press but are shared by many in the general population.

In *The Scarlet Letter*, Nathaniel Hawthorne reflected on the English ancestry of those who persecuted Hester Prynne and her daughter, noting that 'the beef and ale of their native land, with a moral diet not a whit more refined, entered largely into their composition'.[48] Unfortunately, things seem to have changed so little in certain respects, and certainly in attitudes to children, that, if Cotton Mather returned today, he could probably find himself a job as a leader writer for the *Mail*.

NOTES

1. William Blake, *The Complete Poems*, c.1803 (London: Penguin, 1977), p. 502.
2. Blake Morrison, *As If* (London, Granta, 1997), p. 240.
3. Marian Allsopp, 'A triptych for our times', in *Index on Censorship*, 26 (2) March/April 1997: p. 122.

4. Diana Gittins, *The Child in Question* (Basingstoke: Macmillan, 1998), p. 111. For a detailed study of those images see Patricia Holland, *What is a Child? Popular Images of Childhood* (London: Virago, 1992).

5. Jean-Jacques Rousseau, *Emile*, 1762 (London: J.M. Dent, 1993), p. 39.

6. Marina Warner, *Six Myths of Our Time: Managing Monsters* (London: Vintage, 1994), p. 41.

7. Warner, *Six Myths*, p. 43.

8. See Philippe Ariès, *Centuries of Childhood* (London, Cape, 1973).

9. Sabine Büssing, *Aliens in the Home: the Child in Horror Fiction* (Connecticut: Greenwood Press, 1987), p. xiii.

10. Peter Coveney, *The Image of Childhood* (Harmondsworth: Penguin, 1967), p. 31.

11. Heinrich Hoffman, 'Cruel Frederick', *Struwwelpeter*, 1845 (London: Constable, *c.* 1995), p. 3.

12. Nathaniel Hawthorne, *The Scarlet Letter and Selected Tales*, 1850 (London: Penguin, 1986).

13. Reinhard Kuhn, *Corruption in Paradise: the Child in Western Literature* (Hanover: University Press of New England, 1982), p. 41.

14. Hawthorne, *The Scarlet Letter*, p. 116.

15. See Tzvetan Todorov, *The Fantastic: a Structural Approach to a Literary Genre* (New York: Cornell University Press, 1975).

16. Gittins, *The Child*, p. 170.

17. Stephen King, *Danse Macabre* (London: Warner, 1993), p. 210.

18. Wolcott Gibb quoted in William Paul, *Laughing Screaming: Modern Hollywood Horror and Comedy* (New York: Columbia University Press, 1994), p. 477.

19. Paul, *Laughing*, p. 273.

20. Paul, *Laughing*, p. 270.

21. Mervyn LeRoy quoted in Paul, *Laughing*, p. 280.

22. Raymond Durgnat, *A Mirror for England: British Movies from Austerity to Affluence* (London: Faber and Faber, 1970), p. 222.

23. Vivian Sobchack, 'Bringing it all Back Home: Family Economy and Generic Exchange', in Gregory A. Waller (ed.), *American Horrors: Essays on the Modern American Horror Film* (Urbana and Chicago: University of Illinois Press, 1987), p. 178.

24. Sobchack, 'Bringing it all', p. 182.

25. Lucy Fischer, 'Birth traumas: parturition and horror in *Rosemary's Baby*', in Barry Keith Grant (ed.), *The Dread of Difference: Gender and the Horror Film* (Austin: University of Texas Press, 1996), p. 413.

26. See Robin Wood, *Personal Views: Explorations in Film* (London: Gordon Fraser, 1976) pp. 164–8.

27. Samuel Willard quoted in Tony Williams, *Hearths of Darkness: the Family in the American Horror Film* (London: Associated University Presses, 1996), p. 28.

28. Paul, *Laughing*, p. 333.

29. Paul, *Laughing*, p. 288.
30. Paul, *Laughing*, p. 484.
31. King, *Danse*, pp. 196–7.
32. Williams, *Hearths*, pp. 114–15.
33. Cotton Mather quoted in Chadwick Hansen, *Witchcraft at Salem* (London: Hutchinson, 1969) p. 20.
34. Mather, *Witchcraft*, p. 25.
35. Mather, *Witchcraft*, p. 175.
36. Mather, *Witchcraft*, p. 181.
37. Paul, *Laughing*, p. 304.
38. Williams, *Hearths*, p. 112.
39. Paul, *Laughing*, p. 307.
40. Paul, *Laughing*, pp. 316–17.
41. See Piers Handling (ed.), *The Films of David Cronenburg* (Toronto: General Publishing Co. Ltd, 1983), p. 93.
42. Robin Wood, *Hollywood from Vietnam to Reagan* (New York: Columbia University Press, 1986), pp. 101–2.
43. Robin Wood and Richard Lippe, *The American Nightmare* (Toronto: Festival of Festivals, 1979), p. 80.
44. Phil Scraton, 'Whose 'Childhood'? What 'Crisis'?', in Phil Scraton (ed.), *'Childhood' in 'Crisis'?* (London: UCL Press, 1997), p. 167.
45. John Pitts, 'Youth crime', in Polly Neate (ed.), *Scare in the Community: Britain in a Moral Panic* (London: Community Care, 1995), p. 6.
46. For a full analysis of the press coverage of the Bulger case see Bob Franklin and Julian Petley, 'Killing the Age of Innocence: Newspaper Reporting of the Death of James Bulger', in Jane Pilcher and Stephen Wagg (eds), *Thatcher's Children? Politics, Childhood and Society in the 1980s and 1990s* (London: Falmer Press, 1996).
47. Barry Golding, 'Children in Trouble: State Responses to Juvenile Crime' in Scraton, *'Childhood'*, p. 133.
48. Hawthorne, *The Scarlet Letter*, p. 78.

6

Loving the Technological Undead: Cyborg Sex and Necrophilia in Richard Calder's Dead Trilogy

FRAN MASON

The mapping of desire in representations of cyborgs is rare in cyberpunk fiction, despite the possibilities the cyborg offers for the creation of new desires. The cyborg (any human–machine interface) is a delibidinalised figure in the novels of, for example, William Gibson and Pat Cadigan, promising not new desires but mystical fantasies of transcendence of the body and desire. The body is a prison in these narratives, either because desires of the body entrap the mind or because Corporate capital uses the body to control consciousness (through addictive forms of consumption), as a channel for information (through metaphors of programming), and as a means of identification. Power maps cyborg desire even in the liberated worlds that Bruce Sterling's Shaper/Mechanist narratives articulate in *Schismatrix* and *Crystal Express*.[1] Sterling's cyborgs subsume sexual desire into desire for power. Marriages and partnerships have a rational basis and are governed by politics and strategic alliances rather than by sex and desire (the 'irrational' domain of emotion and feeling). Technology's ability to construct artificial life outside of evolutionary determinism creates narratives that focus on technology's effects on social structures or on whether cyborgs are human or machine. *Blade Runner* (Ridley Scott, 1982) provides an example of the latter. Even while it maps a relationship between Deckard and the replicant Rachel, the film displaces this on to an investigation of 'humanness'.[2]

A perverse sort of cyborg desire can, however, be seen in the film *Star Trek: First Contact* (Jonathan Frakes, 1996) in the form of the Borg Queen. In the television episodes of *Star Trek: the Next Generation*, the Borg had been a virtually invulnerable species of delibidinalised cyborg-zombie who roamed the universe in their cube shaped spaceship looking for new species, worlds and technologies to assimilate into the Borg Collective. The Borg were the ultimate colonial parasites and formed a mirror image of the Federation and its 'benevolent' colonialism. Where the Federation stressed the persistence of difference, the Borg integrated all races into a single homogeneous Collective, with differences obliterated by the prosthetic devices and implants forced upon the unwillingly colonised races. The introduction of the Borg Queen introduces desire, but in a qualified way. She attempts to seduce Commander Data in order to gain access to the security codes of the Enterprise which is the Borg's host and which they are in the process of 'borgifying'. In her seduction of Data the Borg Queen is represented as a powerful sexualised woman; when first seen she has only shoulders, a head and vertebrae which undulate like a snake as she is lowered into her prosthetic body. She is a sinuous serpent-like creature who conjures up images of the Lamia or the Medusa, but she is also vampiric. At one point Data's body is pierced by a probe at the Borg Queen's command, leaving two teeth-like marks on his forehead. Whereas the penetration of the body by the Borg in the act of borgification is unwanted by the victim, here Data's response is presented as one of attraction and of willing submission to masochistic desire. Ultimately Data is not tempted by the serpent Queen and, in refusing to betray his Federation comrades, is revealed not to be Adam (a desiring human) to the Borg Queen's Eve, but confirmed as an android devoid of desire.

THE CYBORG AS TECHNOLOGICAL UNDEAD

In 1992 the first of Richard Calder's *Dead* trilogy, *Dead Girls*, was published.[3] The novel presented a Gothic-cyberpunk interchange which intermingled cyborgs with vampires, zombies with robots, and technology with mysticism, and mapped desire as the central force in the imagined culture of sex and death. Patterns of desire between human and artificial life function as the motivation for the narratives and cultural structures of *Dead Girls* and the novel focuses directly on how new bodies create new desires, new patterns of sexuality and new societies. The subsequent novels, *Dead Boys* and *Dead Things*, have extended this investigation of desire and have established a complex set of representations of desire between human, non-human and post-human;[4] but, because cyberpunk interacts with Gothic, these representations also coalesce around desiring relationships between the living (human), the dead (android) and the living dead (cyborg). The cyborg becomes a paradigm for a culture willing itself towards a future that seems to promise transcendence of the human but which finds itself unable to escape from the ideological and power structures of human history.

The *Dead* trilogy offers an examination of post-human society through the mapping of Enlightenment male discourses of power and desire in opposition to new cyborg desires. The three novels deal with the objectification of desire through the creation of women as machines. Women are created as 'things', subjected to male desire in fetishised and obsessive forms. However, *Dead Girls* also maps the objectification of male desire in the creation of a female sexuality that cannot be controlled. In a neo-Hegelian move the machines, created by male desire, assume a 'life' of their own and the male characters subject themselves to the addictive and parasitic desiring relations that cyborg culture generates. In his mapping of desire Calder demystifies male structures of desire and power, firstly, by suggesting that power is necessary for the creation of male desire (women must be objectified in order for desire or sexual arousal to occur) and, secondly, through the articulation of male desires in terms of parasitic, vampiric and, in *Dead Boys*, fascistic signifying systems. Calder's trilogy creates a complex nexus of male and female desiring structures in which men are both dominant, in the creation of the cyborg dolls, and dominated, in that the dolls will bite back because their mutation into cyborgs also creates them as vampires. A parasitic desiring relationship is developed in which both male and female feed off each other. Parasite feeds off parasite, a relationship driven by consumption, through which Calder envisions a death-driven culture of negativity fed by vampiric, addictive and necrophiliac pleasures.

Dead Girls tells the story of the metamorphosis of women into dolls through the narrative of Primavera Bobinski (a young girl in the process of becoming a doll) and her teenage lover Ignatz Zwakh (the narrator of the novel). Ignatz is addicted to the taste of Primavera's cyborg body which is both solid and fluid: dolls are hard technology (mechanical beings) created out of soft technology (new nanoengineered biochemical forms). Spalanzani, the scientific expert of the novel, says of the dolls' creation:

Toxicophilous would first have engineered nanomachines on the molecular scale, programmed with the rules of a cellular-automaton universe. The nanomachines would replicate, each time making a smaller model of themselves, until tiny, so tiny, hardware became software, machine became information, mimicking the quantum effects involved in the firing of neurons in the human brain. (*Girls*, p. 128.)

The process of women turning into dolls (or Lilim as they are later known) begins with the manufacturing of Cartier automata by the East European refugee, Dr Toxicophilous, whose secret is then stolen by the emergent economies of the Pacific Rim (specifically Thailand) who produce imitations of the Cartier automata in the form of 'gynoids'. In response, as Calder's earlier short story 'Mosquito' relates and which *Dead Girls* initially proposes, the Western powers release a virus among the gynoids that renders impotent any man who has sex with them.[5] In a counter move, the Thais (in the form of the pornocrat, Madame Kito) develop a virus which will reverse the effect and cause priapism among the Western men who exploit the gynoids. The novel, however, suggests initially that this virus (the doll virus) does not work as Madame Kito expects it to and instead transmutes itself within the male hosts, lying dormant until they transmit it to women through sex. All female children born of infected women turn into dolls or cyborgs in their teenage years, the end result being the destruction of the reproductive systems of Europe, an apocalyptic scenario that will lead to the extinction of the West.

The dolls are female cyborgs created by a parasitic nanoengineered viral infection, the result of which is that the host (the female body) is embedded with the parasite virus so thoroughly that the human flesh on which the virus feeds is recreated in the virus's image. The dolls' DNA recombines and, as Spalanzani says when talking of Primavera:

Living tissue has adopted the structure of polymers and resins, metals and fibres. It is difficult to perceive in what sense she is actually alive . . . I don't think we'd find any DNA in *this* . . . The entire body chemistry has been altered, reorganized at the atomic level. Mechanized, you might say. By every definition I can think of she *is* dead. (*Girls*, p.101.)

The dolls are both living and dead, organic and inorganic, human and non-human, thus raising the question: are they machines that look and act like humans or humans that look and act like machines? The issue here is the question of alterity: are the dolls 'human' or are they 'other'? As 'other' they can be positioned as aberrant, specifically in terms of male histories of feminine deviation from male 'normality', as testified by the frequent application of the term 'witch' to describe them by the proto-fascist organisation, the Human Front. As witches the dolls can be controlled and destroyed without reference to human morality. The dolls are also 'mechanized' and therefore fail the 'human' test in vitalist and Cartesian discourses which attribute a soul or a mind to humanity.[6] As mechanical entities they are perceived to be all body. Any 'mind' that they might have is produced by the viral programmes that cause them to come into existence. The dolls are the female body to the male mind and are coterminously depicted as the animal-machine, an instinctual unthinking creature mapped by its programmes and acting solely on its desires; in the discourses of the Human Front, they are irresponsible beings incapable of judgement or morality.

The dolls, therefore, inhabit a more complicated matrix than is usually associated with the cyborg because of Calder's focus on the body, specifically the female body, as a site of pleasure and desire in its 'dead' form. The dolls are a 'technological undead', constructed at the interface between cyberpunk and Gothic or horror fiction. To cyborg, animal, machine and witch can be added the description of nanoengineered vampire, the dolls becoming sexual creatures whose bite transmits the virus that has created them: '[d]oll bite man, man fuck lady, and lady have baby turn into doll' (*Girls*, p. 11). The matrix of cyborg-vampire places the dolls at the interface between the past and the future. They inhabit a metaphorical domain between patriarchal histories of women (and their exploitation in masculine power structures) and utopian fantasies of liberating technology. An example of the latter is the postmodern alchemy of nanotechnology, the technology that creates the dolls. Nanotechnology, as described by Eric Drexler, allows engineering at the atomic level by altering molecular structures in order, for example, to turn mineral into vegetable or animal into mineral.[7] Nanotechnology offers a future in which food is limitless, buildings can be 'grown' and in which humans are liberated from work. Its application to the body might produce other results. If Drexler's conjectured future becomes actual it is theoretically possible to create cyborgs without having to implant microchips (such as a memory chip) or graft prosthetic devices on to the body.[8] Instead, body modifications could be 'grown' inside or on the body simply by introducing nanomachines into the body and programming them to re-engineer protein, muscle or bone into the desired chip or prosthetic device. The nanomachines that made this possible could then either remain in the body to maintain the unit or could be removed from the body they have just modified. It would be possible in this way to transform the body entirely into something else.

This is the fantasy that Calder's novels articulate. Teenage girls are nanoengineered virally into dead girls. Where Drexler imagines a future radically separated from history (and its forms of social organisation, cultural behaviour and desire), Calder's vision is one in which history cannot be escaped, only destroyed – because history not only comes back to haunt the future but directly creates it. Specifically, the future is haunted by the male death wish. The dolls represent a potential apocalypse. Because infected males can only produce daughters, who subsequently turn into dolls, the complete infection of the male population would produce a species of sterile dolls unable to replicate and who themselves die in their early twenties. Calder links this to the death wish of European society as represented by its fear of, and desire for, demonic females. The 'virus' that creates the dolls is not a virus at all, but information transmitted as a virus. It is a literalisation of male fears and desires transmitted to the Cartier automata by Dr Toxicophilous in their creation. What is transmitted through the proliferating chain of automaton (or robot), gynoid (or android) and doll (or cyborg) are the fears, paranoias and desires about women that have underpinned male domination of European history and which were thought to have been repressed into the male unconscious by the scientific and rational enterprise of the Enlightenment, of which the Cartier automata are the embodiment. However, it is the Enlightenment that is presented as the cause of the virus and Enlightenment science that is the means of its application. Technology, male fear and male desire are seen as ineradicably intertwined and the cyborgs or dolls are the material manifestation of this matrix, literalised in *Dead Girls* by the physical matrix that exists in the dolls' womb and which signals their continued enslavement to male desires. Irrationality, the supernatural and superstition create the dolls and generate a virus that loops out of control, threatening to destroy the people who created it.

THE CYBORG VAMPIRE AND NECROPHILIA

Desire between cyborg and human is mapped in vampiric and parasitic relationships in *Dead Girls* in which host and parasite consume each other. Ignatz is addicted to the doll body, contaminated by the fluids he ingests, but consuming the female body at the same time. As vampires, the dolls also feed off their lovers' flesh through the image of the *vagina dentata*, a traditional male image symbolising fear of female sexuality: '[b]etween Primavera's depilated thighs her labia opened with the terrible grin of a prehistoric fish. The *vagina dentata* gnashed and snapped' (*Girls*, p. 56). The relationship is parasitic, a circular narrative of desire which is self-consuming: the principle of production and reproduction disappear from human history with the creation of the cyborg and are replaced by a culture that is destroying itself.

These vampiric desires are articulated in the mapping of women by reference to the contradictory Gothic relationship between fear and desire. Of this relationship Barbara Creed has said: 'the female vampire is monstrous – and also attractive – precisely because she does threaten to undermine the formal and highly symbolic relations of men and women essential to the continuation of patriarchal society'.[9] The female vampire represents a reversal of existing gender power relations – male fascination with the female vampire causes male subjection to the hypnotic effects of female desire and sexuality. This subjection is both willed (desired) and unwilling (feared) and represents the death of male will (which desires its own subjection and dependency) as an effective guarantee of both existing gender power relations and of male individuality or autonomy. The female vampire, however, is not as powerful a figure as she initially seems. The female vampire's power is given to her by the male discourses that create her and these discourses enunciate her ideologically as a symbol of the destructive effects of an unfettered female desire (which is also represented by the *vagina dentata*). The female vampire, therefore, is written ideologically by male discourses to legitimate male fears of the feminine and to justify the continued containment of women by men.

In *Dead Girls* male desires create the dolls as an embodiment of the cultural and ideological category of woman who is 'rendered as the *body-matter* for man and philosophy'.[10] Like the female vampire, the dolls are written ideologically by male discourses as the cause of the very male fears and desires that created them in the first place. The dolls are created as mythic and philosophical texts by

Dr Toxicophilous who has unwittingly programmed his automata with his own unconscious desires for sex and death; and these desires are themselves the result of Toxicophilous's programming by modern decadent writers, who:

'sought new themes, a new purpose. The worst of them glorified the old demons that were again racking their homelands: nationalism, populism, the paranoia of the non-existent foe: madness they embodied in a revival of folk tales and images. 'The Second Decadence' the critics called their movement. I was a boy and their stories of witches and golems, vampires and the eternal Jew riddled my mind.'
'Those stories have invaded reality,' I said. (*Girls*, p. 157.)

The new futures that Toxicophilous writes into his creations are already written and a doll race is created out of already existing male desires and paranoias. Indeed, Toxicophilous is himself created as a product of these already existing fears in Calder's novel, representing the mad scientist who generates disorder through an unwavering 'pursuit of knowledge at the expense of humane values'.[11] As such, he maps a history of the madness of male discourses in which desires for order and system actually create disorder and fragmentation. In other words, the future that Calder maps in *Dead Girls* is one which only has old models of desire to inform it, desires that are based on existing power relations. Calder uses the Gothic to show how it can be seen that 'standing at the threshold separating the human from the posthuman, the cyborg looks to the past as well as the future'.[12]

Calder's cyborgs are not Haraway's political cyborgs who liberate themselves from history through the dispersal of existing ideologies, power relationships and structures of exploitation:

The actual situation of women is their integration/exploitation into a world system of production/reproduction and communication called the informatrics of domination. The home, the workplace, market, public arena, the body itself – all can be dispersed and interfaced in nearly infinite, polymorphous ways, with large consequences for women and others.[13]

Despite the rhetoric of polyvalency and indeterminacy in Haraway's discourse and despite her view that cyborgs are 'compounds of the organic, technical, mythic, textual and political'[14] who cross boundaries of fact, fiction and myth (much as Calder's cyborgs cross genres), these are not the same cyborgs as the dolls in *Dead Girls* or the later books in the trilogy. The *Dead* trilogy does not play with desire as *jouissance*, the liberating movements of

115

desire which free subjectivity from ideology and power. The desires mapped in Calder's novels are implicated in power relations. At first glance there are similarities between Haraway's polyvalent cyborgs and the mutable desiring cyborgs of Calder's trilogy. Both share in the indeterminacy of desires and occupy a 'profusion of spaces and identities' and suggest 'the permeability of boundaries in the personal body and in the body politic'.[15] Haraway's political cyborg, however, offers the possibility for humans, specifically women, to forget their past, to avoid being the cultural texts on which male desire is written. In the forgetting of the ideological and power driven discourses traditionally associated with 'the human' the cyborg breaks out of ideological restrictions and creates a new culture of miscegenation. Entering spaces of hybridity and impurity the cyborg abandons notions of purity in gender, sexuality, class and ethnicity, and opens new spaces for desire in a plurality of 'impure' networks.

Calder's cyborg dolls are not figured as constructive. They do not construct new matrices of desire and identity, but are instead parasitic and modelled on historic and mythic constructions of female desire as articulated by male desires and ideology. Calder suggests that male desire when allied to technology creates dead 'things', whether this be commodities, culture or social organisation; all are based around the principle of exercising power and turning the dominated into objects or aesthetic artefacts that can be controlled. Ultimately, male desire does not result unless this objectifying process has occurred, a necrophiliac desire for dead things that can be seen in two forms in *Dead Girls*. The first is in the form of the 'medicine heads' of the Human Front, such as Captain Valiant, who see their task as ridding the world of the 'impure' dolls; as Valiant says: 'The belly. Corrupt. Malignant. It must be sanitized. Put to the spike.' (*Girls*, p. 94). The impaling of the dolls through the abdomen mimics the form in which vampires are destroyed but, like 'slink riving' in *Dead Boys* (the removal of the female reproductive organs), it represents sexual arousal for the dead thing manifested in a murderous penetration of the doll's flesh. The second necrophiliac desire centres on the 'doll junkies', such as Ignatz, who are addicted to cyborg flesh and to the 'allure' produced by the dolls. This objectification of the female body is most evident in the opening of *Dead Boys* where Ignatz is represented as having bottled Primavera's womb and vagina in order to drain off her allure and inject it into his bloodstream. The fetishisation of the female reproductive organs, which are described as a 'rotting star' around which Ignatz orbits with 'a marvellous fatal steadfastness', is objectification of woman in the extreme, the fragmented body represented by itself rather than a substitute fetish (*Boys*, p. 2, p. 1). Ignatz's sexual relationship with Primavera's fragmented cyborg body is also addictive: desire becomes need as the user's physiology modifies both body and mind. Ignatz calls the bottled Primavera 'cunt-for-brains' (*Boys*, p. 14), but because he is subject to addictive and parasitic desires it is unclear whether it is Primavera's mind that is being reduced to her sexuality or whether this refers to Ignatz's addicted consciousness.

Necrophilia is literalised in these examples, but Calder suggests in his mappings of desire that any sexual relationship within power relations takes the form of necrophilia. The dolls symbolise this and represent a distillation of desire into its basic forms of power and exploitation. Exercising desire through power means that men are always necrophiliac; as Primavera says, 'they're all robofuckers' (*Girls*, p. 62). In *Dead Things*, Ignatz, who during *Dead Boys* meta-morphoses into the vampire Dagon, looks at a world that 'dreams it is James Bond of Her Majesty's Secret Service, a secret agent stalking runaway cats on Mars, leading them into ill-lit alleyways, killing them . . .' (*Things*, p. 141). The image of James Bond hunt-ing 'cats' (renegade dolls) suggests a masculinity of glamorised violence while the 'ill-lit alleyways' suggest not only danger but a tryst in which death is a sexual encounter: the penis is a knife or gun and all sex is deathly. Necrophilia goes beyond the sexual and becomes a paradigm for all forms of desire, expanding to become a metaphor for a deathly cyborg culture in which '[d]esire is death. Living death' (*Girls*, p. 38). The desires that cyborgs release create a culture that can only perpetuate itself by also consuming itself.

CONSUMING CYBORGS

The consuming cyborg appears at the end of a history of death-driven technologies of commodification and can be seen at work in the construction of the dolls as commodified objects. The Cartier automata are created by Toxicophilous as aesthetic objects ('*bijouterie*') and represent Enlightenment attempts to repress the primal and animalistic desires of the body that ultimately produce the dolls. They are created as ideal women, objects designed to exist solely within the domain of the gaze. In the form of the gynoid or doll they become commodified objects, with Calder remapping history as a history of desire and the body. Where the

Cartier automata represent Enlightenment desire and the sublime body, the gynoids represent the mass production of twentieth century modernity, an industrial body and desire that is material, mechanised and automatic. In the form of the doll, desire is post-modernised. Like the gynoid, the doll is a commodity, but she is a fetishised commodity governed more by desire for her image than her materiality:

> Was she beautiful? No; like all her kind she possessed, not beauty, but the overripe prettiness that is the saccharine curse of dollhood. Beauty has soul. Beauty has resonance. But a doll is a thing of surface and plane. Clothes, make-up, behavioural characteristics, resolve for her, into an identity that is all gesture, nuance, signs. She has no psychology, no inner self, no metaphysical depths. She is the glory, the sheen of her exterior, the hard brittle sum of her parts. She is the ghost in the looking glass, the mirage that, reaching out to touch, we find is nothing but rippling air. She is image without substance, a fractal receding into infinity, a reflection without source and without end.
> She is her allure. (*Girls*, pp. 53–4.)

The doll is a paradigm of postmodern consumption, in which an object's intrinsic functionality is replaced by extrinsic desire. The dolls are nothing but the desires they generate in others, desires that are excessive and superficial, overpowering and unfulfilling. They are all image. However, the doll-as-image also represents a purifying of desire. The dolls are an image of an absolute male sexual desire, but because a doll has 'got no free will' (*Girls*, p. 68) and cannot, as image, respond to that desire, the initial desire becomes unreal; and without it the desiring male becomes aware of his own unreality in the need for an object to embody his desire. They desire for an affectless age: an 'unreal' desire which is not 'really' felt by 'unreal' subjects for 'unreal' objects. The dolls have a similar contradictory experience of desire. They exist only because of desire, through their sexualisation as dead things, but this desire is channelled upon them – they are unable to feel desire themselves and are positioned as desiring cyborgs unable to desire and as consuming cyborgs unable to consume.

Consumption images recur in the trilogy, references made to the gynoids and dolls as creatures to be eaten or consumed. These occur in *Dead Girls* but are exaggerated in the two succeeding novels of the trilogy in order to symbolise the culture of consumption created by male configurations of desire. *Dead Boys* charts the story of the creation of immortal male vampires called 'the Elohim' through the transformation of Ignatz into the Inquisitor Dagon.

The Elohim are transformed by Meta, an informational matrix existing in the doll virus which reshapes and rewrites the course of history, programming male and female alike to accept the brutal conditions of a male dominated culture. Calder rewrites the vampire as a Nietzschean or fascistic *ubermensch* in *Dead Boys*, reading against interpretations of the vampire novel that see the male vampire as a sexual and desirable creature transgressing against bourgeois morality and releasing female sexuality into culture. The aestheticisation of the male vampire here ignores its position of power which the representation of the male vampires, or Elohim, in *Dead Boys* does not. The Elohim are brutal, and even fascistic, killers who enslave and consume the dolls in order to survive. Similarly, Calder identifies the self-destructive nature of the liberation of female sexuality that vampire stories configure through the transformation of renegade dolls into 'cats' whose blood is transformed into the green allure that the Elohim feed off: '"So many girls are going the Way of the Cat." Trebly true. If they didn't, how would Meta control its numbers? he thought. How would our species [the Elohim] survive?' (*Boys*, p. 25). Male power is not threatened by rampant female sexuality but sustained by it. The Elohim 'can only be satisfied by meat that's gone bad, the green, rotten girl-meat of the traitress' (*Things*, p. 72). Without the aberrant female that the Lilim represent, the Elohim would die or be rendered powerless. The deviant female is necessary not only for male power to be enacted, but to be seen to be enacted: the submissive female implies male power but masculinity demands that power be rendered a spectacle.

Masculine narratives of desire want a controllable female body, not the unpredictable cyborg bodies of the dolls of *Dead Girls*. *Dead Boys* creates the male vampire as a way of returning to power alignments that channel the perverse and complex female desires of *Dead Girls* into a parasitism that serves masculinity. The Elohim are rapacious, brutal, necrophiliac men whose desires create a femininity of treachery for the Lilim in their construction as 'cats'. The 'cats' are renegades who are both unpredictable (vicious) and affectionate (desiring) and whose desires lead them to consume others so that they can be consumed themselves. The Elohim use the dolls as food to sustain them and images of eating abound in *Dead Boys* and *Dead Things*: 'girls in cooking pots, roasted on gridirons, spits, fried in coconut oil, stir-fried in woks, subject to the morbid recipes of maniacal gourmands, girls eaten raw, girls eaten alive (oh yes oh yes), their juices warm and their lips begging

119

for mercy and forgiveness' (*Boys*, p. 94), an image that is repeated in *Dead Things* (*Things*, p. 46). Desire works cannibalistically, but where in *Dead Girls* it was the *vagina dentata* that threatened to eat the phallus, here it is men eating women, desiring and consuming them as products. This is part of the culture of consumption that Calder maps which is 'dying of consumption, puking up the contents of the late twentieth century, dying of dying, of a thousand years of eat, eat, eat, eat, eat' (*Things*, p. 58).

Playing on its double meaning, Calder also maps consumption as a disease. Sex as consumption is both necrophiliac and diseased, the doll body symbolised by 'the bouquet of flesh, rotten, bad, that bloomed between her legs' (*Boys*, p. 90). Cyborg desires release obsessions with the diseased or polluted body. Men who have not been affected by the doll fluids are 'faecal' while the dolls are also presented in terms of disease and dirt. The diseased body is a body without autonomy, a body infected by external agents. The dolls are positioned as a disease, aberrations from the (male) human norm, infected bodies lacking in autonomy because they are diseased and because of the parasitic relationship they occupy in relation to human male and Elohim. The dolls see human men as 'junk food' (*Boys*, p. 53) and 'brood stallion[s]' (*Things*, p. 66), host bodies to be consumed and infected in order for the Elohim to survive. Calder, however, suggests that the idea of the autonomous human body is a myth and, indeed, that the body as a site of difference is a myth. The dolls and Elohim represent an apocalypse of homogeneity, the parasitic relationships consuming difference until, in *Dead Things*, culture is a 'universal film set' (*Things*, p. 43) where all girls are 'standardised into a universal *objet* of desire' (*Things*, p. 11) and where sexual violence is normalised as style: '[s]ome girls even have the hilts of SFX knives protruding from their umbilici' (*Things*, p. 33).

The lack of difference is not a symptom of the cyborg culture Calder maps, but a historical product of diseased male systems of power. All bodies are bags of virus and excrement, as indicated by references to human males as 'boy slime' (*Girls*, p. 36). The body is not something that is infected by diseases which can be purged. Both the human body and the doll body are already made up of diseases and viruses and the similarity between human and doll body indicates that they are both already artificial. In other words, not only do the dolls reveal that the human body is also artificial but the dolls are revealed to be no different from the human that wants to purge them from society. Cyborg desires are the same as human desires, created by histories of oppression and exploitation in the image of the male mind. The dolls are only diseased because of male discourses of purity and contamination which, as Mary Douglas points out, are based on ideological principles: '[w]here there is dirt there is system. Dirt is the by-product of a systematic ordering and classification of matter insofar as ordering involves rejecting inappropriate elements'.[16] The human body is already contaminated and Calder demystifies histories that claim notions of purity and natural humanness.

Calder, therefore, shows how the cyborg rereads history to reveal that human life and ideas were always artificial: '[e]verything in nature is a machine' (*Things*, p. 122). Indeed, the cyborg doll and the Elohim are the 'natural' end product of a history of parasitic, necrophiliac, and artificial desire: they are the paradigm of humanness and human desire, not its inversion. The dolls are cyborgs not because they have artificial nanoengineered bodies, but because they are constructed by male desire. They are 'things' not because they are dead, but because they are only allowed to act as 'things' by male desire. This is demonstrated by the Human Front's appearance in *Dead Girls* (and later by the Martians in *Dead Boys* and *Dead Things*, the Martians representing a pure humanity untouched by, and invulnerable to, the doll disease). The Human Front, who act as the voice of Enlightenment ideology, see things in entirely binary terms of living-dead, real-artificial and pure-impure and see the dolls as artificial. Calder, however, reveals the Human Front to be the symbol of necrophiliac desires such as those manifested by Captain Valiant. Putting dolls to the spike is not simply an enactment of male power through a murderous penetration that will destroy the 'artificial' female principle in the doll. The act also involves the removal of the matrix that Toxicophilous has unconsciously created within the dolls' womb, the matrix of technology, male fear and desire, symbolised by the myths of women in Toxicophilous's unconscious. In putting dolls to the spike, the Human Front are extracting maleness from the doll body. They are purifying male history by destroying women but are in effect also destroying themselves. The Human Front's spiking of dolls is both a repression of masculinity and its destruction, and the Human Front are taking pleasure in their own death, committing necrophilia with themselves, but using the dolls as agents of this sexual and cultural genocide. In the name of domination and the exercise of their own power they are consuming themselves.

CYBORG HISTORIES

The cyborg, for Calder, becomes a metaphor of the deathly and nihilistic history that male Western culture has produced. Necrophilia and consumption are not only metaphors for cyborg culture but for history as a whole. Rather than looking to the future, Calder uses cyborgs to rewrite the past and to demystify male human history by revealing it to be a 'little boy's fantasy' (*Girls*, p. 157). The narrative of *Dead Boys* is premised upon this process: the Elohim colonise time and use it to rewrite history materially. Events that Ignatz thought had happened have never occurred. The Elohim flatten out history and write into it their perpetual domination of culture and society, as Ignatz-Dagon explains to a revived Primavera: 'It's impossible for us to escape destiny, for me to be anything more than a killer, for you to be anything but a victim. Human history is being retrofitted. To accommodate Meta.' (*Boys*, p. 116). Meta, male information systems or male ideology and desire, refigures history to show how men have always had unchallenged power and how they have naturalised structures of domination in which women desire their own destruction and consumption in order to perpetuate the male species.

For Calder this is fascism and his trilogy sees in the cyborg the ultimate combination of male power structures and technology. The doll-as-cyborg represents a history of the exploitation of femininity through technology; the boy-as-cyborg represents an unimpeded expression of male power in technology. Scott Bukatman writes of a similar process when discussing the fascistic implications of the cyborg body in *The Terminator* (James Cameron, 1984):

Under fascism the body almost explicitly becomes part of a machine, delibidinalized through the imposition of boundaries drawn from the outside by the massive deployment of disciplinary and military technologies. The ego is further delibidinalized through pain, severed from the weakness and frailty of the flesh.[17]

Where Bukatman sees delibidinalised cyborgs, Calder sees a sexual fascist cyborg. Calder's cyborg comes about not because of the loss of libido but as a direct consequence of the unleashing of desire in conjunction with technology and male power, a matrix already implicit in history (in Nazism), but, because the cyborg exists in a late capitalist postmodern culture that enables the unleashing of desire in all its forms, it is here made open and celebrated.

Towards the end of *Dead Things*, Meta is shown to be so entwined with capitalism as to be identical to it. Ignatz-Dagon eavesdrops on a meeting of businessmen who, he realises, are 'buying and selling the transformation of consciousness into flesh, flesh into meat, meat into pure, diseased alterity; the transformation of men and women into images' so that, as one of the merchants says, 'Everybody profits . . . You get our protection, we get the pornography and the human race gets to buy death. And the beautiful thing is, it's all justifiable. With Meta, we can sell *anything*' (*Things*, pp. 160, 164). Meta becomes a capitalist release of existing male desires into a culture that will accept any activity no matter how violent, deathly or perverse, and the cyborg as the technological undead becomes both its symbol and its mode of fulfilment.

For Calder, the cyborg confirms history as a history of power and violence which not only survives in the future mapped by the *Dead* trilogy but is also celebrated. At one point, as history is being rewritten by the Elohim, Ignatz-Dagon notices a disparity between his history, in which Toxicophilous created the dolls, and Elohim history in which television is 'showing a documentary – *Heinrich Himmler, Nazi Toymaker*' (*Boys*, p. 102), refiguring history so that Fascism creates the dolls. History writes the future and violence and power are aestheticised and normalised, history recreated as a boy-doll conflict in which eroticised power fantasies are presented openly as normal and legitimate. By *Dead Things*, the boy-doll power structures are so normalised that necrophilia becomes a part of style and Nazism becomes a necessary indication of chic for the fashion-conscious sex killer, who drives a 'Mercedes-Benz 1936 bright-red five-seater type 540K Cabriolet (the sort favoured by Nazi leaders)' (*Things*, p. 38), indicating an eroticisation of masculine technology and sexual violence.

Dead Things does however, ultimately, reverse the narratives of the previous two novels. The violence and sexual murder is so excessive that even the Elohim want to get out of the sex-death cycle and therefore set out to detonate a 'Reality Bomb' which will reconfigure history once again so that the doll virus will never have existed. There is a potential nostalgia for the 'human' here, except that the novel ends with the revelation that the events of the trilogy have taken place in worlds parallel to 'Earth Prime' which itself has only just been affected by the doll plague. In the context of the trilogy as a whole, however, this does not signal a new beginning but rather a return to the beginning of the cycle. Calder has not rooted his mapping of the cyborg in histories of fascistic male power structures and their culmination in the technologies of capitalism just to dismiss them in the end. The ending of *Dead Things*, therefore, becomes a way of rationalising the trilogy's problematic representation of male violence which, even while critiquing it, also reaffirms it.

Calder ends his cycle at its beginning to enact the processes by which history is revealed as inescapably governed by masculine necrophiliac desires and an obsession with death. *Dead Girls* is not a break with the past but an archaeology of the destructive desires at work in history and the necrophiliac pleasures it produces. While the Human Front maintain that it is the dolls, like Eve, who have introduced evil and perverse desire into culture, the novel itself suggests that it is the Human Front and the forces that shaped it which is 'in love with pain and death' (*Girls*, p. 91). The novel's narrative also hints at this. From the perspective of the twenty-first century, Primavera and Ignatz attempt to understand the source of the doll plague through an investigation of historical moments. Initially they see it as part of a postmodern capitalist struggle between old capitalism (Europe) and new capitalism (Thailand), but gradually, as more is revealed, they work back through modernity (the gynoids as viral carriers), the Enlightenment (Toxicophilous programming the Cartier automata with the virus) to the Medieval period which produced the desires and fears that Toxicophilous programmed into the doll matrix. In effect, although the novel maps changing patterns of desire (the aestheticised desire of the Enlightenment automata, the industrial, unfettered desire of the modern gynoid and the perverse, parasitic and necrophiliac desire of the postmodern doll), the novel suggests that nothing has actually changed: desire has always been perverse, parasitic and necrophiliac. The cyborg does not presage a break with history and its masculine ideologies, as Haraway suggests, but offers instead a way of re-reading history to reveal that the past will create the future and masculine power systems will be there to contain the transgressive desires of the female cyborg. The cyborg does not announce the death of history but its confirmation. *Dead Boys* and *Dead Things* confirm this and overturn the suggestion in *Dead Girls* that the doll virus will cause the extinction of both male and female by showing that male and female will survive in the future and that it will be business as usual.

NOTES

1. Bruce Sterling, *Schismatrix* (New York: Ace Books, 1985); *Crystal Express* (London: Arrow Books, 1991).
2. See Stephen Neale, 'Issues of Difference: *Alien and Blade Runner*', in James Donald (ed.), *Fantasy and the Cinema* (London: BFI, 1989), pp. 216–20 for a discussion of the replicants as 'more human than human'.
3. Richard Calder, *Dead Girls* (London: HarperCollins, 1992). Hereafter referred to in citations as *Girls* with page number.
4. Richard Calder, *Dead Boys* (London: HarperCollins, 1994) and *Dead Things* (London: HarperCollins, 1996). Hereafter referred to in citations as *Boys* and *Things* with page number.
5. Richard Calder, 'Mosquito', in John Clute et al., *Interzone: The Fifth Anthology* (London: Hodder and Stoughton, 1991), pp. 128–45.
6. See Georges Canguilheim, 'Machine and Organism', in Jonathan Crary and Stanford Kwinter (eds), *Incorporations* (Cambridge, Mass: MIT Press, 1992), p. 52, for a discussion of Cartesian vitalist discourses of the 'living machine'.
7. See K. Eric Drexler, *Engines of Creation: The Coming Age of Nanotechnology* (London: Fourth Estate, 1990).
8. The T-1000 in *Terminator 2* (James Cameron, 1991) is an example of a nanoengineered cyborg, his programme existing in every molecule, thereby allowing him to recombine or modify his shape as his programme determines.
9. Barbara Creed, *The Monstrous-Feminine: Film, Feminism, Psychoanalysis* (London and New York: Routledge, 1993), p. 61.
10. Sue Best, 'Sexualising Space', in Elizabeth Grosz and Elspeth Probyn (eds), *Sexy Bodies: The Strange Carnalities of Feminism* (London and New York: Routledge, 1995), p. 187, original emphases.
11. Andrew Tudor, *Monsters and Mad Scientists: A Cultural History of the Horror Movie* (Oxford: Blackwell, 1989), p. 137.
12. N. Katherine Hayles, 'The Life Cycle of Cyborgs: Writing the Posthuman', in Chris Hable Gray (ed.), *The Cyborg Handbook* (New York and London: Routledge, 1995), p. 322.
13. Donna Haraway, *Simians, Cyborgs, and Women: The Reinvention of Nature* (London: Free Association Books, 1991), p. 163.
14. Donna Haraway, 'When Man™ is on the Menu' in Crary and Kwinter, *Incorporations*, p. 42.
15. Haraway, *Simians*, p. 170.
16. Mary Douglas, *Purity and Danger: An Analysis of the Concepts of Pollution and Taboo* (Harmondsworth: Penguin, 1970), p. 48.
17. Scott Bukatman, *Terminal Identity: The Virtual Subject in Postmodern Science Fiction* (Durham, NC and London: Duke University Press, 1993), p. 303.

7

Post-feminist Futures in Film Noir

BARBARA KENNEDY

SYNAESTHESIA, JOUISSANCE AND NEW MODELS IN FILM THEORY

This chapter intentionally weaves contradictory philosophical positions culled from French Feminist psychoanalysis, through post-modern cyberdiscourses, in an exploration of the condition which is and is not the logic of twentieth century capitalism. I intend to explore how such philosophical paradigms may provide useful scenarios for a reconsideration of the erotogenics of the filmic experience and, most specifically, film noir. I use the term 'experience' rather than spectatorship as I wish to contend that screen culture, particularly in a contemporary scenario, articulates more than just the pleasures of scopophilia and voyeurism. Identities and subjectivities are experienced, created or negated through wider affective and sensual frameworks outside the notions of vision and the gaze. Nonetheless, vision, the scopic and the fetishistic are still paramount within such debates. Terminology such as 'female' inevitably foregrounds a discourse premised upon structuralist and epistemological oppositions. One immediate contradiction might be that this chapter, although purporting to offer new models in film theory, invites simultaneously a negation of the universal categories which therefore delegitimates any political conclusions around gendered subjectivity.

My defence is that my intention is not to offer an empiricist position within feminist politics, but rather, following on from Rosi Braidotti and Teresa de Lauretis, to open up, liberate and rearticulate post-feminist and contradictory considerations within debates around the active dynamics of female pleasure, desire, fetishisation,

126

love, melancholy and the synaesthesia of *jouissance*. *Jouissance*, abstractly speaking, becomes the 'temporary' pleasure afforded by our recognition of otherness, the undifferentiated. Along with death, *jouissance* lies outside the confines of any knowable construct; it lies outside positionality within the realms of the unfixed, the infinite, the fragmented, the dispersed, one might say, to quote Kristeva, the 'abject'. Indeed, it is the abject which fascinates desire. Kristeva writes, in *Powers of Horror*, of abjection's effect on subjectivity: '[w]e may call it a border; abjection is above all ambiguity. Because, while releasing a hold, it does not radically cut off the subject from what threatens it. On the contrary, abjection acknowledges it to be in perpetual danger'.[1]

The pleasures which are *jouissancial* lie not within the text, but, as Roland Barthes has indicated, at the 'conjuncture with the reader'.[2] Histories of Capitalism and Christianity have positioned pleasure outside the boundaries of the acceptable while pleasure has offered an arena for the transgression of dominant ideological constructions of the self and the role of the self(ves) within culture. Indeed, Bakhtin's theory of the carnivalesque is an exploration of the transgressive potential of the pleasures of the popular, outside the legitimate discourse of bourgeois culture.[3] *Jouissance* may be defined as pleasures, bliss, ecstasy or orgasm, experienced through the heightened sensualities that connect it to human nature rather than to culture. *Jouissance*, then, lies outside of culture; the signified is distanced from materiality. Rather, *jouissance* may be located in the sensuality of the body of the reader. It is perpetually erotodynamic, it climaxes as orgasm at the moment culture breaks down. The sensualities of the body lie outside subjectivity, the pleasures lie outside any fixed positions of subject and the construction of the subject within culture by ideology. Thus, the intention of this chapter is to explore where *jouissance*, flowing as it does as an undifferentiated stream, resides in the cyberotic discourses, specifically in relation to cinematic experiences. If *jouissance* lies without, outside of culture, within the abjection of the other, such loss is experienced in the body as a loss of subjectivities/objectivities. It is within the fluidity of the process, the liquidity of the dynamics of the process, that *jouissance* is experienced.

Woman's role as fetishist has been socially and culturally delegitimated and marginalised, but female fetishism has much to offer in a postmodern landscape where desire and pleasure offer transgressional potentialities. Mary Douglas has argued that culture has maintained a purity of ideas within which the sacred and the profane have been upheld within binary discourses in Western epistemology. Such binary oppositions about sexual difference are breached through a valorisation of the female fetishist. Cyberotics enables an articulation of theories around film spectatorship not focused solely upon representation, the mode through which spectatorship has until now been considered. French Feminist ideas, through a remodelling of psychoanalytic categories, reposition female desire and female libido outside of fixed positions through a non-positionality of *jouissance*. In collaboration with cyberdiscourses emanating from postmodern considerations of challenges to epistemological universals, we can accommodate a new theoretical cyberscape for a journey through the discourses of psychoanalysis: Freudian, Lacanian, French Feminism and postmodernism, discourses upheld as non-compatible and contradictory. The intention of this chapter is to offer a set of interconnecting discourses, through which to discover a *jouissance* outside the phallic closure of a linear and phallic text. Irigaray's epistemology is pertinent to this multiplicity of debates. Like Deleuze and Guattari, Irigaray sees the Lacanian prioritising of the phallus within the Symbolic Order as insignificant to a desire which lies outside the dichotomies of opposition. Deleuze and Guattari relocate desire outside any notion of a sentient subject. Indeed, their work has provided new and exciting possibilities for film theory premised on the materiality of the film as matter and desire as processual.[4]

Female sexuality, desire and pleasure have traditionally been framed within masculine parameters. Woman's sexual pleasure has been perceived within a masculine paradigm whereby pleasure is encoded within the traditional masculine 'clitoral activity' or the female 'vaginal passivity'. Woman's erotic and erotogenic zones have been negated, her pleasure repressed within a male economy based upon her position as 'lack' within the Symbolic Order. Psychoanalysis in Freudian and Lacanian stasis has merely proliferated a discourse premised upon woman'-as-lack' whereas French Feminist psychoanalysis has opened up a consideration of female pleasure outside such constructs.

FRAMEWORKS, FETISHISM AND FRENCH FEMINISMS

Feminist film criticism throughout the 1980s sought to define an arena for thinking about female subjectivity, desire, phantasy and pleasure within the merely 'scopic' articulations of the cinematic.

Laura Mulvey's position in her seminal 1975 article 'Visual Pleasure and Narrative Cinema'[5] has been challenged and criticised by a new wave of post-feminist film discourse which seeks to articulate, through the work of Irigaray, Kristeva and Cixous, a theory of pleasure for the female spectator. Their writing takes both Freudian and Lacanian psychoanalysis as a starting point for an exploration of pleasure which lies outside phallocentrism. The Laws of Castration and Sexual difference have been unchanging organising principles of Western patriarchy, but the work of these French Feminists has provided an attempt to remodel the underlying phallocentrism of psychoanalysis.[6] Their work offered a consideration of 'difference' as liberatory. The 'politics of differenciation' offers women liberating and radical ways of interpreting meaning, different from and alternative to classical phallocentric discourses of which 'gaze theory' is essentially a part. As Josette Feral has said: '[t]he task of woman remains to inscribe in the social body, not so much difference itself as a multiplicity of differences'.[7] French Feminists then, have consistently negated Enlightenment epistemology and Cartesian philosophy. Cartesian ideas were premised upon binary thinking whereby ideas may only have validity in contrast with an opposite; for example: male/female, animal/machine. Such binary thinking is too restrictive and formulaic to sustain a process of thought which is more fluid, mobile, contingent. Similarly, humanism, and with it the 'role of the artist' have been questioned and critiqued. French feminist theory allows us to rewrite the female erotic outside the binary logic of phallocratic discourse. *Jouissance* is attainable outside the oppositional discourses within a framework of differences. Thus we can move towards a model of a new economy in terms of pleasures, desire and erotogenics. Women undoubtedly do fetishise. However, their fetishism is not necessarily scopic, but based upon tactility, as Luce Irigaray states in *This Sex which is not One*.[8] Such an acceptance of female fetishism challenges the very signifier of desire. Any concept of penis envy is an attempt by man to deny the possibility that women might have another form or other forms of desire. The negation of the phallus as signifier of desire would, according to Cixous, also open up an economy of desire to men too. She writes: 'by allowing woman to speak of her pleasure would phallocentrise the body, relieve man of the phallus, return him to an erogenous zone and libido that isn't organised around that monument, but appears shifting, diffused, taking on all the others of oneself'.[9]

Through French Feminist theory women can claim a temporality, a space, a subjectivity or a look to reclaim and demarginalise women. However, to suggest a binary opposite to the 'male gaze' theory is merely to replicate patriarchal binaries and further marginalise the feminine. What is significant about French Feminist theory is the articulation of a 'politics of difference' based upon pleasure, the female libidinal economy, rather than confrontation.

CYBEROTICS AND CYBERSPACE: THE JOUISSANCE IN THE CYBORG

If postmodernist theory is going to offer useful arenas for feminisms, one of its major considerations will be in supporting heterogeneity. In a cultural climate where multi-media and cybernetic technologies proliferate our everyday experiences from digitalised financial transactions to audio-visual, sensorial experiences of video games, virtual reality and cyberspacial simulations, what future is there for a post-feminism no longer positioned within the radical politics of feminism *per se*? Indeed, how can those of us who have accepted feminist theories over several decades now begin to see liberatory arenas which lie outside conventional paradigms with political positionings? The term 'cyberfeminism' is an articulation of a new form of language and philosophy which offers alternatives to those Enlightenment ideas of subject, identity and selfhood, and as such is more liberatory than an epistemology based upon phallocentric systems of language. Phallocratic discourses, through an Enlightenment tradition, have remained dichotomous with the female always considered as other. Such ideas are well known in feminist critique. The postmodern landscape allows for a valorisation of the fractal, the non-linear, for organicity rather than linearity, through a new visualisation encoded through computer technologies which have enabled us to see what the human senses cannot. Consequently, we have developed a new evaluation and respect for chaos theory within which non-linearity displaces positionality and binary thinking through a respect for the random and the fractal. The media, and specifically digitally-controlled media, offer a viral immixture whereby the image becomes almost a virus; contingent, dynamic, dissolutory and disseminatory. Television images become reality, there is dissolution of television into life and, I would argue, of the filmic experience into life.

The media are thus no longer extensions of man/woman, but, instead, the human body/mind has become an extension of them, through a 'terminal of networks'.[10] A terminal culture where digitality replaces tactility, where the sensual 'tactility' of the feminine has been eclipsed into a synaesthetic cyberscape with flows of multiple, distilled and fragmented data. Cyberspace, and along with it cyberfeminism, offers the dissolution of ontological boundaries. How then is this seen as valid to a post-feminist project within film spectatorship? One of the main concerns of any valorisation of postmodernist pretensions for women and feminists has been what potential there might be for a breakdown of patriarchal myths and trajectories. Cyberfeminism, in its articulation and development of a new language premised on difference and affinity, not on identity and opposition, far from appropriating phallocentric structures within culture, breaks down these boundaries which have maintained oppositional discourses in favour of polysemy. Meaning emanates from difference. Cyberfeminism offers a new exploration of the 'subject' through new subjectivities, new identities and new affinities. Chela Sandoval envisages a postmodern culture where there is a new consideration not so much of the notion of 'identity' but of 'affinity' through what she refers to as 'oppositional consciousness'.[11] Oppositional consciousness is perceived as a fusion of identities, a fractured postmodern identity which is characterised through negation. As Donna Haraway has suggested, 'one may be confined to an identity but may choose an affinity'.[12]

However, the term cyberfeminism must be explained in terms of its technological roots. 'Cyber' as a prefix is used to denote almost anything in our contemporary technological information society. The society of the spectacle becomes the society of the digital from cyberkids to cyberpunk (and even cybermomas – which seems a contradiction in terms, since the term 'cyber' distanciates the fixity of terms like mother, in itself replete with stereotypical and essentialist concepts). The prefix is replete with connotations of control and empowerment. Derived from the Greek word for pilot, its Hellenic origins reflect Greek traditions of independence and self-reliance. Timothy Leary talks of the 'cyberbreed' thus: '[s]elf assured singularities of the cyberbreed have been called Mavericks, ronin, free lancers, independents, self-starters, non-conformist, oddballs, troublemakers, kooks, visionaries, iconoclasts, insurgents, blue-sky thinnners, loners, smartallecks . . . clever, creative, entrepreneurial, imaginative, resourceful, talented, eccentric'.[13]

Donna Haraway's work is perhaps the most significant in terms of the development of cyberdiscourse and cyberfeminism. Her 'Cyborg Manifesto' is particularly important as a critique of epistemological dichotomies and its call for new identities through what she refers to as 'cyborg heteroglossia'. Her work offers a 'utopian re-definition of the "cyborg" as a figure that might elude the racial, gendered or class-based dichotomies of western culture'.[14] Her call for a cyborg politics poses the possibility of technological symbiosis as a progressive alternative rather than a simple masculine fantasy of 'natural' mastery and domination. She explores two specific scenarios which are useful for developing new ideas which may be used in determining new models of spectatorship for feminist and post-feminist film theory. Firstly, the valorisation of non-fixity around subject/object positionings allows for a reconsideration of spectatorial positions in terms of the viewing subject. Secondly, the image of the cyborg provides both a symbolic and literal figure of transgression and subversion particularly pertinent to a feminist politics.

An attempt to offer a contribution to a socialist feminist culture while simultaneously challenging Enlightenment epistemologies, Haraway designates her work as an 'oppositional utopian myth for socialist feminists'.[15] The manifesto endeavours to contribute to cultural theory within a postmodernist and post-structuralist landscape by considering the significance, within an advanced technological society, of the interrelationship between humankind and machine, together with a consideration of cyborg manifestations literally, metaphorically and symbolically. The image of the cyborg offers an alternative to male or female in that, firstly, it is genderless and, secondly, not entirely human: 'a cyborg is a cybernetic organism, a hybrid of machine and organism, a creature of social reality as well as a creature of fiction'.[16] As an oppositional myth, Haraway's cyborg has no place of origin or sense of Western creation and, as such, challenges Western humanist myths of original unity, wholeness and sanctity (found in the master discourses of Marxism and psychoanalysis). She presents a rejection of Enlightenment ideas of duality: man/animal, organism/machine, physical/spiritual, male/female. This non-positionality, Haraway claims, **is** a position that 'feminists must code'.[17] Thus, for feminism, there is the possibility of a liberation from notions of opposition into an arena of heterogeneity, difference, multiplicity and transgression: 'nature and culture are reworked, the one can no longer be the resource for the appropriation by the other'.[18] Haraway therefore sees the cyborg myth as offering the possibility of transgression of established boundaries.

The refusal of the old nineteenth-century debates then is based upon the technological revolution within which the digital and the electronic are significant and within which the integrated circuit provides for the locus of analysis. We are already 'cyborgs' given that the industrial world of the nineteenth century has been replaced by a twentieth century global system of domination, whereby all those dualisms that I mentioned earlier have become entwined and indistinguishable. The cyborg becomes an image of our imaginations and our realities. The question then is, how do such philosophical underpinnings relate to our experiences of filmic culture? Given that the traditions of Western politics and science have been predominantly white, male and middle class with a concern with the 'self' and the 'subject' and the 'autonomy of the self', Haraway's manifesto for the transgression of such ideas provides a useful framework for filmic analysis.

CYBERSPACIAL STRUCTURATIONS IN FILMIC SPECTATORSHIP

Cyberspace exists as a malleable arena of fluid and evanescent data structures where diachronic time is accounted for in nanoseconds. Spatially it exists both invisibly and globally. It accommodates a 'womb-like' environment, according to cyberculturalist Doug Rushkoff, with its series of passageways and pathways providing a cocooning through which new forms of socialisation are taking place.[19] Films like *Blade Runner* (Ridley Scott, 1982) and neo- and tech-noir films like *Romeo is Bleeding* (Peter Medak, 1993) and *Natural Born Killers* (Oliver Stone, 1994) may be read as consisting of a series of interfaces between the human subject(s), cyberspaces and terminal spaces, thus providing new terminal identities. Terminal identity may be explained as a double articulation in which we find the end of the subject and also a new subjectivity(ies), new identities and new affinities. William Gibson, in a short story entitled 'Burning Chrome', uses the metaphors of new technologies to express the indeterminate and fragmented nature of the self. This is demonstrated through the idea of a hologram, which he calls the 'Fragments of a Hologram Rose':

> A hologram has this quality, recovered and illuminated
> each fragment will reveal the whole image of the rose.
> Falling toward delta, he sees himself the rose, each of his
> scattered fragments revealing a whole he'll never know . . .
> but each fragment reveals the rose from a different angle . . .[20]

In popular cultural texts, when we as humans interact with media technologies, the process consists of more than just adding machinic or robotic prostheses to the human form. Rather, it involves a splitting, a fragmentation or a distillation of the self much as Gibson's metaphorical hologram rose, outside notions of the Cartesian self. Human subjectivity, while not totally abandoned, is irretrievably altered in a fractal erosion of its 'oneness'. Much of my recent work has therefore been an exploration of Hollywood movies with particular reference to current noir and neo-noir thrillers. Postmodern theories project a concern with the blurring of boundaries; the boundaries between popular and high culture have been legitimately eroded and transgressed. The conventions of classical generic categories no longer hold legitimation within a contextual framework that rejects, transgresses and subverts boundary distinctions. Film noir becomes horror, horror becomes science fiction. Feminist film theory has traditionally been premised upon a negation of classical Hollywood narrative which, according to some writers, has prioritised pleasure in masculine terms. The scopic regime has been evinced through a consideration of the male gaze. Within postmodern theory, several arenas seem to have significance outside of 'gaze theory'. The body, space, dance, movement, performance, style and fluidity provide new paradigms for spectatorial desires. Such theories are located within postmodern and cyborgian politics. What I am offering is a new way of thinking about the pleasures of the Hollywood movie through discourses of cyborg theory, through reconsidering dance, movement and embodiment. Susan Bordo, commenting on Derrida, has said that: 'metaphors of dance and movement have replaced the ontologically fixing stare of the motionless spectator. The lust for finality is banished. The dream is of "incalculable choreographies" not just the distant mirrorings of nature from the heights of nowhere'.[21]

The body thus becomes an epistemological metaphor for our locatedness and within cyborg theory offers a consideration of shifting subject/object positioning in relation to the filmic text. The cyborg invites us to take pleasure in the confusion of boundaries. In the fragmentation of the notion of the 'self', we can run, dance, play, our sensualities within and outside of the text. The cyborg offers us cultural polyvocality. In other words, there is a multiplicity of spaces, locations and voices through which we can explore cultural formations through theory. We can trace the cyborg, her/him/it, through filmic and media texts from *Metropolis*

(Fritz Lang, 1926) to Madonna. Madonna's music video *Justify My Love* embodies a range of sexual personae: the mythological trickster is both Madonna and not Madonna, inviting and providing pleasures for the audience across a wide range of sexual orientations. The dance becomes the trickster; the trickster becomes the dance, as Carol Smith-Rosenberg writes: 'the trickster is of indeterminate sex and changeable gender who continually alters his/her body, creates and recreates a personality . . . and floats across time from period to period and place to place'.[22]

I want now to exemplify much of this theory with reference to several contemporary films. It seems that during the late 1980s and 1990s there has been a proliferation of neo-noir or après-noir films formulated within the generic cycles and conventions of the traditional Hollywood noir movement of the 1940s and 1950s.[23] My choice of contemporary tech-noir, horror, and science fiction for analysis is within the framework of ongoing research, and attempts to relocate new paradigms in feminist film theory. Films such as *Damage* (Louis Malle, 1992), *Body of Evidence* (Uli Edel, 1992), *The Hand That Rocks the Cradle* (Curtis Hanson, 1992), *Fatal Attraction* (Adrian Lyne, 1987), *Single White Female* (Barbet Shroeder, 1992), *Sliver* (Philip Noyce, 1993) and *Romeo is Bleeding* offer women wider pleasures outside the boundaries of phallocratic and modernist notions of identity. New pleasures may be experienced by reading these films through the politics of French Feminist and cyberfeminist discourses with a concern for a 'politics of difference' rather than confrontation. Criticism of this work will inevitably be targeted at my use of contradictory discourses. My defence is to argue for theoretical positionings which do not locate fixed ideas but heterogeneously combine oppositional discourses in a system of non-synchronicity. Women may claim subjectivities which demarginalise them from patriarchal positions of oppression. To suggest binary opposites to the male gaze is purely to perpetuate patriarchal discourse. What I want to propose here is an aesthetics of heterogeneity rather than confrontation. This will ultimately displace or relocate the 'politics of representation'.[24]

ABJECTION, LOVE AND MELANCHOLY: WHY ROMEO IS STILL BLEEDING!

How do theoretical perspectives such as the above have any validity within spectatorship of a film like *Romeo is Bleeding*? Like Bataille, Kristeva emphasises the attraction as well as the horror of the undifferentiated. The undifferentiated, as I have indicated, may be encapsulated within what we might call the 'cyberotic'. How then is the cyberotic experienced in *Romeo is Bleeding*?

Peter Medak's film has Jack Grimaldi (played by Gary Oldman) as a New York cop intrigued with the world of double-dealing gangsters and their illegitimate rewards. In his inevitable search for identity, Jack is ensnared along the way by the charms and machinations of the traditional femme fatale, Mona (Lena Olin). He is caught up within a tripartite relationship with three women, each of whom becomes a parallel, within a field of feminine identities.[25] This array of feminine identities confuses and disorientates Jack's fixed and phallocratic masculinity to the point of madness.

The film reads as a contemporary parody of traditional film noir conventions. Parodic signifiers include the exaggerated ironical voice-over, which permeates the text. As a New York cop, Jack gets involved in double-dealing and double-crossing in his desire to feed the 'hole', a hideaway where he deposits cash for his future 'dreams'. His double-dealings with Mona (Lena Olin) and Don Falcone (Scheider) provide the narrative trajectory of the plot. *Romeo* is epitomised through Jack's involvement with women: Natalie (Anabella Sciorra), his dutiful, submissive but dangerously bored wife, Sherry (Juliette Lewis), his childlike and alluring mistress and Mona, the cyborgian fatale. In terms of literal representation, Mona is cyborgian in that she is both woman and machine in several ways which relate to Haraway's depictions. Both in literal and metaphorical terms she serves to both confirm and yet disorientate traditional signifiers of the femme fatale.[26] She is both woman and machine: woman in the sense that she feels, as a fleshly orientated human entity, the wound from a gunshot which obviously causes immense pain and suffering. She is machine in her dislocated and static body movements, angular, cold, hard and mechanistic in several sequences, for example, in the dance at the end of the film. At the same time, she lacks the polymorphous fluidity of Sherry's rhythmic dance movements. This is, however, parodied by the flash forward to the nightmare sequence which juxtaposes the femme fatale, Mona, to the 'good wife'.

The contrasting pleasures of movement, musical notation and tactility offer a range of scenarios for the female spectator. Mona oscillates between both positive and negative trajectories. Jack's private little dance on the rooftops emphasises his auto-eroticism and, narratively, his apparent role as trickster and manipulator. This is set into disequilibrium by the multiple fascinations of the female protagonists, Mona, Sherry and Natalie. Jack's dance on the lawn with Natalie very soon becomes the nightmare scenario within which he is unable to maintain positionality. Both Natalie and Mona are juxtaposed, neither is singular, and they serve to disorientate Jack's sense of his own masculinity and sexuality. Within this sequence the pleasures are narratively expressed in that Natalie is controlling the gaze, and this symbolically has phallic associations of power. She holds her camera up to 'shoot' Jack, while Mona holds up a gun, again a signifier of both the phallus and power, mocking and threatening, in parodic fashion, to shoot Jack. Natalie with her camera and Mona with her gun thus serve to destabilise Jack's masculinity and identity. Both camera and gun symbolise the gaze, the scopic manifestations of power over a fetishised image of woman, here reversed. Jack's power is relinquished.

In one specific sequence Jack imagines, through a nightmare hallucination, a fearful encounter with the cyborg/Mona. Within this sequence, both women become Madonna and whore, neither is prioritised. Mona takes centre frame surrounded by a multiplicity of characters from sadomasochistic fantasies and fetishistic pleasures. Colours and textures from red silk to black fur provide pleasurable sensations. The music here has very quickly changed from child-hood dream-like chords to discordant and grating rhythms. The body of the viewer is bombarded with a cacophony of pleasures. Fluctuating camera angles project Jack's increasing sense of disori-entation. This sequence is then followed by Sherry's exhibitionist display which is erotically charged and voyeuristically shot so that the scene serves to re-establish Jack's voyeuristic control. However, the pleasures of the scopophilic gaze here are neither male nor female but genderless. The music, rhythm and sensuality of the *mise-en-scène* allow for a pleasurable engagement with fluctuating subject and object positionings. Jack's dance with Mona finally has him relinquishing all power. Mona encapsulates cyberotic control through body language, style and fetishistic pleasure.

Dance, within the narrative diegesis of *Romeo is Bleeding*, func-tions as a dynamic for tactility and sensuality outside the scopic regime of classic film theory. Similarly, in other noir movies, for example *Basic Instinct* (Paul Verhoeven, 1992), dance functions as an arena for *jouissancial* pleasures. In *Basic Instinct*, it serves as a display of the fluidity of desire and an escape from positionality, in terms of object/subject positionings. In the dance sequence in the disco in the film there is an immense diegetical display of eroticism for the female spectator across a range of object/subject position-alities. The central protagonists, Catherine (Sharon Stone) and Nick (Michael Douglas), are in a disco with Catherine's lesbian partner Roxy. Within the narrative, this sequence comes as a climactic sce-nario to the shifting power games played between Catherine and Nick. Catherine has played with, cajoled and disorientated Nick's masculinity throughout the film. She teases and allures, like the femme fatale of 1940s noir, but consistently maintains control in a cat and mouse detective game. The game is a metaphor for the psy-choanalytical Law of the Father, the Symbolic Order of patriarchy and the Law of Society (Nick as cop) with an emphatic structuring of 'order' out of chaos.

Nick's constant frustration, both physically and intellectually, has been played upon by Catherine. Metaphors of movement and dance are a means of replacing that fixed stare of the voyeuristic gaze, through a matrixial web of intensities and speeds. This pro-vides a multiplicitous sensuality through movement, rhythm and tactility, evinced in the *jouissance* of the female away from the politics of the 'look'. The 'lust' for a final, fixed identity is replaced with a Derridean desire for detachment and disembodiment. There is in *Basic Instinct* a celebration of the feminine ability to enter into the perspectives of others, to accept change and fluidity as features of a 'reality'. The pleasure lies in the confusion of boundaries. Thus, as women, we may be able to choreograph our own *jouissance* through the metaphors of cyborg heteroglossia. In the fragments of the self, we dance, run and play our sensualities within, across and beyond the confines of the text. The literal dance sequence then provides pleasures for the female spectatrix through visual, tactile, sensual, aural and cyberotic methods.[27]

Similarly, in *Romeo is Bleeding* dance serves to allow for sensual experiencing of a visual text through the *jouissance* of cyberotics. We are introduced to the narrative through a deserted landscape, haunted only by a strange music, silence, disorientation. Along with more contemporary films like *Basic Instinct, Sliver, Body of Evidence* and *Single White Female, Romeo is Bleeding* offers an experience outside the stereotypical representations of 1940s and 1950s noir films. The femme fatale has something more sinister. She has emerged out of and beyond the 'monstrous feminine', the 'abject', within which lies a new philosophical arena for the consideration of non-fixed gendered identities and subjectivities. Representational debates within traditional feminist film theory would consider the role of the femme fatale as the crucial criterion of consideration.

138

Such critique might indicate a perceived 'negative' portrayal of woman, as Mulvey indicates, as stereotypically encoded with to-be-looked-at-ness, fetishised, contained and appropriated within the phallic Symbolic Order by virtue of her appearance: tight black clothes, stockings, stilettos and the inevitable cigarette. Such critique negates a female fetishistic pleasure in the sensuality of exhibitionism, tactility and display that the film offers, specifically in the climactic escape scene and, as indicated earlier, the dance sequences. Dot Tuer discusses the significance of the pleasures of the exhibitionist in woman's *jouissance*: '[i]f women display femininity perhaps it is not masquerade they are constructing, but a simple direct access to pleasure through exhibitionism'.[28]

In the escape sequence from *Romeo is Bleeding* we can explore the fluctuating pleasures of object/subject oscillation. In this sequence, where is the pleasure for the female spectatrix? Mona is captured, shot in the arm and bound by Jack, and thrown into the back of his limousine, because she tried to double-cross him. While driving the car away from the dockland where this sequence takes place, Mona writhes and struggles to escape, only to use the rope to then attempt to strangle Jack while he is driving.

Filth and defilement exist at the borders of identities. Mona's metamorphosis from a classically dressed, demure and pure image is fragmented through this scene in which she is transformed outside of the gendered body, through the signifiers of filth, defilement, blood and strangulation, the threat of death and mutilation. Her arm is destroyed through the ravages of Jack's gun, she writhes uncontrollably, an image of undifferentiation, transgression and horror. Psychoanalysis here provides an interesting frame of reference to the phallic reconstructions through signifiers of arms, guns and their interrelationship. However, psychoanalysis is too reductionist in its spaces for exploration of the pleasures of the text. The sequence continues with her vengeance, obtained through similar horrific conventions, until she ultimately breaks through the screen, not only of the car windscreen, but also the fixed position as gendered female. Hence, *jouissance* in the cyborg. Contemporary critique through an engagement with cyborg discourse would suggest that within the monstrous-feminine lies a creature outside gendered positioning, outside abjection, within the cyberotic, which encapsulates the fluctuating fetishistic desires: neither male nor female, but cyborgian.

In *Powers of Horror*, Kristeva articulates the similarity of three familiar structurations of subjectivity or emotional states. Such

139

states are symptomatic of a twentieth-century *fin-de-siècle* existence: horror, love and melancholy. All three are evident in *Romeo is Bleeding*. The mythical tale of sixteenth-century courtly love and melancholy that was *Romeo and Juliet* is transformed into a post-modern landscape where ideological categories of gender and subjectivity are no longer fixed or static. The real becomes the image; the image the real: the simulacra of a viral immixture. In one sequence in the film, Jack is confronted with an imaginary scenario, trapped in the domestic kitchen, with the two faces of the monstrous feminine: Natalie the wife, Mona the cyborgian fatale. His dream is both real and unreal; his wife is mythical whore, madonna and trickster, as is Mona juxtaposed, while simultaneously the cyberotic. Neither can be immobilised for the fixed stare of the spectator. Both are fluctuating and morphologically transient identities, dancing across fixed object and subject positions, in relation to which Jack tries to accommodate some sense of his own experience. The pleasure for the female spectatrix lies in the matrixial web of choreographed spaces of engagement, through the non-positionality of Mona/Natalie. The mythical, romantic tale of *Romeo and Juliet* displays within its ideological and narrative spaces the horror, love and melancholy that exist in a simulacra of twentieth-century experiences. *Romeo is Bleeding* may be read as an exploration of classic mythology around masculine/feminine identities within *Romeo and Juliet*: the nature of romantic love; the hero, the seducer and the transgressor of all such positions of masculine identity. However, such a reading reduces the text to a humanist exploration of Enlightenment ideas. Gary Oldman's role as Jack Grimaldi shows Romeo cajoled, parodied and ultimately powerless and bleeding through his experiences with not the new Eve but the new Juliet. Juliet no longer resides outside the binary closure of self and other, but she epitomises the abject non-positionality of gender or sexuality, thus cyberotically destabilising fixed gender positions, particularly masculinity. Hence, by the end of the film, Romeo truly is still bleeding!

In conclusion, the intention of this chapter has been to open up feminist film criticism from its traditional staging within humanist debate and to engage with critical theory in a multi-discursive choreography, a cyborgian heteroglossia which explores wider scenarios of social/psychological and cybernetic identities and subjectivities. Those spaces have only just appeared – beyond the confines of conspiratorial images and representational discourses lies a new and post-feminist engagement for film theory with the intensities of movement, dynamism and vitalism; a post-feminist engagement which destabilises the subject and argues for a micro-political and contingent situated ethics of film theory.

NOTES

1. Julia Kristeva, *Powers of Horror: An Essay on Abjection*, Leon S. Roudiez (trans.) (New York: Columbia University Press, 1982), p. 9.
2. Roland Barthes quoted in John Fiske, *Television Culture* (New York: Methuen, 1987), p. 228.
3. See Mikhail Bakhtin quoted in Fiske, *Television*, p. 100.
4. The author wishes to acknowledge that her work has undergone new and challenging directions through an engagement with Deleuzian philosophy and new structures of desire which are not located in representation: the 'politics of difference' emerging from this chapter is replaced with a 'politics of becoming'. See Barbara Kennedy, *Deleuze and Cinema: The Erotics of Sensation* (Edinburgh University Press, forthcoming) and chapters in I. Buchanan, (ed.), *Deleuze and Feminism* (Edinburgh University Press, 1998).
5. See Laura Mulvey, 'Visual Pleasure and Narrative Cinema', *Visual and Other Pleasures* (London: Macmillan, 1989), pp. 14–26.
6. See Toril Moi, *Sexual/Textual Politics* (Oxford: Polity, 1985).
7. Josette Feral, 'Powers of Difference', in Hester Eisenstein and Alice Jardine, (eds), *The Future of Differences* (Boston: Hall, 1980), p. 88.
8. See Luce Irigaray, *This Sex which is not One*, Catherine Porter (trans.), 1977 (Ithaca, New York: Cornell University Press, 1985).
9. Hélène Cixous, 'Castration or Decapitation', Annette Kuhn (trans.), in *Signs*, 7(1) Autumn 1981: p. 51.
10. Jean Baudrillard, *The Ecstacy of Communication*, 1987 (New York: Semiotext(e), 1988), p. 16.
11. Chela Sandoval quoted in Donna Haraway, 'A Cyborg Manifesto', *Simians, Cyborgs, and Women* (London: Free Association Books, 1991), p. 155.
12. Haraway, 'Manifesto', p. 155.
13. Timothy Leary quoted in L. McCaffrey, *Storming the Reality Studio* (London: Duke University Press, 1991), p. 246.
14. Haraway, 'Manifesto', p. 156.
15. Haraway, 'Manifesto', p. 151.
16. Haraway, 'Manifesto', p. 149.
17. Haraway, 'Manifesto', p. 163.
18. Haraway, 'Manifesto', p. 151.
19. See the television documentary *Visions of Heaven and Hell*, 1997 (Leanne Klein and Mark Harrison, 1995).
20. William Gibson, *Burning Chrome* (New York: Ace Books, 1986), p. 42.
21. Susan Bordo, 'Feminism, Postmodernism and Gender-scepticism',

in Linda Nicholson (ed.), *Feminism/Postmodernism* (London: Routledge, 1990), p. 143.

22. Carol Smith-Rosenberg, *Disorderly Conduct* (Oxford: Open University Press, 1985), p. 291.

23. The terms après-noir and tech-noir are recent terms within film theory. Après-noir I here define as a description of contemporary films which display a cross-generic use of iconography blended from traditional noir, but located within contemporary post-industrial settings. *Romeo is Bleeding* is a good example. Tech-noir, similarly, is a term which describes the infusion, or coagulation of styles found within many contemporary movies. Such films as *The Fifth Element* (Luc Besson, 1997) or *Strange Days* (Kathryn Bigelow, 1995) display a wide array of such iconography as to be labelled tech-noir. Of course, *Terminator* (James Cameron, 1984) is the epitome of tech-noir movies.

24. See aforementioned (note 4) forthcoming work by author of this chapter which engages with Deleuzian concepts of immanence and becoming as ways of rethinking the experience of cinema outside of representation. It thus engages with philosophical concepts of affect, modulation, intensity and the materiality of the filmic process.

25. In Deleuzian terms, one of three 'lines of flight'.

26. See E. Ann Kaplan, *Women in Film Noir* (London: BFI, 1978).

27. The term 'spectatrix' with its feminine suffix 'ix' defines the specifically female spectator. The connotations of matrix/spectatrix/dominatrix imply an empowerment through a specifically fluid reading position.

28. Dot Tuer, 'Pleasures in the Dark: Sexual Difference and Erotic Dev-iance in an Articulation of Female Desire', in *Cineaction*, 10, 1987: p. 57.

8

Blood is the Drug: Narcophiliac Vampires in Recent Women's Fiction

ANNA POWELL

The connection between vampires and drugs is becoming more frequent in popular horror fictions. In Abel Ferrara's recent film *The Addiction* (1995), for example, it forms the central image and we see the newly made vampire, Kathryn, injecting herself with stolen blood. I will be exploring narcophiliac imagery in vampire novels by Poppy Z. Brite and Freda Warrington, highlighting thematic relations between vampirism and drug use and considering the implications of this recent foregrounding. Whereas Warrington favours traditional, historical romance for her tale of decadent desire, Brite uses a streetwise countercultural self-reflexivity in her novel of vampire degenerates, influenced by Goth youth culture. I will consider their representations of specific drugs as used by vampires or their acolytes and, in order to theorise the dynamics of these fantasy scenarios, I will draw on psychoanalytical concepts of intense pleasure, or *jouissance*, as delineated by Jacques Lacan.

The Gothic novel has a long tradition of eroticism displaced by dread, anxiety and taboo, and women writers have historically been amongst its foremost practitioners. Creative writing inspired by drug use, or overtly exploring the effects of narcotics, is still predominantly masculine, despite the growing numbers of women drug users, and countercultural gurus have been mainly men. This situation is currently changing, particularly in the USA where women writers of fiction, such as Kathy Acker, are counterculturally identified and explore previously taboo areas of experience. The

143

novelists I will be considering here use the displacement devices of Gothic to emphasise the allure of psychoactive drugs as well as the traditional sexual appeal of the vampire lover. Indeed, their descriptions of narcotic use are as libidinally cathected as the erotic scenes. Now that women horror novelists dominate the market, narcophiliac fantasy presents them with new challenges while maintaining generic parameters.

Although blood is the main drug used by vampires, they also partake of a variety of stimulants and hallucinogens, adding chemical combinations to their own bloodstreams. Mortal vampire-lovers are addicted to acts which drain them of their own blood and may involve receiving vampire blood in exchange. If this occurs, they are reborn into the immortality of Undeath. Certain vampires drink the blood of humans who have recently ingested drugs, which thus provides a doubly charged 'hit'. In *The Gilda Stories*, Jewelle Gomez describes her lesbian vampire hero, Gilda, drinking the blood of a young man who has just popped a pill: 'the drug that diluted his blood pulsed through Gilda's veins, light exploded in her head, and her breathing raced dangerously'.[1] As well as sharing the nourishment of the victim's life fluid, the vampire here samples drug-induced pleasure by proxy. This process is mirrored by the 'safe' reader who imaginatively shares the experience of drug ingestion by a fictional surrogate.

As Dracula's acolyte Renfield reminds us, blood is, literally and metaphorically, the life.[2] Religious symbolism of sacrifice and communion, as well as the shedding of blood in war, punishment and murder, have historically invested the substance with a potent mixture of desire and dread. Blood is also the habitat of viruses fatal to humans. The dangers of transmitting the AIDS virus through bodily fluids exchanged during unprotected sex and intravenous drug use are defied in fantasy by the vampire's relish for drinking blood directly from the host's veins. Sexual promiscuity and forbidden acts of perversion have traditionally been the vampire's operational field in the displaced imagery of the Gothic. That fantasies of blood-drinking have wide popularity and circulation underlines the transgressive function of the vampire figure for contemporary readers and viewers. To enjoy drinking blood laced with drugs adds increased impact to their breach of taboos.

The two novels I will focus on are Warrington's *A Taste of Blood Wine* and Brite's *Lost Souls*, both published in 1992.[3] They differ considerably in style and narrative structure and as adaptations of the vampire genre. They also evince specific generational attitudes towards their drug content. An established Sci-Fi/Fantasy writer, Warrington's Jungian approach to vampires as archetypes of the Collective Unconscious is explored in a sequel to *Blood Wine – The Dark Blood of Poppies*.[4] Her quotations from early 1970s rock lyrics, by Fleetwood Mac and Horslips, plus her use of LSD as preferred drug scenario (albeit masked as cocaine and opium) place her attitude within late 1960s/early 1970s hippy contexts; while her style is laden with transcendental and mystical imagery – glittering crystals, kaleidoscope patterns and lurid colours. Vampiric rapture transports characters into a parallel universe which coexists and interacts with normal reality. Becoming a vampire, and entering the Crystal Ring at will, seems to involve living in a permanent 'trip'.

Brite writes of contemporary Goth/Grunge/Biker counterculture in the USA. Her mode of address combines hip cynicism with a self-reflexive Goth romanticism evoking 'incense, green chartreuse and altars'.[5] Concerned to construct a rebellious public image, she confides her youthful excesses in press interviews with a mock nonchalance which is clearly relish. She admits to 'extreme depression and alienation at the height of her Goth involvement, and says that she was "into cutting my wrist for fun, playing with blood, and all that"' to authenticate her subcultural credibility.[6] When her vampire characters do drugs, it forms one more sensation in their catalogue of hedonism. Drugs are ingested for their own sake rather than being a guide on a transcendental voyage of self-discovery. In Brite's work, drug references are straightforwardly explicit and use insider terminology, such as crucifix blotters of acid and popacatepetl purple marijuana. She makes much play with the rituals and paraphernalia of the ingestion process, which lends authenticity to the descriptions. As well as relishing the hit of specific drugs, the Goth vampires Zillah, Molochai and Twig use them to intensify their pleasures in sex and sadism. Narcotics facilitate total enjoyment of nefarious practices and loosen the last shreds of inhibition felt by the neophyte vampire, Nothing, who has retained some elements of morality from his mortal mother.

Warrington and Brite represent a recent bifurcation in vampire fiction. Broadly considered, the two identifiable types are traditional romantic Gothic, with purple prose, high flown moral sentiments and religiosity,[7] and the other sub-genre which features the vampire as Goth/street-punk/night-person. The latter type, originating in American countercultural fictions, owes much to the 'road' genre, featuring willing hitch-hikers, violent casual killings and quick getaways. Belonging to this group, which is rapidly gaining in popularity, are the novels of Nancy Collins, Melanie Tem, Laurell K. Hamilton and Poppy Z. Brite. Examples of their cinematic counterparts include *Near Dark* (Kathryn Bigelow, 1987), *Vamp* (Richard Wenk, 1986) and *The Crow* (Alex Proyas, 1994). Seedy bars and strip-joints, roadhouses and motels are the setting for drug use, gang war and ultra-violence. Their appeal lies in visceral excess and violent action rather than in the etherealised elisions of traditional Gothic. Nevertheless, the recent generic transformation still bears romantic appeal. Both types often rework the same motifs in different contexts. Aficionados of the vampire fantasy may well use and appreciate both types of fiction.

Unlike the historical romance of Warrington's nostalgic 1920s London Bohemia, Brite's writing records Gothic iconography as manifested in the specific cultural capital of disaffected WASP youth. Contemporary American Goths recycle British music and fashion trends from the early 1980s and combine them with the fantasies coined by Anne Rice and her followers.[8] This amalgam draws on existing rock and drug cultures in the USA, such as punk, hippy and grunge, and is grounded in the subcultural milieu of particular cities. The novel's epilogue sequence, set 'Fifty Years Later', features decorative scarification, live S/M and a vampire rock band of a resplendent grunge glamour. I would now like to offer a closer examination of how each author depicts the consumption and effects of drugs in a vampiric context and to foreground their stylistic and attitudinal differences to narcophilia.

NEEDLES, BLOTTERS AND BLOOD WINE

These vampire novels are vehicles for their female authors to express an interest in drug-induced modes of ecstasy in a displaced, romanticised form. Like Anne Rice's homoerotic vampires, Brite's characters prefer making out with their own gender, as well as sharing drugs with them. Zillah takes casual female partners, such as Anne, and gets them intoxicated with opium to aid the seduction process. Not only do the boys have better sex scenes with each other in *Lost Souls*, they also do more drugs together. Again, the female actant is displaced on to the sidelines and the female reader's fantasy participation is gender-displaced.

Charlotte, in *A Taste of Blood Wine*, affords an appealing, although somewhat clichéd, vehicle for female readerly identification. Exquisite sensations and spectacular hallucinations are presented from her viewpoint first as an addicted mortal, then as a vampire-addict on a permanent high. Her sister, Fleur, a Bohemian artist, is also a user of cocaine and enjoys the narcotic nibbles of the vampire twins, Stefan and Niklas. Both writers refer to psychedelics in their depictions of vampiric ecstasy – Brite's vampire crew devour LSD blotters with relish; Warrington's Crystal Ring, although not overtly drug-induced, is clearly based on accounts of LSD trips. Blood is the drug which transports the user into heightened states of consciousness.

The contrast between Brite and Warrington's attitude towards drugs is evident in their descriptions of the characters 'coming up' or beginning to register the drug's effects. Warrington uses images of alcohol but the ecstatic hallucinations are different to drunkenness. Karl, the vampire, drinks his own blood for survival and ingests the narcotic substance found within his own veins: '[h]e drank with steady intensity, eyes wide open to keep his head clear as he fought the rising tide of pleasure. And as he drank, he watched the auras glittering against the strange shadow-shapes of the Ring'.[9] Again, when Charlotte decides to accept Karl's gift of Undeath, her sensations are described in rapturous adjectives evoking acid visions as the energy 'entered in a thousand different ways, it pierced her with ruby lines of light, and with curling, white-gold tendrils of fire'.[10] Such synaesthesia is a frequently recorded effect of hallucinogens as the customary sensorium is extended.

Compared to this glowing purple rapture, Brite emphasises the physical, tactile sensations, mixing pleasure and discomfort, as the tab of acid melts on Nothing's tongue and begins to enter his bloodstream: '[t]housands of tiny fingers came alive inside him, crawling. The spit ran down his throat, syrupy, slicking its way along the passages of his body'.[11] Here, the sentences are short and economically concise when compared to Warrington's lengthy clauses. They employ repetitions and sibilants to evoke the excessive tactility of the hypersensitive nervous system. An urbane reference back to other trips serves to demystify the special status of the acid experience. This trip will be more intense for Nothing because the chemical mix is stronger, not because of any mystical revelation. Nothing's Foucauldian emphasis on bodies and pleasures describes a good hit for its own sake, without any metanarrative of transcendentalism.

There is only one brief reference to acid hallucinations in *Lost Souls*, as LSD is just another 'buzz' to Brite's streetwise hedonists, whereas *A Taste of Blood Wine* contains pages of sublime visions. Warrington's visionary sequences endorse the 1960s view expressed by Huxley and Leary of psychedelics as the key to transcendental experience.[12] She describes how Kristian, the domineering 'father' of the vampire brood, travels through the Crystal Ring early in the narrative of *A Taste of Blood Wine*. He passes through a realm of shifting light and flowing patterns which is in a state of constant flux and reversal, familiar from accounts of LSD effects:

Overhead a vast range of mountains soared upwards, purple-black and glossy; a paradox; solid, yet insubstantial as thunderheads. A rich, deep glow spilled down between them, turning their walls to fire. Kristian ascended a floorless canyon, light flowing violet and amber around him.[13]

As well as patterns and colours, Warrington's descriptions feature light in various forms, with the prismatic glint of crystal forming the central image. Synaesthesia is used to suggest a tactile quality of the light. When she becomes a vampire, Charlotte supposes her body to be transformed into crystal, the ultimate light-reflecting substance. Vampiric transformation is like religious revelation and she feels that her former mortal vision was limited and fogged. Light imagery is a traditional staple in the aesthetic representation of ecstasy and connotes mystical enlightenment. Undeath is here depicted as becoming godlike and leaving mortal limitations behind. Vampires exist in a higher state of being than humans do and are capable of more exquisite sensations. Users of psychotropics also consider them to afford a sense of more than mortal bliss. This Nirvana-state of simultaneous absence and plenitude is a goal of the hallucinogen user, who imagines glimpses of eternal immutability. As Leary enthuses: '[t]he glory of the psychedelic moment is the victory over death won by seeing the oscillating dance of energy and yielding to it'.[14] The collapse of constraining concepts, such as time and space, is a central element in both vampiric and narcotic states of bliss.

In *A Taste of Blood Wine*, a transcendentalist discourse is clearly evident. The drug-induced ecstatic states are presented in a tone of reverential sublimity reminiscent of the Coleridge/De Quincey strand of Romanticism which values opiates as a magic key to unlock the creative imagination. Brite's attitude to acid is, in contrast, 'cool' in a studied posture of world-weary decadence. She foregrounds the mechanics of the drug business, street prices and brand names. A self-reflexive joke has these vampires getting high on crucifixes rather than being exorcised by their sacred power. Nothing's third ever trip is heralded by the minutiae of drugspeak:

[A]round lunchtime, Zillah passed out tiny squares of paper-blotter, he said 'Crucifix' from New York. Molochai and Twig gulped theirs down. Nothing looked thoughtfully at his. He had only taken acid twice, weak stuff called Yin/Yang, bought off Jack for three dollars a hit.[15]

LSD use is a regular feature of the gang's lifestyle. Brite's depictions at once play down and retain its romantic connotations. Her streetwise style operates on the possession of inside information forming part of her youthful readers' cultural capital. The slang is a shorthand decipherable by *cognoscenti*.

Parallels between vampire bites and intravenous drugs are overt. Each acts to breach the body's boundary and inject alien fluid that causes exquisite sensations. Both bear the risk of addiction, physical deterioration and premature death. The vampire could be viewed as a fantasy of addiction with impunity, for the vampire is an addict for whom a regular 'fix' of blood is necessary. Like the heavy heroin user, the vampire exists in Undeath rather than in life, sampling a kind of death before final death. William Burroughs has noted that 'the addict exists in a painless, sexless, timeless state',[16] all of which are achieved by the vampire, but the vampiric will to power demands a degree of sadistic agency not desired by Nirvana seekers. A vampire's preying upon an addict is a sadistic refinement of the victim already being preyed upon by a vampiric drug. Brite aligns vampirism and heroin and, similarly, Warrington's 'Bright Young Things' could equally be morphine injectors when they 'take' the bite of the vampire twins.

In *Lost Souls*, Brite explores the erotic cathexis of the junk shooter's habit in a complex interchange when Nothing is picked up by the junkie biker, Spooky. Brite's vampires seek to experience the multiple effects of simultaneous stimuli rather than savouring them one at a time. Narcotic overkill enables higher flights than the use of single drugs. In this sequence, Nothing allows Spooky to 'fix' him. When the biker 'nods-out', the neophyte vampire reopens the puncture wound and sucks. This combines the effects of blood with secondhand heroin, in the most transgressive combination possible: 'the junk-laced blood tasted so good, so pure', he enthuses over his cocktail.[17] Again, Brite emphasises the mechanics of drug taking, combining the exotic and the sordid in the ambiguous vignette of Spooky's habit. She simultaneously acknowledges and deflates the romantic connotations of heroin as:

[Spooky produces] a flat, lacquered box inlaid with a bright scene of tropical birds. He opened it reverentially; Nothing half expected silver light to spill out, bathing Spooky's face, engulfing him. But inside the box was only a plastic bag full of little foil packets, seemingly hundreds of them. And there, innocuous as a dull, gray viper, the syringe.[18]

The cheap tackiness of the plastic bag, and the ugly, toxic connotations of the 'dull, gray viper' deflates the exotic promise of the lacquered box. The 'silver light' image echoes the transcendental, romantic tradition of opiate use. Wry humour is added when Nothing accepts Spooky's offer after brief deliberations: '[d]ead rock stars flitted through his mind, William Burroughs chided him'.[19] This countercultural self-reflexivity adds to the multiple registers of Brite's novel, whereas Warrington's story is 'straight' single register romance.

Unlike LSD, heroin affords a short cut through sensory distortions and hallucinated visions to a desired void of a prolonged bliss and loss of subjective agency. As a trainee vampire, however, Nothing's first-time heroin experience does not numb but energises. He 'felt the junk spreading through him, tendrils venturing into his hands and legs, turning his blood as clear and pure as water. He didn't feel sleepy at all. His mind was sharp, cold. He felt as powerful as a god'.[20] Later, Brite compares the vampire's bite to the fix when Christian gives Nothing a love-bite 'as gently as a junkie slides a hypo into a vein'.[21] In the epilogue sequence Molochai injects Nothing with a blood-filled syringe directly into his tongue to heighten the sensation, and some of the blood also trickles down his throat 'rich and sweet'.[22] These references to careless injection intensify the transgressive impact of the vampire crew. Along with unprotected sexual promiscuity, vampires are free to indulge in the most taboo acts in our current society without risk or anxiety. They offer the reader a fantasy of invulnerability as well as eternal youth and superhuman strength.

As part of her period detail, Warrington's 1920s Bohemian set use cocaine to intensify artistic creativity as part of a self-consciously cultivated decadence. It is easy for the vampire twins to infiltrate this set and to introduce the jaded aesthetes to the new sensation of bloodsucking. The twins practise psychic as well as physical vampirism, invading the imaginations of their hosts. In the early stages, artists such as Fleur produce visions of dark splendour on canvas, but these degenerate into gruesome horrors as psychosis predominates. Stefan is fully aware of the narcotic fantasy they fulfil and explains that their victims 'seek eagerly the clouded nightmares and the daydreams that our bite can bring. We are supplying a need if you like . . . like an addiction'.[23] The effect of their bite is modelled on their habitual drug, cocaine. Fleur echoes the same phrases she used earlier to describe the pleasures of the stimulant: 'Fleur lifted her hand, ran her thumb over the pale crescent marks. They only take a little. Makes one feel so light-headed and wonderfully creative'.[24]

Brite, who is superficially more of a realist in her images of drug use, chooses the most 'romantic' drugs for her hard-headed vampires, eschewing cocaine for hallucinogens and opiates. Goth culture prizes solitary or small group activity and holds itself aloof from large festival or 'rave' type gatherings, so that a social and group-oriented stimulant like Ecstasy would not appeal. Its happy, euphoric effects would be anathema to the angst-ridden, gloomy Goth psyche and disturb its élitist posturing.

The use of pure opium in paste form rather than its derivatives is comparatively rare in the West nowadays. Of all the psychotropic drugs it is the one most heavily laden with romantic connotations and a long documented history of use by artists and poets. Smoking opium today bears a self-conscious identification with the heritage of Romantic decadence and a rejection of contemporaneity; historical nostalgia too is now a hallmark of the Goth subculture. Anne is impressed by Zillah's invitation to a pipe of opium as well as by his stunning green eyes. Nothing is also intrigued by the offer of his 'second new drug in two hours':

Zillah lit a tiny pipe carved in the shape of an ebony rose and passed it to Nothing. The substance in the bowl was dark, sticky. When Nothing sucked at the pipe, a sweet, strange taste came into his mouth. It was like smoking incense. 'What was it?' he gasped, trying to hold the smoke in.

Zillah gave him an evil, heart-stopping smile. 'Opium'.[25]

Brite's vampires use drugs as a seductive ploy as well as being a pleasure in their own right. They take opiates and hallucinogens, alcohol and blood. Only mortals smoke marijuana with its low-level euphoria, providing *plaisir* rather than *jouissance*. The fey singer, Ghost, smokes to help him 'chill out' and escape the pressures of his psychic gift, while Brite's vampire crew would consider the drug's mild effects as insufficiently transgressive to interest them. Having thus considered how a variety of drugs are represented in each novel, I will now suggest the commonality between vampiric and narcotic *jouissance*.

151

NARCOTIC JOUISSANCE

As consciousness shifts from cerebral to physical centres in ecstatic states, the Cartesian valorisation of mental cognition is undermined and the mind/body dichotomy of modernity is temporarily negated. The baser urges of the senses and the libido become the centre of awareness and the focus of exquisite sensations, resulting in a narcissistic cathexis antithetical to both Christian and Enlightenment frames which foreground external object relations and social responsibility. Lacan uses the term *jouissance* to denote ecstasy, with its associations of sexual orgasm. According to his account, *jouissance* is more easily accessible to women or 'perverts' than to phallic men, due to their being situated outside the symbolic order, in an 'opaque place'[26] of otherness beyond the limitations of the phallic economy. This 'supplementary' *jouissance* has been depicted in Bernini's statue of St Teresa. For phallic man, Lacan argues, desire employs fantasy to over-invest objects as other and these seduce him by the promise of a plenitude from which he is excluded. Phantasy forms a 'supple, yet inexhaustible chain'[27] which keeps *jouissance* situated in otherness for the desiring subject. Drug ingestion would seem able to afford egress to the plenitude of this imaginary space and fantasy depictions of vampires suggest that they are able to access such a state.

Leary claimed that LSD trippers 'turn off the conditioning, and experience afresh the hardly bearable ecstasy of direct energy exploding on their nerve endings'.[28] Such a positive embrace of sensuality is paralleled by the vampiric rebirthing of the chosen mortal lover. According to Freud in 'Beyond the Pleasure Principle', the Death Drive originates from the libidinally bound destructive instinct, a portion of which remains inside the organism as the 'original, erotogenic masochism'.[29] Rather than fearing this instinct, vampiric neophytes embrace the Death Drive with positive will, freeing themselves from anxiety in the face of fate. As they pass over to the 'other side' they experience an ecstatic breakthrough and 'come to their senses' anew, unfogged by the limitations of mortality and moral compunction.[30] They are transfigured not by complete change but by functioning at their highest capacity, and with the kind of pristine vision induced by certain narcotics. Warrington details this apotheosis when Charlotte 'passes over' and perceives familiar surroundings from her new vampiric perspective:

It was dark, but nothing seemed to be hidden from her. The street-lights were diamonds, brushing everything with soft colours. Shadows were as deep as velvet, yet she could see into them quite clearly. Far away beneath the trees, she heard and saw a mouse scuffling through fallen leaves.[31]

Vampiric vision is both microscopic and telescopic and the processes of perception are libidinally charged to an intensely pleasurable degree. Familiar, everyday objects can trigger *jouissance*-states and the environment is full of potential turn-ons in unlikely places – like Burroughs's junkie staring at his shoe for hours on end in a state of rapture.

Vampiric addiction is twofold. Vampires are addicted to mortal blood and also feed off emotions and psychic energy. They may form strong erotic bonds with mortal 'lovers' whose desire and adoration serves to fortify their already powerful egos. Mortals become addicted in turn to vampiric congress and are prepared to risk death to ensure its continuance – ironically, however, vampires tend to prefer living mortal partners. As with hard drug use, vampiric sex inevitably entwines pleasure with pain, their mutual interrelation intensifies feeling. Narcotics may transport the user into states of extreme bliss but toxins cause physical pain and discomfort. Addiction to hard drugs is an illness which inevitably hastens bodily disintegration as well as mental and psychological disturbance and weakened ego defences.

The vampires of *Lost Souls* are not affected by pain apart from the pleasure of causing it in sadistic relation to others. When they use drugs, illness or nausea from narcotic poisoning is accepted, even enjoyed, as an integral part of the trip. This impermeability to suffering is assisted by their remarkable powers of regeneration. Toxins are rapidly expelled or absorbed, just as wounds heal almost immediately. The novel's mortals, however, are prone to physical and emotional pain, and illness caused by both sexual and intoxicant over-indulgence.

As well as specifically sexual pleasure, vampiric blood sharing as initiation brings potent rapport and a sense of group unity, particularly to the neophyte vampire. A feeling of universal love is frequently symptomatic of LSD and Ecstasy use. In Brite's novel, this feeling of oneness is overtly connected to sharing the blood and wine cocktail between Nothing and his new friends. His feelings of bonding, commonality and group membership are clarified during his acid trip. The easy rapport and rapid intimacy between narcotic users involves, like romantic love, outward projection of narcissistic libidinal drives and consequent lowering of ego defences. Nothing has moved beyond the early stage of the narcotic-induced tension and paranoia into rapport and emotional bonding. This sense of a group identity and loyalty against outside threat is also character-istic of the formation of subcultures, with their group narcissism and ego-identity, strengthened by shared specificities which serve to differentiate them from 'straight' society. Here, Nothing has passed his tribal initiation ritual:

A moment ago he'd been getting tied up in mind-knots, half afraid of his new friends. His friends who were more exciting than anyone he'd known before, their company more intoxicating, because somehow they were more like him. They accepted him. This is what he had wished for on nights alone in his room.[32]

In *A Taste of Blood Wine*, Karl enthusiastically recounts his close-ness to the vampires who 'birthed' him, in terms which recall 1960s encounter groups. Andreas and Katerina, whom he previ-ously distrusted, have now become his 'loving friends' and 'formed a circle . . . Energy flowed between us. It was like love; perfect happiness, no doubts . . . these are alien creatures, but they've made me one of them'.[33]

The act of vampiric blood sharing acts out in symbolic form a recognition of human commonality beneath individual specificities. Although shared drug experiences and vampiric kisses negate differences between Self and Other, both depend on the identifi-cation of a new 'other' in repressive 'straight' society. Not everyone is considered worthy of love, trust and sharing and the Gothic world-view is undemocratic in its construction of a vampire élite. The only egalitarianism practised by vampires is their view of all mortals as a potential food source. According to the structuralist psychoanalysis of Lacan, the Symbolic Order depends on an active subjecthood under the patriarchal Law of language, which interacts with others and performs actions to affect environmental change. Vampires and frequent narcotic users might prefer to be positioned outside the Symbolic Order, in a state of Imaginary plenitude, but they are both empirically dependent on it and active within it. Vampires, indeed, have very potent egos which they impose on others without compunction.

When we read about the activities of vampires, we experience abandonment and excess by surrogate. The characters within the diegesis may believe in the reality of the Gothic world, but readers regard it as a pleasurable imaginative fantasy stimulated by aesthetic consumption. Psychoactive drug users move more deeply into fan-tasy engagement, adopting a temporary or long-term position of psychosis or 'primary disturbance of the libidinal relation to reality'.[34] They allow fantasy scenarios greater veracity than does the reader or film viewer, and cede to them a more extreme subversion of the Reality Principle. The willing 'suspension of disbelief' is radical until the tripper comes back down into the more objective mode of mundane awareness. Fantasy fictions, on the other hand, seem to offer a relatively safe form of narcotic effect. They stimulate the imagination, temporarily suspend the reader's external relations for the duration of the novel, and can become addictive in the sense of generic fan culture. The individual book or the favourite genre pass in print through the pupil into the physical brain circuitry, stimulating a shift in consciousness and feeding subjective fantasy life, in a process which parallels penetrative injection.

The vampires of *Lost Souls* do not step into parallel universes of elevated sensibility. Brite's depiction of the world inside the black van is concise and relatively low-key. It is a 'drugged dreamland of wine and song where the graffiti writhed on the ceiling and the stars sped by all night long'.[35] This imagery and rhyme echoes rock lyrics, and the lifestyle resembles accounts of wild rock bands 'on the road' – sex, drugs, booze, violence and homosociality. Blood, their favourite hit, functions in the narrative like an illegal drug enmeshed in the criminal underworld and which can only be obtained through extremes of violence. This vampire gang are like serial killers on the run.

In prolonged narcotic ingestion, permanent psychological deteriorations occur, such as memory loss, confusion and the inability to make decisions. Flashbacks disrupt usual activities with a psychotic element and paranoia may ensue. The debate continues around issues of legalisation and information circulation to protect the health and safety of users – the adulteration of 'cut' drugs undoubtedly increases toxicity as a by-product of profit motives. Some of these anxieties around drug use are expressed by Warrington when Charlotte is racked with guilt in a typically Gothic blend of desire and dread felt by a heroine. Her desire for the guilty pleasures offered by Karl is fraught with fear expressed with camp melodrama as the writer echoes the register of the genre's nineteenth-century moral framework: '[i]t's been the same cry down the ages. How can something so beautiful be wrong? The cry that precedes ruin!'[36] After becoming addicted to Karl, her vampire lover, Charlotte's physical appearance becomes marked by her dreadful secret indulgence. Her pallor and listless languor are reminiscent of the drug abuse warning leaflets to parents and teachers: 'Charlotte stared at her reflection in the mirror; eyes rimmed with tired shadow, lips too dark against her drained skin. She pressed powder on her cheeks in the hope of disguising her paleness, but she felt desolate.'[37]

As well as physical illness, vampiric drug addiction incurs psychological damage to the victim's mind as a result of psychic energy loss. The vampires warn that: '[o]ur victims suffer mental derangement, which may take the form of irrational terrors, delusions or outright insanity. Depending on the victim, the madness may last only a few days, or it may be permanent.'[38] This psychological degeneration is similar to prolonged narcotic poisoning. The vampires are themselves prone to illness and torpor if they abuse the pleasures of the Crystal Ring by over-indulgence. They become cold and exhausted, then fall into a kind of hibernation. Being too greedy for *jouissance* can cause burn-out when it takes back the pleasures it gave. The immunity of most fictional vampires is part of their appeal. They manage to enjoy the most excessive hedonism and stay young and beautiful, and can live forever unless they meet nemesis in the form of stakes, garlic, crucifixes, etc. Brite's vampires have no qualms about pleasure-seeking. Nothing, as a novice, rapidly overcomes his loyalty to his former friend and lover Laine when the group decides to torture and devour this unwary hitchhiker. The vampires' relation to pleasure combines lust and cruelty, which themselves induce additional intoxication. One of the characteristics of vampiric *jouissance* is its rejection of moral and social convention. Vampire lovers require their partners to cast aside decorum and restraint which shocks their more proper family and friends and leads to the disapproval with which drug users and 'drop-outs' are regarded by the staid. Having established the nature of narcotic *jouissance* for vampires, I will attempt some evaluation of the subversive potential of the vampire/drug connection, both within and without the fictional diegesis of Brite, Warrington and other Gothic novelists, and its social resonance.

FANS, USERS AND FANTASY

The Goth youth culture in Britain and the USA has considerable longevity in subcultural terms. It began in the late 1970s and is still surviving, albeit in decline, with special clubs and fanzines. Fanzines such as *The Velvet Vampire* and *For the Blood is the Life* reveal them to have a highly participatory vampire fan network, ranging from academic interest to blood sharing.[39] They also express an interest in paganism, sexual fetishism and sadomasochistic imagery. Despite their non-confrontational reputation compared to other subcultures such as 'Crusties',[40] they espouse a distinctive sartorial image combining vampire, punk and Victoriana which uncompromisingly asserts the predominance of fantasy in their lives. One reason for the success of recent Gothic film and literature is their provision of voyeuristic 'decadence' to readers who would never risk offence by public avowal of their fantasy life.

Brite's gang fulfil the traditional role of fantasy 'folk devils' of youth culture 'satiating themselves with blood, torture, raucous music, candy and a cornucopia of drugs'. They are 'not so much traditional vampires (no sleeping in coffins) as immortal fantasy Goths with "their dark blots of make-up" and hair in "great, tangled clumps".'[41] They combine the appeal of countercultural debauchees with the current serial killer vogue.

Warrington's vampires and their 'groupies' are an even safer prospect for readerly voyeurism. They come wrapped in a series of distancing devices: the 1920s, the generic formulae, the parallel universe of the Crystal Ring, the period detail of when particular vampires were 'made'. Warrington's early 1970s psychedelic framework, like old hippies, seems relatively safe and reified by 1990s cultural and commercial hegemony, particularly in its respectable 'New Age' guise. The 'Age of Aquarius' now has period charm and its own nostalgia industry, and is likely to disturb none but the most conventional. The novel's fantasy diegesis is the escapist period romance and its style is purple, decorative prose. Some survivors of psychedelia would still endorse the romantic enthusiasm of Warrington's altered states and her endorsement of the ecstatic quest. Her Jungian transcendentalism seeks to disavow materialist rationalism. She validates *jouissance*, despite its perils. As with drug-induced ecstasy, vampiric bliss enables mortals to realise their *ubermenschen* potential in fantasies of total empowerment and enlightenment. The eternal return of Undeath involves accepting mutability and physical death, by entering into a corporeal form of eternal bliss.[42]

Vampirism and altered consciousness through drug use share considerable commonality. Both involve a precarious balance between death/Undeath and life. For the fortunate, each may afford dazzling vistas, exquisite sensations and levels of blissful awareness. Both practices involve interaction with others by symbiosis. The vampire needs the victim's blood and so is addicted to mortals, and the smitten mortal is hooked on the thrills a vampire's kiss can provide, despite the attendant risks. If they become Undead in turn they exchange one addicted relation for another. Regular users of addictive drugs are dependent on their dealer, the fellowship of other users, and possibly other support workers such as doctors and counsellors. The user may have an entirely drug-oriented lifestyle, with its own slang, music and fashions, forming a hermetically-sealed world. Like fictional vampires, the world of narcotics addicts has its own sense of time, its own mystique and a lack of interest in the values of 'straight' society which it self-consciously rejects and inverts. Heavy addicts are regarded by the outside world with a mixture of pity, disgust and horror.

The *raison d'être* of both drug users and vampires is a particular kind of *jouissance* over which they imagine, at least at the 'honeymoon' stage, they have a measure of control, before ingestion becomes compulsive and habitual. This state of bliss shares characteristics with mystical or religious ecstasy, but without a deity. It involves a narcissistic hedonism which marvels at the capacity for pleasure, insight and hallucinatory creativity. The economic and power relations of drug supply, however, undermine these imaginary projections.

Hallucinogens and Gothic texts each foreground vivid fantasies and enable the user's imaginative engagement with them, but fiction readers retain an awareness of their illusory nature. This enables both the sublimation and the catharsis of intense and disturbing matter. Formal aesthetic conventions maintain egoic parameters and a sense of subjective unity so that horror and excess are distanced, and differentiation between fantasy and empirical materiality is facilitated. The use of fantasy according to this model, would then act in support of the Reality Principle, which, according to Freud, modifies the Pleasure Principle *vis-à-vis* conditions imposed by the outside world and accepts the consequent transformation of free into bound energy. Restraining the sexual instinct sublimation 'places extraordinarily large amounts of force at the disposal of civilised activity'.[43] By supporting the process of reality-testing, Art assists in the maintenance of psychological wholeness and thus is instrumental in maintaining both subjective and societal cohesion.[44]

Simultaneously, however, the spectator's responses elude this restraint. Exciting subject matter and seductive style can penetrate the consciousness to cause emotional and physical responses in the apparently detached user. Increased pulse-rate, rapid breathing, even sexual arousal may result from textual stimulus. The reader may compound this by later fantasising or dreaming about the material, perhaps choosing to repeat and reinforce the response by reading or viewing more of the same; hence the success of series or follow-ups such as the vampire chronicles of Anne Rice, Chelsea Quinn Yarbro, Nancy Collins and Freda Warrington. Formulaic consumption involves reliving the particular diegesis by spending time apart from the usual daily round in reading or film-watching processes. Despite the intense absorption in these activities, when we read Gothics we experience transgression by surrogate only. The characters may accept the actuality of vampires but the reader maintains a distance from them as enjoyable fantasy figures.

Narcotic users engage with their fantasies at a deeper level and choose to stimulate an expansion or distortion of consciousness. They may adopt a temporary or longer term psychotic position, what Laplanche and Pontalis characterise as a 'primary disturbance of the libidinal relation to reality'.[45] They seek to subvert the Reality Principle and allow their fantasising greater veracity than the film viewer or novel reader does. Their 'willing suspension of disbelief' becomes convincing when in deep narcosis and seeks to exclude more analytical or rational modes of cognition. Mundane levels of awareness are regarded as part of the 'straight' world's repression and intoxication is valorised.

Films, stories and role-playing games seem to afford a relatively safe and recoupable form of hallucinogen. They stimulate the imagination, arouse bodily affect and suspend many of the user's social relations for the duration of their consumption. Art acts like a drug whose effects are conveyed through the sense organs into the brain circuitry, simulating sensations of fear and desire. Physical residues and toxins are avoided, the use is legal and, generally, socially and morally acceptable, although perhaps viewed as obsessive or slightly maladjusted when carried to excess. For the committed 'fan', fantasy activity may become an addictive 'repetition compulsion' with a considerable amount of time devoted to it. Like regular drug users, fantasy aficionados may develop a lifestyle oriented towards their obsession, with its own cult status, fanzines, slang, music and fashion. Vampire fantasies appeal to both types of subculture, as a romantic projection of their own group image, élitist, secretive and with access to a special kind of knowledge for *cognoscenti* only.

Hallucinogens subvert familiar cognitive processes. By their foregrounding of fantasy and the subjective imagination, they appear to transform empirical reality by altering responses to it.

159

Reading fictions about countercultural excesses involves a voyeurism in which the aroused but protected reader transgresses by proxy. Drug fictions may have social realist elements, like Irvine Welsh's *Trainspotting*, or foreground surreal fantasy, as in Burroughs's work, but their matter is undoubtedly grounded in events possible in the empirical world and the subjective consciousness.[46] Hallucinations occur in historical, social and temporal contexts and, for the drug user, form part of the lived experience, however this may be mediated. The growing street availability of drugs, and their increasing high social visibility, renders their fictional depiction a trajectory grounded in actuality. With vampires, however streetwise and culturally situated their diegesis might be, supernatural and metaphysical frames persist. Although they relate metaphorically to lived experience, our consumption of them is a fantastic game.

When vampires and drugs occur together, the stimulus each provides is doubled. At the same time, the drugs content is distanced and elided by its connection with mythical beings who are immune to their poisons and experience their pleasures unharmed. They are also free from the threats of gangsters, cut drugs and social stigma, as well as financial problems. Drug consumption with impunity is a further superhuman attribute of vampires. For women writers and readers, fictions of vampiric narcophilia extend the catalogue of transgressive pleasure offered by the Gothic diegesis. Increased drug use and changing gender patterns of consumption ensures these fictions' appeal and the growth of this generic hybrid. The problematic relations between the ecstatic body and aesthetic simulacra of pleasure lie at the interface between those narcotics of fiction and those in a user's bloodstream.

NOTES

1. Jewelle Gomez, *The Gilda Stories* (London: Sheba, 1991), p. 182.
2. Bram Stoker, *Dracula*, 1897 (Harmondsworth: Penguin, 1979).
3. Poppy Z. Brite, *Lost Souls* (Harmondsworth: Penguin, 1992); Freda Warrington, *A Taste of Blood Wine* (London: Pan, 1992).
4. Freda Warrington, *The Dark Blood of Poppies* (London: Macmillan, 1995).
5. Poppy Z. Brite quoted in Elizabeth Young, 'And a Very Good Fang Too', *The Independent on Sunday*, 13 March 1994: p. 31.
6. Young, 'Good Fang', p. 31.
7. Literary and filmic examples include: Anne Rice, *Interview with the Vampire*, 1976 (London: Futura, 1977) and its sequels; Chelsea

Quinn Yarbro, *Hotel Transylvania*, 1978 (London: New English Library, 1981) and its sequels; Francis Ford Coppola, *Bram Stoker's Dracula* (1992) and Neil Jordan, *Interview with the Vampire* (1994).

8. For a recent survey of the British and American Goth scene see Mick Mercer, *The Hex Files: Goth, Fetish, Pagan* (London: Batsford, 1996).

9. Warrington, *Taste*, p. 471.

10. Warrington, *Taste*, p. 498.

11. Brite, *Lost*, p. 153.

12. See Timothy Leary, *The Politics of Ecstasy*, 1965 (London: Paladin, 1970) and Aldous Huxley, *The Doors of Perception and Heaven and Hell*, 1955 (New York: Harper and Row, 1968).

13. Warrington, *Taste*, p. 41.

14. Leary, *Politics*, p. 37.

15. Brite, *Lost*, p. 152.

16. William Burroughs, 'From the British Journal of Addiction', in John Calder (ed.), *A William Burroughs Reader* (London: Picador, 1982), p. 35.

17. Brite, *Lost*, p. 134.

18. Brite, *Lost*, p. 136.

19. Brite, *Lost*, p. 134.

20. Brite, *Lost*, p. 135.

21. Brite, *Lost*, p. 228.

22. Brite, *Lost*, p. 358.

23. Warrington, *Taste*, p. 356.

24. Warrington, *Taste*, p. 352.

25. Brite, *Lost*, p. 138.

26. Jacques Lacan, 'Encore: Le Seminaire XX', Jacqueline Rose (trans.), in J. Mitchell and J. Rose (eds), *Feminine Sexuality: Jacques Lacan and the Ecole Freudienne* (Basingstoke, Hampshire: Macmillan, 1982), p. 153.

27. Jacques Lacan, *Ecrits: A Selection* (New York and London: Norton, 1977), p. 323.

28. Leary, *Politics*, p. 29.

29. Sigmund Freud, 'The Economic Problem of Masochism', *The Standard Edition, XIX*, p. 163.

30. Leary, *Politics*, p. 29.

31. Warrington, *Taste*, p. 503.

32. Warrington, *Taste*, p. 154.

33. Warrington, *Taste*, p. 267.

34. J. Laplanche and J. B. Pontalis, *The Language of Psychoanalysis* (London: Karnac, 1988), p. 370.

35. Warrington, *Taste*, p. 40.

36. Warrington, *Taste*, p. 158.

37. Warrington, *Taste*, p. 194.

38. Warrington, *Taste*, p. 251.

39. See *The Velvet Vampire*, published by The Vampire Society, Keighley,

West Yorkshire and Allen J. Gittens (ed.), *For The Blood is the Life*, Chippenham, Wiltshire.

40. Crusties are an anarchist-influenced, heterogeneous group who may squat in inner cities or be on the road. They tend to be ecologically conscious, vegan and micropolitically active in anti-motorway and airport campaigns.

41. Young, 'Good Fang', p. 30.

42. For a postmodern approach to drugs and vampires which uses the concept of bifurcation, from chaos theory, see Jalal Toufic, *(Vampires) An Uneasy Essay on the Undead in Film* (New York: Station Hill, 1993).

43. Sigmund Freud, '"Civilised" Sexual Morality and Modern Nervous Illness', *Standard Edition, Volume IX*, James Strachey (ed. and trans.), 1908 (London: Hogarth Press, 1959), p. 187.

44. An alternative model of this process is offered by Nietszche's concepts of the Apollonian and the Dionysian in Friedrich Nietszche, *The Birth of Tragedy*, 1872 (Harmondsworth: Penguin, 1993).

42. Nietszche, *Birth*, p. 103.

43. Nietszche, *Birth*, p. 421.

44. Nietszche, *Birth*, p. 540.

45. Laplanche and Pontalis, *Language*, p. 370.

46. Irvine Welsh, *Trainspotting*, 1993 (London: Minerva, 1994).

PART III

Marked Risks

9

Only Skin Deep? Tattooing, Piercing and the Transgressive Body

PAUL SWEETMAN

I enjoy the whole process of booking it, finding a design, going up there, chatting to the artist, you know, getting in there. Getting it done, obviously, is brilliant, [you] get a real buzz off it and everything, and then afterwards you've got all the healing and looking after it. And then, obviously, after that [. . .] you've got the tattoo there, and . . . you're like, 'Yeah, brilliant, I've got [. . .] a piece of artwork that I really, really enjoy'. (Mark, 25: multiply-tattooed and pierced interviewee.)

INTRODUCTION

Recent years have seen a considerable resurgence in the popularity of tattooing and body piercing in the West, leading not only to a remarkable growth in the numbers involved in such practices, but also their spread to an ever wider clientele.[1] The stereotypical image of the tattooee as young, male and working-class is becoming increasingly outdated as more and more men, but also women, of various age-groups and socio-economic backgrounds, choose to enter the tattoo studio. Piercing too, although previously associated with certain marginal subcultural groups, is now more popular amongst an increasingly diverse range of enthusiasts.[2]

Although these trends date back to the 1960s[3] they have accelerated markedly since the mid- to late-1980s, a period which also saw a growth in the popularity of new styles of tattoo and piercing, and the partial incorporation of both forms of body modification into the world of fashion. Numerous celebrities now sport tattoos and piercings and related imagery is frequently featured in advertising copy, as well as in the work of designers such as Jean-Paul Gaultier.[4] Their increased popularity, combined with the developments outlined above, has led some to dismiss contemporary tattooing and piercing as little more than a fashion trend.[5]

The rising popularity of tattooing and piercing has been matched, however, by the steady growth of more 'conventional' modificatory practices such as dieting and 'keep-fit' and, within academia, by an explosion of interest in the body among social and cultural theorists. From the perspective of writers such as Giddens and Shilling, the popularity of such practices as aerobics reflects a growing tendency to treat the body as a 'project' through which a sense of self-identity is constructed and maintained.[6] Whereas in traditional or pre-modern societies identity was relatively fixed and the size, shape and appearance of the body accepted more or less as given, in late-, high- or post-modernity, identity is increasingly fluid and the body is mobilised as a plastic resource on to which a reflexive sense of self is projected in an attempt to lend solidity to the narrative thus envisaged. We are, in other words, assuming increasing responsibility for the design of our bodies and selves.[7]

From this perspective, the rise of dieting, 'keep-fit' and other corporeally-oriented practices or activities is a manifestation of the increasing tendency to treat the body as constitutive or expressive of the reflexively-constructed self and the growing popularity of 'nonmainstream body modification'[8] could be seen as a reflection of this trend. Like the more conventional forms of 'body project' considered by Shilling, for example, tattooing and piercing also have the effect of transforming the exterior surfaces of the body 'in line with the designs of its owner' and can allow a 'wholesale transformation' of the body along these lines.[9] However, in contrast to the more mainstream activities such as dieting and 'keep-fit', tattooing and piercing arguably move the body further away from, rather than closer towards, the hegemonic Western ideal of the youthful, slim and *unmarked* body which lies at the heart of Western (consumer) culture.[10]

This is important from the perspective of those various theorists who, following Foucault and others, have argued that the body is a primary site of disciplinary power relations in contemporary society, and is perhaps of particular importance from a feminist perspective given the greater pressure on women to conform to this hegemonic ideal. Bartky, for instance, has argued that '[n]ormative femininity is coming more and more to be centered on woman's body . . . [and] more precisely, its presumed hetero-sexuality and its appearance'.[11] For Bartky, women's bodybuilding may be seen as an example of the 'experimentation with new "styles of the flesh"' that is needed in order to resist 'conventional standards of feminine body display'.[12]

Tattooing and piercing might similarly be argued to resist 'conventional standards of body *display*', particularly, although not exclusively, where female body modifiers are concerned.[13] Rather than focus on the tattooed or pierced body as text, however, I intend here to concentrate on the 'lived-body' or the 'body-in-use': that is, on the process of *becoming* tattooed or pierced and on the effects that such modificatory procedures can have on the 'corpo-real subjectivity' of those concerned.[14] Tattooing and piercing do not simply and magically transform the appearance of the 'outer body';[15] they are invasive procedures involving pain, blood and the penetration of the skin in a non-medicalised setting. Piercing, moreover, can be 'functional' as well as decorative, significantly affecting bodily sensations during sex or other activities.

These points are significant not only because of their potential importance to those involved, but also because they suggest that tattooing and piercing may be seen as transgressive practices rather than simply procedures constitutive of resistant or subversive outward appearances. As several writers have recently emphasised, the construction of the disciplined body-subject involves not only an adherence to gendered modes of appearance, but also the 'material acculturation' of the body into 'habitual practices of "femininity" and "masculinity"'.[16] Activities such as aerobics, for instance, may be dedicated towards the transformation of the body's surface in line with 'normativized image[s] of femininity', but they also comprise '*a set of practices constitutive of that femininity*', prac-tices which, for Lloyd, 'produce female-feminine subjects with an agonistic relation to their bodies'.[17] As I intend to demonstrate below, it may be that tattooing and piercing disrupt such 'habitual practices', whilst also leading to the creation of new 'bodies and pleasures'[18] – outside of the realms of normalised sexual discourse – in the manner that theorists such as Foucault have advocated.

Drawing on interviews with a variety of men and women,[19] the following looks first at the modificatory process itself in order to demonstrate its importance to those involved. Comments from various body modifiers suggest that, far from being inconsequen-tial, the process of acquiring a tattoo or piercing can instead be seen as a moment (or period) of heightened reflexivity, a liminal

encounter which demands that the '*corporeal* subjectivity' of the tattooee or piercee is acknowledged and experienced to the full.[20] I
will then move on to consider the ways in which their experience
of this procedure affects the tattooee or piercee's sense of subjectivity – and the way in which becoming tattooed or pierced can, for
example, act as a means of regaining or reclaiming control of the
body – before examining the extent to which piercing, in particular,
can lead to a remapping or reintensification of the body's 'erotogenic sensitivities'.[21]

The penultimate section of the chapter considers whether, in
light of the previous discussion, such forms of body modification
might indeed be described as transgressive, while the conclusion
addresses the wider significance of the article as a whole. To para-
phrase Jack Katz, it is suggested that 'only through awareness and
analysis of the phenomenological foreground of' contemporary
body modification, 'of the intricacies of its "lived sensuality"', can
we understand not only its 'moral and sensual attractions', but also
its wider cultural significance.[22] Only through an examination of
the modificatory process itself, and its corporeal and subjective
effects, can one understand why people become tattooed and
pierced and assess the status of such procedures as potentially
transgressive practices.

THE MODIFICATORY PROCESS

That certain body modifiers very much enjoy the process of being
tattooed or pierced was confirmed by several of those interviewed
during the course of this study, with one young male tattooee, for
instance, telling me: 'I loved it. [. . .] I just didn't want him to stop.
You know, the longer it took the better.' Having found that there
was 'something quite sexual' about the process, the informant in
question 'went back and had [his tattoos] filled in again' soon after
their initial application, in spite of the fact that 'they didn't really
need filling in': 'I just wanted to have it done, 'cause it was enjoyable'. Another, heavily-tattooed female, interviewee told me that
she too 'gets off' on getting tattooed, and that that is 'probably
[. . .] three quarters of the reason' she gets them done: 'I think the
whole process is gorgeous [. . .]. I mean even if I can't get a new
one, [. . .] I'll go in and get them touched up [. . .] just 'cause I like
the needle on the skin'.

Certain informants also told me that they enjoyed the process
of becoming pierced, although not, perhaps, to the same extent as

Myers's interviewees.[23] One, older, female interviewee remarked that this enjoyment was a large part of her motivation, although she also noted that she would not get pierced solely for this reason: 'I don't think I would get pierced with a view to taking the jewellery out immediately, but [. . .] I'd get pierced just about anywhere [. . .] to see what it was like.'

That is not to say that all contemporary body modifiers enjoy the process of becoming tattooed or pierced. When, for example, one middle-aged man was asked how he found getting tattooed, he told me: 'I find it uncomfortable. [. . .] I know some people do enjoy a bit of pain, but no, I definitely don't fall into that category'. Other, more heavily-tattooed, interviewees stressed that the degree of pain associated with the process depends upon the area being tattooed. One multiply-tattooed female interviewee, for instance, noted that being tattooed on the shoulder was fairly easy to cope with, but described the acquisition of a large design on her abdomen as 'gut-wrenching'. Seeing the process itself simply as a means to an end, she noted that, were it practicable, she would 'probably' make use of some form of anaesthetic to control the pain. As another interviewee pointed out, however, surface anaesthetic has its limitations: 'it only works for about an hour and a half, so [. . .] you can get shock if you come out of the anaesthetic and you're still being tattooed.'

As a general rule, such anaesthetics are seldom used in tattooing but are applied for the majority of piercings. One heavily-tattooed and pierced interviewee told me that there was 'no way' he would consider acquiring a genital piercing without some form of anaesthetic, adding that he 'hates' the pain associated with both forms of body modification and would 'rather it didn't hurt'. As the same interviewee pointed out, the use of anaesthetic in piercing not only alleviates the pain, but also 'makes for a better piercing [. . .] 'cause you're not wriggling around as much'.

That is not to say, however, that piercing is necessarily non-traumatic. Compared to tattooing, the piercee still has to cope with the more invasive nature of the process itself, and as one interviewee pointed out: 'you don't really appreciate it until you see it done, what's actually involved, and how thick the skin is [. . .]. It does take a hell of a lot of force to push it through sometimes.'

A further contrast between tattooing and piercing is that the pain, discomfort or 'heightened sensation' associated with the former, whilst initially more prolonged and intense, tends largely to be confined to the tattooing process itself: any soreness is generally shortlived, and, as several interviewees pointed out, the healing process is relatively straightforward.[24] Piercing, on the other hand, may be less painful in and of itself, but once any anaesthetic has worn off, the healing process is far less predictable and can involve a considerable degree of pain, not to mention bleeding, soreness and general discomfort. Having already noted that his tongue piercing meant he was unable to eat properly for 'about a week', for instance, one interviewee also referred to the unexpected amount of bleeding associated with the first of his genital piercings:

[T]he Prince Albert[25] bled like mad the night I got it done. The anaesthetic wore off, and I woke up about three in the morning absolutely saturated in blood, [. . .] it was gushing out. And you could feel it, 'cause obviously there's, you know, soreness with the piercing. And that was like, 'Shit, what have I done?' [laughter], you know, 'Fucking outrageous! I've just stuck something through my knob, I'm either gonna get done or it's gonna fall off' [laughter]. So that was quite scary.

To greater or lesser degrees, then, both tattooing and piercing can involve a considerable degree of pain, discomfort and/or 'heightened sensation', both during their initial application and – in the case of piercing – during the subsequent healing period. The manner in which this is experienced varies considerably, however: some tattooees and piercees spoke of their enjoyment of the process, while others saw the pain as something to be endured. That is not to say that those in the second group gained nothing from the process, however. Both sets of body modifiers frequently referred to the high that can follow a new tattoo or piercing. When asked how he felt immediately after being tattooed, for example, one interviewee replied as follows:

Totally euphoric. I mean [. . .] you're releasing tons of endorphins into your blood, and it's rushing around at God knows what speed [. . .] and all of a sudden your body's not hurting any more, [. . .] and it's like, 'Shit!', and it just hits you. And most of the time [. . .] I [. . .] could run around all over the place, and [. . .] jump up and down and stuff when I have 'em done, I just feel that good.

Several piercees described their experiences in similar terms, with one young, heavily-tattooed and pierced interviewee noting that she was 'sky-high for about a day' after having her clitoris-hood pierced and another, older interviewee telling me that all her piercings leave her with a 'natural high [. . .] that lasts for several days': 'I always feel absolutely great afterwards [. . .]. It's better than drugs'.

170

Whether as a result of the initial process or the subsequent high, certain body modifiers find the acquisition of a new tattoo or piercing to be a cathartic experience, again illustrating that, for some, the necessary physicality of the process is key to their over-all motivation. As one heavily-tattooed interviewee explained:

I usually get tattooed if I'm bored or depressed, and that [. . .] wakes your system back up again. [. . .] I like the finished [tattoo], the fact that [. . .] you're making a permanent marking at the end of it, but the actual process seems to kick your system back in a bit, if you're feeling down.

In a statement which, for the most part, refers equally well to piercing, the same interviewee also noted that a complete or finished tattoo cannot simply be bought:

[Y]ou can't like, go to the shop and try it on and say, 'I'll have one of them', and just walk out with it. You've gotta sit there for hours and put up with the pain. So even if you're really rich, if you can't stand the pain, you can't get tattooed.

Far from acting as a passive consumer, then, the tattooee or piercee is necessarily positively involved in the production of the 'corporeal artefact' in question. Not only does he or she have to 'put up with the pain and the process' and in a very real sense com-plete the 'product' through attention to the appropriate healing procedure, but the tattoo or piercing *only exists as part of the lived-body of the tattooee or piercee*.[26] In this sense the tattooee or piercee might be described as both subject and object of the modificatory procedure, worker and raw material, and – to some degree at least – 'artist and . . . work of art'.[27]

This last point is not intended to downplay the role of the tattooist or piercer in the modificatory process, but rather to emphasise the inherently collaborative nature of the procedures involved. That both tattooing and piercing involve pain, blood and the penetra-tion of the skin in a non-medicalised setting also implies a degree of intimacy and trust absent from most commercial transactions.[28] This is most directly evident in the relationship between tattooist and tattooee, or piercer and piercee, but can also allow the forging of intimate links between the client and others in the studio. Noting that his girlfriend had been present while he had his nipple pierced, one interviewee told me:

I do feel it's, sort of, bonded us a bit because of that. [. . .] because it was me sort of, exposing [myself], and being [. . .] fully vulnerable at that point. You know, me sitting there letting myself have this dirty great needle put through me.

CHANGED SUBJECTIVITIES?

Given their involvement in what is a necessarily painful, invasive and intimate procedure, it is perhaps unsurprising that many body modifiers speak of a sense of accomplishment after acquiring a new tattoo or piercing. As one heavily-tattooed and pierced interviewee put it: '[i]t's quite an achievement I suppose [. . .]. You get through [. . .] a long session of tattooing, and you think, "Yeah", you know, "I've got through it, and I feel really good."' This sense of accomplishment can also manifest itself in greater self-confidence. Echoing the comments of several other informants, one needle-phobic interviewee, for instance, told me that he felt 'a lot more confident' after having his nipple pierced:

I still have a problem with needles, but it's [. . .] kind of, 'I've gone [. . .] through that, it hurt like hell for a week', you know, [. . .] 'I can consciously and wilfully submit myself to this, of my own free choice [. . .] and come out of the other end [. . .] liking it'.

In this particular case, the positive effect on the piercee's confidence arose in part from his endurance of the process itself, but also because the piercing was something to which he had 'consciously and wilfully' submitted himself. Others similarly stressed the importance of choice in this regard, with one young interviewee arguing that both tattooing and piercing 'build up your self-confidence' because they are something 'that you've *chosen* to do'. For the interviewee in question, this meant that having a tattoo was an act of self-creation. When asked what she most liked about being tattooed she replied that, although most people have 'got two arms and two legs and all the rest of it', her tattoo was something that she had 'decided to have [. . .] done': '[y]ou know, I didn't decide on the shape of my legs, or [. . .] even the colour of my hair, [. . .] but this is definitely my decision, and you know, [. . .] I was creating myself somewhat by doing that.'[29]

Certain interviewees also saw the act of becoming tattooed or pierced as a means of asserting control of the body. One young female tattooee, for example, argued that tattooing was 'part of wearing what you want, and looking how you want, and, yeah, doing [what you want], that's part of it as well'. Another young male tattooee told me that he thought 'having a tattoo done' was a way of saying:

If I want to brand my body, if I want to stick something through my ear, [. . .] or [. . .] put ink underneath my skin so I have a picture on my body for the rest of my life, I will 'cause it's my body, and you can't tell me otherwise.

Like certain of Sanders and Myers's informants, some interviewees felt that this assertion of control could also act as a means of reclaiming the body.[30] Such comments were more or less specific. When asked whether he thought tattooing could be described as 'subversive or anti-establishment', for instance, one heavily-tattooed interviewee replied: 'I think a bit, 'cause you're like reclaiming your body, and [. . .] making the statement that it's yours and you can do what you want with it'. The comments of an older female interviewee, on the other hand, implied that in her case becoming tattooed and pierced was a way of reasserting control of her body following adolescence and motherhood:

I've been through [. . .] all the adolescent things, and I've had my children, and now my body's just mine [. . .] to do what I want with. And [. . .] it's like a way of [. . .] asserting control. And I'll do what I want, and I don't care if other people find it unpleasant or whatever.

Echoing the comments of one of Sanders's informants, and confirming the observations of the piercer Raelyn Gallina,[31] another interviewee told me that she had become tattooed and pierced following the dissolution of a 'violent marriage' which had seen her denied the freedom to be who she 'really was':

I've always been [. . .] a very masculine type of person, and he made me change into like a [. . .] girlie bimbo type, with dresses and [. . .] long [. . .] permed hair, and all that. And [. . .] when I left him it was like freedom, you know. I could do exactly what I wanted to do again, and be the person I've always wanted to be.

That the timing of the tattoo or piercing event, and thus the process itself, can be central to such 'declarations of independence' was confirmed by a number of interviewees, with one young informant, for example, telling me that while she had wanted a tattoo for some time, she finally decided to get it done on her twenty-first birthday, both as a mark of adulthood and as a celebration of the event itself. Her eyebrow piercing was similarly intended to mark and celebrate a specific event, in this case the offer of her first full-time job and the financial independence this brought her.

The way in which tattoos, in particular, may be chosen not only to mark particular periods or events but also to act as indelible reminders of more or less specifically defined episodes was emphasised by several interviewees. As one young tattooee explained: 'it's something that [. . .] connects me with certain people, and with certain times of my life. [. . .] It connects me with like, my [. . .] teenage years really'. Once again, it is the process of acquiring the tattoo that is important in this regard, not simply its status as a permanent mark. Having already pointed out that becoming tattooed 'was [. . .] a way of marking a point in [his] life where everything was perfect', and explained that 'when things get bad it reminds [him] of that time and sorts [him] out', another young interviewee went on to elaborate these points as follows:

By marking myself I thought I could [. . .] keep [. . .] what I felt when I was eighteen, nineteen, for the rest of my life, 'cause I'd always remember the time. *Because having a tattoo done is such a special thing.* There's the pain to begin with, then there's like the high you get afterwards when you first have it done [. . .]. But, just looking at them reminds me of that time, and hopefully it will stop me from forgetting who I am, when life starts to get, you know, kick the door in a bit more. The older you get, mortgage, kids, whatever.

On the one hand, then, becoming tattooed or pierced can act as a powerful mnemonic device, connecting the tattooee or piercee with their past, in part through the permanency or 'semi-permanency'[32] of the mark thus acquired, but *also* as a consequence of the invasive nature of the process itself. At the same time, however, the process can also lead to significant changes in the body modifier's understanding and experience of the (embodied) self. That many body modifiers report greater self-confidence as a consequence of having undergone the tattoo or piercing process has already been discussed and the sense in which such self-inscription can lead to a remapping and extension of the body's 'erotogenic sensitivity'[33] will be considered below. At this point, however, it is worth noting that the interviewee quoted above, who saw his tattoos as an indelible link with his nineteen- year-old self, also noted that his enjoyment of the tattoo process had caused him to rethink certain fundamental attitudes towards pain, blood, emotion and his own interiority:

You know, the whole being bled process as well, the bleeding, and the pain, which I'd never really associated with a beneficial experience before. You know, blood and being cut, and pain had always been falling over when you're a kid in the street, or getting smacked on the way home from the pub. That was never like, something you'd look forward to. But this is quite an enjoyable, creative process, that involved, like, the pain. I think that brought me to the realization that every emotion in life is just the same, whether it's the emotions hate [and] love, pain and happiness, it's all the same. It's just an emotion and they can be used for beneficial purposes, and pain can be controlled, and blood shouldn't be looked upon as something to be scared of, do you know what I mean? It's just what's pumping around your body all day, and we just don't get to see it till it comes out, then you're scared of it.

NEW BODIES AND PLEASURES?

Once they have healed, the primary effect of tattoos is to alter the body's visual appearance. Piercing, however, can be 'functional' as well as decorative, enhancing and potentially remapping the body's 'erotogenic sensitivity' through the creation of newly sensitised surfaces, edges, ridges and orifices in a three-dimensional interplay of metal and flesh.[34] The act of piercing quite literally creates holes in the body and the subsequent insertion of jewellery exerts pressure against these 'interior surfaces' whilst at the same time affecting the exterior dimensions of the body through the raising and stretching of the pierced area and/or the protuberance of the jewellery itself. The latter means that some piercings do not only alter physical sensation for the piercee – whether during sex or otherwise – but can also be a direct source of pleasure to the piercee's sexual partner.

Certain effects of the more obviously 'sexual' piercings have already been documented elsewhere[35] and several of the body modifiers interviewed for this study confirmed the pleasures associated, for example, with 'male' genital piercings, such as the Prince Albert, and 'female' piercings such as the clitoris-hood or labia.[36] For the purposes of this discussion, however, it is important to note, first, that a number of interviewees also referred to the physical pleasures and sensations associated with certain more innocuous or fashionable piercings such as the tongue and labret.[37] Referring to his tongue piercing, for instance, one heavily-tattooed and pierced male interviewee told me:

Yeah, I mean, it's [. . .] brilliant for, you know, any kind of stimulation, wherever you want it really. [. . .] French kissing or whatever's brilliant.

175

And obviously fellatio or anything else is just as good as well. So, yeah, [. . .] very much more sensitive, [and] it's better for the other person as well.

Of the more explicitly 'sexual' piercings that are shared by both male and female piercees, it appears that the gender of the piercee can significantly affect the way in which the physical or 'sensational' effects of the piercing are experienced, explored and received. While female piercees tended to refer to nipple piercing, for example, as enhancing sensations associated with already existing erogenous zones, several male interviewees referred to the unexpected consequences of piercing this part of the body, suggesting that certain piercings can lead to the 'creation' or 're-discovery' of previously unexplored areas of erotogenic sensitivity. As one male interviewee put it: 'the nipples [. . .] were amazing. I never realised [they] were so bloody sensitive until I got them pierced, and then it was like, "Shit, I just wanna play with these all the time."'[38]

As well as potentially remapping the body's sites of erotogenic sensitivity, piercings also create new holes, channels or orifices, which can in themselves lead to new sensations and ways of using or experiencing the body. This is particularly true of those 'male' genital piercings which connect with the urethra, thereby affecting the flow of semen and other fluids.[39] Referring to his Prince Albert and ampallang[40] piercings, one interviewee told me:

[I]t's even good when you take [the jewellery] out, because you've still got the holes. So when you come, you've got like, what, I dunno, there's one for the Prince Albert, one through your urethra, and two for the ampallang. So you've got four holes in there. And it comes out everywhere. Like a bloody sprinkler [laughter]. So that's quite interesting as well.

That is not to say, however, that the pleasures or sensations associated with genital or other piercings are confined to explicitly sexual activity. The same interviewee also noted that when he is wearing jewellery in his genital piercings he gets 'a sensation off the weight' which is pleasurable throughout the course of his day-to-day activities: '[i]t bounces around a bit, so it's quite good'. Women's genital piercings can be equally, if not more, pleasurable. While none of the women interviewed for this study told me of quite such intense effects, the author Kathy Acker apparently noted that, following her labia piercing, she had been 'coming at random in theatres and cafes ever since'.[41]

176

TRANSGRESSION?

The above has considered the modificatory process and its subjective and corporeal effects, in part to indicate that the procedures involved, and their 'sensational' consequences, are central rather than peripheral to many body modifiers experiences and motivations. The following will now examine whether, in the light of this discussion, such practices might indeed be described as transgressive.

In the first place it might be suggested that, in celebrating the modificatory process itself, contemporary tattooees and piercees challenge the meaning and cultural evaluation of pain. As was noted above, certain tattooees and piercees very much enjoy the procedures involved, and in enjoying rather than enduring the process, may be said to subvert the firmly drawn dichotomy between pleasure and pain. Even those for whom the pain is something to be endured rather than enjoyed tend to emphasise the positive effects of having undergone the process, whether in terms of the immediate 'high' that follows the procedure or, for example, the increased confidence that can ensue.

Tattooing and piercing also violate the integrity of the body, subverting the 'deep-rooted ideal of "the natural"' that lies at the heart of the 'Western body-image'.[42] Tattooing, for example, has been described by Seaton as a practice that involves 'visibly defiling boundaries, mixing ink with skin, shattering frames',[43] and in this sense the practice can be said to raise serious questions over such fundamental oppositions as nature/culture, naked/clothed and, in relation to the body, inside/outside.

Piercing too, in its penetration of the body with inert substances, which may then become, in a felt sense, part of the body,[44] can be seen to question such distinctions as organic/inorganic, body/technology, natural/artificial. In both cases, as 'matter... out of place',[45] tattoos and piercings can be argued to represent 'dirt' as defined by Douglas, their disquieting effect in this respect helping to explain the strong distaste they both commonly arouse within Western culture, and why they are widely 'conceived of as a profanation of the flesh'.[46] As Grosz points out, 'dirt', for Douglas, is anything 'that... is not in its proper place, that... upsets or befuddles order' and thus 'signals a state of possible danger to social and individual systems'.[47]

Mixing ink with skin, or flesh with steel, is not the only way in which contemporary body modification violates corporeal integrity, however. Although tattoos and piercings may be sought as a means of sealing the body, serving, perhaps, as a form of psychic armour,[48] the act of becoming tattooed or pierced opens up the body – at least temporarily – through the invasive nature of the procedures involved. In this sense, the modificatory process might also be argued to transgress a fundamental tenet of modern individuality – that of the foreclosed and bounded self.[49] In modernity, the (free) individual is surrounded by a 'zone of inviobility',[50] but tattooing and piercing can be argued to collapse this boundary in the context of an act which – unlike a medical examination, for example – is neither officially sanctioned nor prescribed.

To the extent that this is the case, opening one's body up to the tattoo or piercing needle might be seen as a way of regaining control of the boundaries of the self – reclaiming one's body from the experts – in an act of deliberative, creative, and non-utilitarian '(self-)penetration'. It was noted above that several interviewees regarded the modificatory process as an act of self-creation and a means of asserting control of the body, and this is, perhaps, additionally significant given, first, the increasing penetration of the body by corporate, governmental, medical and scientific interests[51] and, second, the way in which the boundaries of the individual body serve, at least to some degree, as a metaphor for the boundaries of the social.[52] In an era when the body is invaded and policed as never before[53] and where fears of pollution, contamination and indeterminacy reflect precisely such concerns at the level of society or culture as a whole,[54] attempts to reassert control of the boundaries of one's own corporeality are arguably of increasing importance.

Whether or not becoming tattooed or pierced is seen as a way of regaining control of the boundaries of the self, opening the body up in this way certainly demands a degree of intimacy between tattooist and tattooee, or piercer and piercee, and, as was indicated above, can allow for the forging of intimate links with others who are present during the tattoo or piercing process. This is perhaps of particular interest where male body modifiers are concerned, given that, while women's bodies have commonly been represented in the West as 'leaky', 'as lacking not so much or simply the phallus but self-containment',[55] the 'phallicization' of the male body has involved the construction, or representation, of a 'sealed-up, impermeable' corporeality.[56]

The act of becoming tattooed or pierced might thus be seen as contrary to the process of 'phallicization', implying as it does a

178

certain level of exposure, vulnerability and permeability. Flows of body fluids are also important in this regard: by controlling or denying their own fluidity, 'men demarcate their ... bodies as clean and proper'[57] in contrast to women's leaky, formless and dangerous corporeality; also, the bleeding associated with tattooing and piercing – but more particularly the latter – might again be said to question the notion of a tightly-bounded, impermeable self.

This is also true, of course, of certain effects of male genital piercing. Although directed towards the reintensification of sensation associated with the most heavily valorised zone of the phallicly-oriented body and appearing, perhaps, to seal the urethra with an invulnerable metal prosthesis, in practice, piercings such as the ampallang and Prince Albert perforate the end of the penis, creating new holes, channels and orifices, and rendering flows out of the body unpredictable and uncontrollable: 'it comes out everywhere [. . .] Like a bloody sprinkler'.

In remapping and reintensifying the body's erotogenic sensitivity, other piercings might similarly be argued to subvert phallicised corporeality, in this case through challenging the subordination of 'the rest of the body to the valorized functioning of the penis'.[58] It was noted above, for example, that several male piercees saw nipple piercing as leading to the 'creation' or 'rediscovery' of a previously under-used or unexplored erogenous zone, and that apparently 'decorative' piercings such as the labret could also intensify pleasures and sensations associated with otherwise 'desensitised' areas of the body. Like certain gay men, according to Grosz, male piercees may thus be said to challenge the notion of the 'sexually binarized body'[59] in their assertion of 'bodily regions' other than 'those singled out by the phallic function' and their willingness to 'explore the rest of their bodies ... taking on pleasure of a different order ... [and] reclaim[ing], reus[ing], and reintensify[ing], body parts, zones, and functions that have been phallicly disinvested'.[60]

Women's piercings too, may be said to lead to the creation of 'new bodies and pleasures', which, although not directly challenging 'phallicized corporeality', can nonetheless remap the female body in a manner which questions or subverts the 'genito-penetrative' orientation of normative heterosexuality. Tongue, nipple and even genital piercings, for instance, might be said to reassert the piercee's right to pleasure and to direct attention away from the penetrative act, resubjectifying a potentially objectified corporeality. As with certain 'male' piercings, women's genital piercing can also

179

allow for heightened and pleasurable sensation during everyday activity and not simply in the course of a sexual encounter.

In contrast to men's nipple piercings, women's nipple piercings – like genital piercings for both men and women – appear to be experienced as heightening sensations associated with what is already experienced as an area of erotogenic sensitivity. In light of certain of the interviewees' comments noted above, however, such piercings might still be described as a reassertion of the piercee's sexuality, which, for some, represents a reclaiming of the body following divorce, motherhood or other significant events in the life-course. To the extent that the breast is discursively positioned as a maternal device,[61] women's nipple piercings might also be said to contrast with men's genital piercings; for example, in sealing off the body rather than opening it up to intensified and less controlled flows. Given the representation of women's bodies as leaky and lacking in self-containment (in contrast to men's tightly bound physicality), however, this might be seen as equally transgressive of the 'sexually binarized' model of corporeality.[62]

Contemporary body modification can thus be argued to be transgressive in its challenge to the Western dichotomy between pleasure and pain (or to the latter's overwhelmingly negative evaluation), in its violation of the integrity of the body through the merging of ink and skin or flesh and steel, and in the way it opens the body up to new vulnerabilities, intimacies and flows. In the remapping and/or reintensification of the body's erotogenic sensitivities, and the creation of new channels or orifices, piercing in particular can also be said to upset the sexual binarism that underpins both normative heterosexuality and the phallic economy of desire.

That contemporary body modification is perceived as transgressive is indicated in part by the way in which it so frequently evokes a visceral response. Several interviewees reported that onlookers commonly responded to their piercings, for instance, with revulsion or disgust. Referring to his nipple piercing, for example, one young male interviewee told me that 'a lot of people have kind of gone, "Ugh, ugh!" [. . .] Like you're showing them some kind of road-kill or something'. Pressures of space prevent any detailed consideration of this but that procedures such as those in question are also considered transgressive from an establishment perspective is indicated by the various condemnatory judgements reached during *R* v. *Brown* in the early 1990s. The 'Operation Spanner' case, as it has become known, saw several gay male S/Mers charged and convicted of assault following their consensual involvement in a variety of sadomasochistic practices.[63]

Although attention was focussed primarily on more unusual acts than those documented above, cases of genital piercing, for example, were included in the charges levelled at some defendants, and although piercing for decorative purposes was judged acceptable, 'piercing for the purposes of sexual pleasure was [judged] an offence'.[64] At least one commentator has suggested that the acts in question were threatening to the legislative establishment because of their 'displacement of the phallus', for '[t]o remove the phallus is . . . a fundamental act of disruption' and such practices can thus be described as 'an acutely political moment of transgression'.[65]

CONCLUSION

Focusing on the modificatory process and its subjective and corporeal effects, the above has indicated first, the importance of the procedures involved to many contemporary body modifiers; and second, the extent to which both process and effects might be considered transgressive. It should be noted at this stage that not all contemporary tattooees or piercees are equally concerned with the processes involved – some interviewees told me that their primary motivation was simply to alter the body's appearance – but the above has indicated that to understand both the meaning of contemporary body modification and its wider cultural significance, one needs to focus on the lived-body of the tattooee or piercee – or the 'body-in-use' – not simply its textual surface.

Despite certain commentators' assertions to the contrary,[66] this discussion has indicated that the painful, invasive and bloody nature of the procedures involved, and their subjective and corporeal effects, are central rather than peripheral to the experiences and motivations of many contemporary body modifiers, and that to focus solely on the effects that tattooing and piercing have on the appearance of the 'outer body'[67] would be to miss much of what constitutes the lived-reality of such practices.[68] It also suggests, again contrary to the pronouncements of certain commentators,[69] that such practices should not be dismissed as 'mere fashion': were tattoos and piercings motivated solely by fashion, then the stress would lie simply with the finished body decoration, as a purely visual signifier, and not with the wounding and healing involved in its acquisition, or its effects on the corporeal subjectivity of the tattooee or piercee. In this context a tattoo transfer, or clip-on

181

piercing, would be as meaningful as the real thing.[70] That this is not the case suggests that the current popularity of 'nonmain-stream body modification', while partially explicable in terms of the increasing tendency to treat the body as a project constitutive of the self, also reflects the resurgent sensuality which, in its opposition to 'the formal rationality characteristic of modernity'[71] is central to emergent patterns of sociality.[72] More pessimistically perhaps, the resurgence of tattooing and piercing may also repre-sent a doomed attempt to re-engender feeling into bodies lost to the 'mediascape',[73] rendered increasingly redundant through technological advance,[74] and insulated from pain to the extent that, as corporeal-subjects, we have been turned 'into unfeeling spectators of [our] own decaying selves'.[75]

Either way, the emphasis that many contemporary body modi-fiers place on the painful, bloody and invasive nature of the procedures involved suggests certain difficulties with Eubanks's criticism of 'Modern Primitivism's' 'naive longing for and reliance on the concept of the "authentic"'.[76] It is true that certain 'hard-core' body modifiers have naively appropriated non-Western forms of body-modification in the belief that this somehow lends greater authenticity to such practices and this is problematic in its reliance on a reified and romanticised conception of the non-Western 'other'. At the same time, however, few of the body modi-fiers interviewed for this study shared such beliefs and, in so far as they positioned tattooing and piercing as in some way 'authentic' practices, referred more to the necessary physicality of the proce-dures involved than to any association with non-Western cultures.

To the extent that contemporary body modification reflects a resurgent sensuality or an attempt to reconnect with 'the disap-pearing body',[77] the same might also be said of other corporeally-oriented practices. According to Bordo, however, activities such as 'keep-fit' or bodybuilding are more ascetic than sensual, and although 'preoccupied with the body and deriving narcissistic enjoyment from its appearance [allow for] little pleasure in the *experience* of embodiment'.[78] Tattooing and piercing, on the other hand, can be argued to assert control *of* the body rather than *over* it and, particularly in the case of piercing, to reintensify the body's 'erotogenic sensitivity' rather than seek to overcome it. Both prac-tices may also be said to be transgressive and, in creating a 'body that is permeable . . . that opens itself up rather than seals itself off, that is prepared to respond as well as to initiate', male piercees, for instance, are arguably engaged in 'a quite radical rethinking of [their] sexual morphology'.[79] Although this is in itself of considerable significance, tattooing and piercing involve more than simply a permanent or semi-permanent modification to the appearance of the 'outer body':[80] both practices are, indeed, much more than skin-deep.

NOTES

I would like to thank Michele Aaron, Graham Allan, Chris Shilling and Terry Sweetman for their comments and suggestions on earlier versions of this chapter, and the Department of Sociology and Social Policy at the University of Southampton for supporting the wider study of which it forms a part. Thanks are also due to the interviewees quoted above, and to all those others who have helped with my research in some way, shape or form. The usual disclaimers, of course, apply.

1. See M. DeMello, 'The Carnivalesque Body: Women and Tattoos', in *Pierced Hearts and True Love: A Century of Drawings for Tattoos* (New York and Honolulu: The Drawing Center/Hardy Marks Publications, 1995) and '"Not Just For Bikers Anymore": Popular Representations of American Tattooing', *Journal of Popular Culture*, 19 (3) 1995: pp. 37–52; M. Blanchard, 'Post-Bourgeois Tattoo: Reflections on Skin Writing in Late Capitalist Societies', in Lucien Taylor (ed.), *Visualizing Theory: Selected Essays from V.A.R. 1990–1994* (New York and London: Routledge, 1994); D. Curry, 'Decorating the Body Politic', *New Formations*, 19 1993: pp. 69–82; M. L. Armstrong, 'Career-oriented Women with Tattoos', *Image: Journal of Nursing Scholarship*, 23 (4) 1991: pp. 215–20 and 'Tattoos on Women: Marks of Distinction or Abomination?', *Dermatology Nursing*, 5 (2) 1993: pp. 107–13; J. Myers, 'Nonmainstream Body Modification: Genital Piercing, Branding, Burning, and Cutting', *Journal of Contemporary Ethnography*, 21 (3) 1992: pp. 267–306; C. Sanders, *Customizing the Body: The Art and Culture of Tattooing* (Philadelphia: Temple University Press, 1989); A. Rubin, 'The Tattoo Renaissance', in A. Rubin (ed.), *Marks of Civilization: Artistic Transformations of the Human Body* (Los Angeles: Museum of Cultural History/University of California, 1988).
2. See Curry, 'Decorating'.
3. See Curry, 'Decorating'; Sanders, *Customizing* and Rubin, 'Tattoo'.
4. See A. Bellos, 'As British as S&M', *The Guardian*, G2 6 November 1996, p. 7 and G. Bradberry, 'Branded for Life', *The Times*, 20 November 1997: p. 21.
5. See V. Steele, *Fetish: Fashion, Sex and Power* (New York and Oxford: Oxford University Press, 1996), pp. 160–1; J. Craik, *The Face of Fashion: Cultural Studies in Fashion* (London: Routledge, 1994), p. 25.

6. See A. Giddens, *Modernity and Self-Identity: Self and Society in the Late Modern Age* (Cambridge: Polity Press, 1991); C. Shilling, *The Body and Social Theory* (London: Sage, 1993).
7. See Giddens, *Modernity*, p. 102.
8. See Myers, 'Nonmainstream'.
9. Shilling, *The Body*, p. 3.
10. See M. Featherstone, 'The Body in Consumer Culture', in M. Featherstone, M. Hepworth and B. Turner (eds), *The Body: Social Process and Cultural Theory* (London: Sage, 1991).
11. S. L. Bartky, 'Foucault, Femininity and the Modernization of Patriarchal Power', in I. Diamond and L. Quinby (eds), *Feminism and Foucault: Reflections on Resistance* (Boston: Northeastern University Press, 1988), p. 81.
12. Bartky, 'Foucault', pp. 83, 78.
13. See DeMello's work and P. Sweetman, 'Marked Bodies, Oppositional Identities? Tattooing, Piercing and the Ambiguity of Resistance', in S. Roseneil and J. Seymour (eds), *Practising Identities: Power and Resistance* (London and Basingstoke: Macmillan, forthcoming).
14. H. Y. Jung, 'Phenomenology and Body Politics', *Body & Society*, 2 (2) 1996: p. 6.
15. Featherstone, 'The Body', p. 171.
16. S. Bordo, 'Postmodern Subjects, Postmodern Bodies' (Review Essay), *Feminist Studies*, 18 (1) 1992: p. 167.
17. M. Lloyd, 'Feminism, Aerobics and the Politics of the Body', *Body & Society*, 2 (2) 1996: p. 91, emphasis added; p. 94. See also S. Bordo, 'Anorexia Nervosa: Psychopathology as the Crystallisation of Culture', in Diamond, *Feminism*.
18. M. Foucault, *The History of Sexuality, Vol. I: An Introduction* (London: Penguin, 1981), p. 157. See also Foucault, 'Sexual Choice, Sexual Act: Foucault and Homosexuality' (interview), in L. Kritzman (ed.), *Michel Foucault: Politics, Philosophy, Culture – Interviews and Other Writings 1977–1984* (London: Routledge, 1988).
19. This chapter forms part of a wider study on contemporary body modification, for which in-depth, semi-structured interviews were conducted with thirty-five tattooed and/or pierced informants, as well as with several professional tattooists and body piercers. The study also draws on observation conducted at a number of tattoo conventions and tattoo and/or piercing studios, as well as analysis of the popular literature devoted to the forms of body modification in question.
20. See M. F. De Monchy, 'The Horrified Position: An Ethics Grounded in the Affective Interest in the Unitary Body as Psyche/Soma', *Body & Society*, 1 (2) 1995: pp. 25–64.
21. E. Grosz, *Volatile Bodies: Towards a Corporeal Feminism* (Bloomington and Indianapolis: Indiana University Press, 1994), p. 139.

22. Jack Katz quoted in J. Ferrell, *Crimes of Style: Urban Graffiti and the Politics of Criminality* (New York and London: Garland Publishing, 1993), p. 167.
23. See Myers, 'Nonmainstream', p. 278.
24. That is not to say that it is not also enjoyable. Curry suggests that there is an erotic element to caring for a new tattoo (Curry, 'Decorating', p. 81) and, as one interviewee put it: 'when you have to wash it the first time, [and do] all the care sort of stuff, it's brilliant.'
25. A ring-piercing that enters through the urethra and exits at the base of the glans. For illustration and further description see Myers, 'Nonmainstream', pp. 300–1.
26. See Blanchard, 'Post-Bourgeois', p. 292.
27. P. Falk, 'Written in the Flesh', *Body & Society*, 1 (1) 1995: p. 99.
28. I. Barfoot, 'If Beauty Is Only Skin Deep . . . Why Was I Born Inside Out?', *Skin Deep*, 4 (4) 1997: p. 6.
29. Or, as another, heavily-tattooed male informant explained: 'everyone's born with roughly the same bodies, but [. . .] you've created yours in your own image'.
30. See Sanders, *Customizing*, p. 43; Myers, 'Nonmainstream', p. 282.
31. V. Vale and A. Juno (eds), *Re/Search #12: Modern Primitives – An Investigation of Contemporary Adornment & Ritual* (San Francisco: Re/Search Publications, 1989), p. 105.
32. See Curry, 'Decorating', p. 73.
33. Grosz, *Volatile*, p. 139.
34. For a similar description of non-Western body marking, see A. Lingis, *Excesses: Eros and Culture* (Albany: State University of New York Press, 1983), p. 34.
35. See the work of Curry, Myers and Vale and Juno.
36. See Myers, 'Nonmainstream', pp. 300–1.
37. A plug- or ring-piercing below the lip.
38. See also G. P-Orridge, in Vale, *Re/Search*, p. 176.
39. Vale, *Re/Search*, p. 175.
40. A horizontal piercing through the glans. Again, for illustration and further description see Myers, 'Nonmainstream', pp. 300–1.
41. K. Acker quoted in E. Vulliamy, 'Outrageous author Acker dies', *The Guardian*, 1 December 1997: p. 3. The continual sensation associated with certain piercings is not experienced positively by all piercees, however. One interviewee told me that she had removed the jewellery from her clitoris-hood piercing soon after having it done: 'it was just [a] continual distraction. And it made me a bit over-sensitive as well'.
42. Falk, 'Written', p. 100.
43. E. Seaton, 'Profaned Bodies and Purloined Looks: The Prisoner's Tattoo and the Researcher's Gaze', *Journal of Communications Inquiry*, 11, 1987: p. 18. See also Blanchard, 'Post-Bourgeois'.

44. As one interviewee explained: 'Well, [. . .] the piercings [are] just [. . .] part of me now. I don't really think of them as accessories or anything [. . .], they're just there'. See also Falk, 'Written', p. 99; Grosz, *Volatile*, p. 91.

45. R. W. Wilson, 'Cyber(body) Parts: Prosthetic Consciousness', *Body & Society*, 1 (3–4) 1996: p. 249.

46. Falk, 'Written', p. 100.

47. Grosz, *Volatile*, p. 192. See also D. Lupton, 'The Embodied Computer/ User', *Body & Society*, 1 (3–4) 1996: p. 110.

48. See J. A. Popplestone, 'A Syllabus of the Exoskeletal Defenses', *Psychological Record*, 13, 1963: pp. 15–25.

49. See M. A. Schneider, 'Sacredness, Status and Bodily Violation', *Body & Society*, 2 (4) 1996: pp. 75–92; also Falk, 'Written'.

50. Schneider, 'Sacredness', p. 78.

51. A. Kroker and M. Kroker, 'Theses on the Disappearing Body in the Hyper-Modern Condition', in A. Kroker and M. Kroker (eds), *Body Invaders: Panic Sex in America* (New York: St. Martin's Press, 1987), p. 28.

52. Grosz, *Volatile*, p. 193.

53. See A. Balsamo, 'Forms of Technological Embodiment: Reading the Body in Contemporary Culture', *Body & Society*, 1 (3–4) 1995: pp. 216, 219; Kroker and Kroker, 'Theses', p. 28.

54. See V. Eubanks, 'Zones of Dither: Writing the Postmodern Body', *Body & Society*, 2 (3) 1996: pp. 73–4; Kroker and Kroker, 'Panic Sex in America', in *Body Invaders*, pp. 11–12.

55. Grosz, *Volatile*, p. 203.

56. Grosz, *Volatile*, p. 201.

57. Grosz, *Volatile*, p. 201.

58. Grosz, *Volatile*, p. 201.

59. Grosz, *Volatile*, p. 202.

60. Grosz, *Volatile*, p. 201.

61. S. Pink, 'Breasts in the Bullring: Female Physiology, Female Bullfighters and Competing Femininities', *Body & Society*, 2 (1) 1996: p. 53.

62. Grosz, *Volatile*, p. 202.

63. See C. Stychin, *Law's Desire: Sexuality and the Limits of Justice* (London: Routledge, 1995) p. 6; L. J. Moran, 'Violence and the Law: The Case of Sado-Masochism', *Social & Legal Studies*, 4 1995: pp. 225–51; L. Bibbings and P. Alldridge, 'Sexual Expression, Body Alteration, and the Defence of Consent', *Journal of Law & Society*, 20 (3) 1993: pp. 356–70; C. Stanley, 'Sins and Passions', *Law and Critique*, 4 (2) 1993: pp. 207–26.

64. Bibbings and Alldridge, 'Sexual', p. 361.

65. Stanley, 'Sins', pp. 221, 222, 226.

66. A. Gell, *Wrapping in Images: Tattooing in Polynesia* (Oxford: Clarendon Press 1993), p. 313.

67. Featherstone, 'The Body', p. 171.
68. See A. Radley, *Body and Social Psychology* (New York: Springer-Verlag, 1991), pp. 112–13.
69. See Steele, *Fetish* and Craik, *Face*.
70. Given that this is not the case, and that the acquisition of such 'corporeal artifacts' inevitably 'disrupts ... the passivity of mediated consumption' (Ferrell, *Crimes*, p. 176) it might further be argued that, to whatever degree tattooing and piercing imagery is incorporated into the fashion industry, the practices themselves are less subject to recuperation. As was noted above, the nature of the procedures involved means that while 'you *can* buy a tattoo, [...] you've still gotta put up with the pain and the process'.
71. C. Shilling and P. A. Mellor, 'Embodiment, Structuration Theory and Modernity: Mind/Body Dualism and the Representation of Sensuality', *Body & Society*, 2 (4) 1996: p. 10.
72. See Mellor and Shilling, *Re-forming the Body: Religion, Community and Modernity* (London: Sage, 1997); M. Maffesoli, *The Time of the Tribes: The Decline of Individualism in Mass Society* (London: Sage, 1996); Jung, 'Phenomenology'.
73. Kroker and Kroker, 'Body Writing', in *Body Invaders*, p. 223.
74. Kroker and Kroker, 'Theses', in *Body Invaders*, pp. 21–2.
75. See Illich in G. Bendelow and S. Williams, 'Pain and the Mind-Body Dualism: A Sociological Approach', *Body & Society*, 1 (2) 1995: p. 99. See also De Monchy, 'Horrified'.
76. Eubanks, 'Zones', p. 74.
77. Kroker and Kroker, 'Body Writing', in *Body Invaders*, p. 223.
78. Bordo, 'Anorexia', p. 98, original emphasis. See also Lloyd, 'Feminism'.
79. Grosz, *Volatile*, p. 201.
80. Featherstone, 'The Body', p. 171.

10

Cicciolina *and the Dynamics of Transgression and Abjection in Explicit Sex Films*

TANYA KRZYWINSKA

We are discontinuous beings, individuals who perish in isolation in the midst of an incomprehensible adventure, but we yearn for our lost continuity. We find the state of affairs that binds us to our random and ephemeral individuality hard to bear. Along with our tormenting desire that this evanescent thing should last, there stands our obsession with a primal continuity linking us with everything there is.[1]

The paradoxical double-bind of transgression is that we are impelled to transgress the limits of self and culture but, at the same time, also impelled to conserve and maintain these limits. Georges Bataille was the first modern philosopher to focus on the concept of transgression in his analysis of the relationship between the social order and the psyche. For Bataille, a cultural system is dependent on transgression for its particular shape and structure. The framework of law provides a culture with its structural logic in relation to which the people of that society define identity. This structure shapes and channels sexuality and desire which constitutes the 'subject before the law'.[2] To become a subject within a given culture is to become a sexed, gendered, 'clean and proper' person within the terms of that culture.[3] Certain aspects of sexuality and desire are remaindered, and thereby repressed, through the processes of socialisation. These processes are closely connected to what Julia Kristeva has called 'abjection'. It is the traces of abjected and repressed pleasures and desires, which may endanger identity, that find their way into Explicit Sex films. When the laws that govern the shaping of identity are violated, the limits of the culture are reinforced and, as such, culturally determined identity is dependent on an individual's direct experience of transgression. When an individual transgresses the limits of a culture, shame or anguish is felt. For sexual subjecthood, this means that the subject has to repress or deny aspects of sexuality and desire which do not conform to the dominant model. However, as Bataille argues, we can never fit the model of identity that culture demands and we are, therefore, forced to test and transgress the limits of culture and identity. For some people the experience produced by transgression is a liberating pleasure of ego-loss, for others the pleasure of transgression is control and power. Through an exploration of the traces of repressed and abjected desires in *Cicciolina in Italy*,[4] this chapter aims to tackle the question of what it means to call Explicit Sex films transgressive.[5] In so doing this chapter will address how Explicit Sex films are symptomatic of, and also employ, conflicts between identity and the body's 'perilous pleasures'.

For Bataille, there are two areas of life that hover on the boundaries of a culture or individual's identity which contaminate or rupture their coherence. These are sex and death, primary cultural sites of taboo and prohibition. The ritualised rhetoric of taboo shrouds prohibition in such a way that these areas as social constructs are hidden from view as God-given laws. These sites work to create anxiety (and mystery) for the subject and it is here that Bataille's work intersects with Freud's work on taboos. For Freud and Bataille, taboos operate to protect the integrity of a culture and the individual from repressed aggressive and sexual desires which are produced and marginalised through the formation of the gendered, sexed, person. To become a clean and proper person within a particular culture is to sublimate aspects of desire that do not conform to the dominant norms of gender and sexuality in that culture.

I will now demonstrate how repression, shame and eroticism are connected, as this will prove crucial to my reading of *Cicciolina in Italy*. Bataille argues that eroticism is borne of shame.[6] His concept of eroticism, which I read as similar to Lacan's concept of desire, is the direct product of repression. Identity is formed through the sublimation of certain formations of desire. When the movement of these desires are felt, shame is experienced and, because these desires are sexual, they also carry with them a certain titillating thrill. It is the exciting residue of repressed desires that constitutes eroticism. This process corresponds to a Christian

189

model of original sin.[7] The intrinsic link between eroticism and shame has many familiar analogues. The concepts of the 'Fall' and original sin underpin many creation myths and purport to answer our questions about the origins of our sexual desires and identity. These myths create prohibitions which shape the boundaries of a given culture thereby determining taboos and transgression within it.

Although lapsarian myths around sexual shame might not be true in the scientific sense, they demonstrate that sexuality has a problematic relationship with ego-identity. The mythic or imaginary answers that are produced to account for sexuality may be negated or proved wrong but they are never lost (and their traces will be examined in detail in my analysis of the opening scene of *Cicciolina in Italy* below). Instead, these traces remain as repressed components of the psyche which re-emerge in a secondary way through fantasy, works of the imagination, and through the organisation of our speech. Transgression, guilt and shame are key foundational components of myths and fantasies. It must be emphasised, however, that transgression has a potent dynamic and experiential force. Acts and thoughts experienced as transgressive, whether in fantasy or reality, lend substance to the cultural system through the placement of otherness and difference. Transgressive acts or thoughts always carry with them an excess (a form of overdetermination) which both problematises and reinforces the limits of cultural practices. What is important here for my analysis is that Explicit Sex films make overt use of transgressive tropes which reinforce cultural boundaries. They do so by depending on sexual desires that have become loaded with transgressive meanings through the processes of becoming a clean and proper gendered, sexed person.

Libertarian calls for the 'free' expression of sex[8] and many pro-censorship writings assume that sexuality can be divested of power. This call for a return to a prelapsarian sexual innocence implies that sexuality has a fixed content, rather than being produced through the channelling frameworks of a given culture. The utopian investment in the lifting of sexual 'repression' – as if it were a dark cloud blocking out the sunlight of human joy – fails to see that repression is intrinsic to the shaping of sexuality. Bataille argues that sexuality is constituted through the taboos and prohibitions that shape a cultural system; for example, incest taboos, taboos around non-heterosexuality, and the child as non-sexual. Following Bataille I would maintain that sexuality cannot be divested of its repressive fetters because it is precisely the product of these prohibitions (even as it breaks them). The desire to remove the perceived constraints on sexuality elides the possibility of using the experience of transgression to help locate the contradictory economies that underpin the logic of the social and psychic matrix. Contradictions within this matrix are glossed over in a hegemonic attempt to preserve the coherent status of a social or psychic system. The heterosexual matrix, for instance, often operates to assign otherness and transgression to lesbian and gay sexualities as a means of drawing fire away from the inherent queer disruptiveness of all sex and sexual desire. This helps to displace the strange workings of abjection and power, which in my non-redemptive 'original-sin' reading lie at the heart of sexual desire, on to an othered group.

Bataille's analysis of eroticism's excess is based on a model of the subject who is structured through continuity and discontinuity. Individual existence is characterised as a discontinuity whereby the subject is split off from others and the absolute, which is experienced as anguish. There is, he argues, a nostalgia for the continuity of an imagined pre-individualised state and this imaginary continuity is petitioned through sex. Following Lacan, I would argue that this is a retrospectively constructed fantasy. Through erotic contact we seek to dissolve the boundaries between ourselves and the Other/other, but as continuity is also aligned with death, it is feared as well as yearned for, as indicated in the opening citation from Bataille.[9] Eroticism provides a foretaste of death in that it is experienced as ego-loss and thereby desecrates the holy ground of unified identity: '[i]n essence, the domain of eroticism is the domain of violence, of violation' and '[t]he whole business of eroticism is to destroy the self-contained character of the participators as they are in their normal lives'.[10] The Bataillean model of continuity/discontinuity is pivotal to the status of transgression in Explicit Sex films in that they destabilise the user's sense of a gendered, sexed self. These films offer a psychological 'laceration' through the depiction of what is not shown on legitimate, mainstream broadcast television. However, the question remains: what does it mean to say that these films are transgressive? An interrogation of their apparent transgressive status reveals that their tempting offer of allowing users to indulge in repressed desires carries with it, following Bataille's model, the negative reinforcement of dominant norms of sexuality as an expression of love between two heterosexual partners. My main task, therefore, is to show that these films are marked by a conflict between transgressive and conservative forces. The films reinforce dominant sexual and gender norms and, even in the least apparently transgressive 'fuck film', the transgressive status of the films is dependent on a universally repressed sexual economy, the traces of which can be seen to invite a pleasurable (but universal) disruption of ego/sexual identity. I am, therefore, arguing that these films trade on the pleasure of a flight from identity and individuation while, at the same time, they operate to bolster the rims and boundaries that shape a given culture.

The aim of the genre of Explicit Sex films is to elicit sexual desire by presenting the film's user[11] with sexual images which are deemed exotic or sinful because they foreground sexual acts other than heterosexual coitus. These exotic sexual images are key to the Bataillean ego-lacerating transgression performed by the films and they take several forms. For the straight-identified user (as the 'intended' users of these films) this is achieved through the use of images of non-heterosexual acts; for example, 'lesbian' sex as in *Punky Girls*, gender-fuck typified by the women with realistic looking penises as in *Kinkorama 14*, sadomasochism as in *Education d'Anna* (Michael Ricaud) and corporal punishment as in *Moral Welfare*. These exotic (extrinsic) images often depend on what may be regarded as repressed economies of sexuality that are produced through the formation of sex and gender identity, as governed by the hegemonic heterosexual matrix.[12] As this matrix is constructed as the legitimate form of sexual activity, the presence of these othered, sinful sexual acts can be regarded in two different ways. First, the status of these acts is construed as an exotic difference with the aim of 'spicing up' the sexual action in a film. Second, they can work to disrupt the heterosexual economy as they betray the operational valency of alternative sexual economies that are often sublimated through the heterosexual matrix. They demonstrate the besieged nature of heterosexual identity by showing that desire often exceeds its 'ideal' and narrow confines (albeit that the elements in the film that might be 'challenging' to users are often couched within a matrix of safety valve devices). Following the logic of Bataille's argument about transgression, these othered or sublated[13] sexual desires are the direct or inverse product of the cultural apparatus of sexuality.

It is through the demands of the heterosexual matrix, as an intrinsic channelling force, that certain desires and acts gain their 'sinful' meaning. These acts are the staple of Explicit Sex films,

including: 'phallic' (genital auto-eroticism) – typified by the preoccupation with images of masturbation and the 'come-shot'; 'anal' –
typified by the frequent depiction of anal penetration in films such
as *Dr Butts II* and *Kinkorama 14*; 'polymorphic' – typified by the
frequent 'orgy' scenes which often act as the closing scene of many
films, such as *Rambone the Destroyer* and *Cicciolina in Italy*. Lesbian
sex as an othered sexual economy is also a staple component of
these films (however, sex between men is rarely directly depicted
in Explicit Sex films that are targeted at a 'straight' audience). It
is important to point out that, in many videos, lesbian sex acts
are frequently bracketed by heterosexual coitus. The full force of
lesbian sex as transgressive is maintained through its juxtaposition
with heterosexual sex. In *Kinkorama 14*, for example, there are several scenes which depict sex between two women. However, these
scenes are always preceded and followed by a scene which involves
heterosexual penetrative sex which operates as a ruse to allow
heterosexually identified women users to experience clandestine
same-sex desires. Heterosexual sexual acts carry with them a
secreted load of othered sexualities and, as such, the heterosexual
matrix is not so simple and 'straight'-forward as it might seem.
There are, then, two levels of transgression at work here. The films
derive an overt transgressive meaning through the representation
of sex acts that do not apparently conform to the heterosexual
ideal, and heterosexual sexual acts carry traces of sublated, and
therefore transgressive, sexual desires.

The contemporary hegemonic ideal of heterosexual coitus is
legitimated as a private domestic exchange between a couple. Scopophilia, Freud's term for the pleasure of looking in a general sense,
which he argues plays a key role in adult sexuality, is sanctioned
within this private space. This sanctioning gains currency because
it is set against the illegitimate public voyeuristic or masochistic
economies of pleasure and desire. It is this illegitimate form of
sexuality that is mobilised by Explicit Sex films as the sex performed
in them is couched as public performance. In the contemporary
discursive hierarchy of sex, the heterosexual committed partnership
of a man and a woman, who orgasm neatly together through gen-
tle and passionate sex, is the ideal. This is the model of sex used in
the legal, and therefore legitimated, multi-media *'Lover's Guide'*-
style books, CD-ROMs and videos. This model is also the criterion
for the 'normalisation' of lesbian and gay people – private sex, sustained loving relationships and marriage. The transgression of
Explicit Sex films inverts this model of sanctioned private sex by

making explicit sexual acts open to a public gaze. One of the effects of this centralisation of the heterosexual, private ideal is to render the user of Explicit Sex films as abject (which can be felt as liberating and/or anguish). If identified, users may, for example, be treated in public/social space with contemptuous laughter and considered 'sad' or perverted. Users of these films are often designated as being unable to achieve a 'real/genuine' sexual relationship (the pejorative term 'wanker' works on the same principle). The use of these films is popularly considered to be a weak substitute for so-called genuine sex, the criteria for which are outlined above. For fear of exclusionary treatment, many users may not admit to their pleasure in watching these videos, while other users may instead see it as an act of bravado, cocking a snook at establishment values – as is often evident in internet/worldwide web discussion groups on sex films. For some users, it may be the very secrecy of clandestine use that adds to a sense of transgressive pleasure.

Heterosexual coitus is often legitimated and reified through reference to the discourse of the biological imperative: reproduction. Explicit Sex films can be considered to be transgressive of the sex-for-reproduction myth as the legitimating origin of sexual desire. Sex for reproductory purposes is completely absent in these films which favour sex for pleasure and spectacle. Some recent videos feature condoms (for example, *Kinkorama 14*), but this is a result of the increased awareness of HIV/AIDS and other sexually transmitted diseases, rather than for the prevention of pregnancy. Because of the absence of sex as reproduction, Explicit Sex films correspond to Bataille's reading of eroticism as transgressive as the sex depicted exceeds production/work. However, as sex in Explicit Sex films is commodified (and is therefore a form of exchange), this might present a problem to the application of Bataille's reading of eroticism as a form of tactile interchange which exceeds production/work. In Explicit Sex films, sex becomes entangled with the processes of work (the exchange of sexual labour within the capitalist system), and it may then lose its potential for exceeding the system of production. Conversely, the association of sex and money gives the films an added sense of transgression.[14] It is the role of abjection in relation to transgression that I want to explore in depth as this corresponds most closely to Bataille's model of transgression as a violation of ego-identity and which will provide the basis for my close analysis of the opening of *Cicciolina in Italy*.

Julia Kristeva's use of the term 'abjection' draws on Mary Douglas's anthropological work but frames it through a psychoanalytic model of the psyche. In *Purity and Danger*, Douglas examines a range of what she calls 'primitive' cultures and looks at the diverse range of taboos around dirt and sex as a means of understanding the role of taboo in contemporary culture.[15] Kristeva takes Douglas's term and uses it to explore its role as a primary mechanism for subject formation; she uses it to describe the process by which we are interpellated as subjects into culture. In order to become a clean and proper person, one must internalise the taboos of the culture and, in so doing, learn a dislike or disgust for certain bodily processes (and their products). This may lead to a repression of the pleasures previously attached to these products. Kristeva maintains that the mechanism of abjection centres around objects that disrupt bodily continuity. These objects include bodily fluids, such as excrement, sexual fluids, scabs, dead skin cells, menstrual blood, mucus and pus. The corpse, the skin of the milk and slimy non-vertebrates also have potential abject status and can be transformed into 'non-objects' through the mechanism of abjection.[16] Through these abjected (non-)objects, the subject as a coherent entity is faced with the conditional borders of embodied existence. All these objects call into question the subject's illusory unity. Bodily fluids, for instance, disrupt or violate the boundaries which constitute the illusion of subjecthood. Bodily fluids are bits of the body which have become unattached from the body. The ambiguous status of these non-objects (are they me or not me?) threaten the subject's illusion of continuity and narcissistic integrity. The problem is that they cannot be 'properly' regarded as either subject or object as they violate or transgress the differential distinction between the two. The experience of these non-objects may be double-edged; disgust may be violated by (an unholy[17]) fascination which disrupts the separation of subject and object and transgresses the boundary through ambiguity. The Bataillean experience of continuity and discontinuity as anguish and liberation is thereby reiterated.

Disgust, through abjection, ostensibly operates as a means of defending the coherent subject from becoming dissembled or violated. This policing function may be contaminated by a fascination with the (non)-object. Here the investment of desire has a double function and both repels and attracts in equal measure. The cry of disgust may then be closely associated with the cry of orgasm, and, as such, the movement of desire, which the subject seeks to control through abjection, is betrayed. The repressed pleasure invested in the object emerges through the intensity of the experience of disgust. The desire for fusion, in Bataille's words continuity, therefore threatens the narcissistic coherency of the subject. Kristeva does argue, however, that the 'avant-garde' preoccupation and fascination with the abject is itself a means of narcissistic mastery of the experience of (non-)objects. Here there is a fetishistic investment in the double meaning of the object of disgust. Disgust carries with it the dual load of fear and desire for annihilation. Abjection's primary function is to enable the subject to maintain the boundaries of ego-identity.

Abjection can then be seen to operate as a defence mechanism as it helps to define what is regarded as 'human' in a given cultural moment. It does so by facilitating the internalisation of the differential boundaries between inside/outside, Other/I, and operates to keep these differences intact.[18] As Kristeva says 'abjection is above all ambiguity';[19] it is therefore key to the mapping of the terrain and limits of the 'human' in a given culture and time. Abjected non-objects, however, have the power to contaminate and corrupt the logic of difference that underpins these mappings. Through the institution of taboos and the individual's experience of the taboo as disgust, the taboo operates to keep the integrity of a structure in place, and subjecthood and narcissism whole. This then links Bataille's notion of the function of the taboo directly to Kristeva's theorisation of the mechanism of abjection.

Fascination with the abject may then ostensibly work to pervert or contaminate the boundaries of language or the subject; but, argues Kristeva, this also helps to strengthen the ego as a means of controlling the anxiety it engenders. By naming the unnameable, the object *non-gratis* is then conferred with the status of an object and the threat to subject integrity is lessened. (Purification rituals can also be seen as a means of helping to name and thereby control the non-object status of a given experience.) Total control through the naming is not, however, possible, as transgression of the distinction between object and non-object is vital to the concretisation of the differences upon which the psychic and the cultural are based. Transgression is not only disruption here, but also acts as a reinforcement of borders. However, ambiguity, engendered through the emergence of repressed desire, can undermine the organisation of differences that give a culture its structural identity.

For Douglas, like Bataille, transgression holds the taboo in place. For Kristeva, however, working with the heterogeneous contradictory complexity of psychic functioning, the status of transgression is far less clear. In my reading of her work on abjection, I assume two kinds of transgression in operation in relation to abjection. The direct experience transgression (as shame, disgust or anguish) maintains the distinction between the object and the non-object and, secondly, the transgressive and mischievous function of desire undermines the operation of difference by contaminating language and identity with a decentralising ambiguity.

My reading of Kristeva's abjection can then be worked as an elaboration of Bataille's model of transgression as an experience which helps to maintain the structure which gives coherency to the subject but which also can operate as a form of liberation from the self. The subject internalises social mores through the experience elicited from the transgression of a taboo. The experience produced through transgression is crucial for it to retain cultural currency, but transgression can also carry within it the capacity to disrupt the stability of a given system through the pressure of repressed desire which produces excess. In Bataille's terms, the transgression carried out through eroticism is bound into the dual movement of the subject in relation to nostalgia for, and also a fear of, an imagined continuity (death). Sex is predicated on the drive to combat the discontinuous isolation of the subject; but this continuity also holds its own terrors, which are primarily the terror and, counterwise, the pleasure, of the annihilation of the subject's boundaries between itself and the Other. Sexuality is then problematically predicated on the oppositional nature of this dual movement. This formulation demonstrates how our own sexual desires and sexuality can be experienced as other to ourselves. Abjection, as a mechanism, prevents the dissolution of subject boundaries, the pleasure of abjection, as 'perilous pleasure' is strongly linked to the desire for a Bataillean continuity (death and the dissolution of identity).

Some feminist analyses of Horror and Explicit Sex films locate abjection around the female body in the male imaginary; I am here referring to the pro-censorship platform and also to Barbara Creed's psychoanalytic reading of the representation of women in the Horror genre.[20] Creed's approach usefully shows how women are constructed as emblematic of abjection in the male imaginary, but this paradigm is problematic in two ways. First, it reduces the abject to 'woman' and fails to address the operation of the mechanism of abjection in a broader sense. Second, within the Bataillean paradigm, this gender-specific approach is reductive as it fails to address the ways in which transgression is experienced as liberation and anguish. That sexuality and desire will always be other to the subject regardless of gender may, as Creed suggests, be projected on to others. Sexuality is, then, always a violation of subject coherency. It is linked with death and challenges the ego's illusion of autonomy. The very violence of sexuality is intrinsic to it and cannot, as the pro-censorship lobby requires, be erased by the imposition of juridical law. Through the same argument the libertarian position, which Bataille calls the 'back to nature' argument, is also flawed, as taboos cannot be simply removed to reveal a 'pure', untainted subject.

The excess of sexuality will therefore always pose a problem for the coherency of the subject and it is this knot of opposing drives that inflects the economy of desire in Explicit Sex films. Desire will always exceed intention and is written into language, gesture and action through the primary process. This further maps on to the notion that desire will always relate to sex and aggression; its inherent contradictoriness, its ambiguous play, affronts the 'clean and proper' subject and, as such, is disavowed through such mechanisms as abjection and the primary process. These processes are what underpin the aesthetic, psychic and social transgressions of Explicit Sex films. These films lean upon conventional models of desire but also demonstrate that the channelling of desire produces an excess which inhabits sexuality and renders it uncanny. Freud defined the uncanny as the emotional effect of an object which was once 'homely' but has become unhomely through repression.[21] He uses this term to describe the effect of the female genitals for the 'neurotic' male: '[t]his unheimlich place, however, is the entrance to the former Heim (home) of all human beings'.[22] My use of the term 'uncanny' in relation to sex, broadens Freud's explanation. I will use it to describe the uneasy feeling (and the frisson) that the representation of sex can produce because it bears with it repressed and othered material that relates to the primal scene (the fantasy of parental coitus). This is because the depiction of explicit sex leans on 'something which is familiar and old-established in the mind and which has become alienated from it only through the process of repression . . . something which ought to have remained hidden but has come to light'.[23] It is this that lends the films part of their transgressive meanings.

CICCIOLINA'S DIRTY–SUBLIME PRACTICES

Cicciolina in Italy is not dated but appears to have been made in the mid- to late 1980s. In the version of the film I viewed, most of the speech is in Italian and the subtitles are in Greek. The film features Cicciolina, the (in)famous blonde, baby-doll, porn-star, one-time member of the Italian government and Jeff Koons's ex-wife.[24] She stars with another porn-superstar, John Holmes, who is infamous for his large penis and his prodigious sexual encounters. Holmes and Cicciolina are cast as themselves, or at least, in their star personas. The video has an atmosphere of friendliness and the sex scenes are bracketed by conversations, hugging and kissing which indicates that the film targets a different audience to the 'teenage' fantasy videos, such as *New Wave Hookers*, *Gang Bang* and *Dr Butts II*. The sex scenes in *Cicciolina in Italy* are, in part, 'normalised' by the absence of parody, there is no misogynist banter between the men and no overt reference to sadomasochism. The sex is then coded as 'normal' heterosexual adult behaviour. For example, the orgy finale is bracketed by a dinner party, Holmes and Cicciolina are cast as 'partners' and they are often seen warmly embracing in bed after having sex with other people. The group sex and the 'lesbian' scenes are then situated within the frame of a loving heterosexual partnership, albeit non-monogamous. This works to attenuate the aesthetic and psychic transgressive dimension of the film.

The music in the film has important diegetic and non-diegetic roles to play. It creates continuity, rhythm and a jolly atmosphere through the various sex scenes. In the first scene it is directly related to the action. Cicciolina takes a tape of a song to a record industry executive. She sings along with the tape while the record executive watches and hears her performance. The song is very sweet, her high voice combines with harps and strings, helping to establish her angelic innocent 'essence'. This opening scene is important to the film and I will spend some time analysing it because it features the one element of the film that relates most closely to abjection, uncanniness and transgression.

The camera is set up directly facing Cicciolina sitting on a chair, an eye-line match from the position of the record executive. The initial shot is a slightly canted medium shot which includes some background and behind Cicciolina is a large mirror which doubles her image. Cicciolina addresses the camera throughout the scene. She is dressed in fairytale princess clothing – her peroxide white-blonde hair and her tiara, which has long silver threads hanging from it, resemble the image of Anita Louise's Titania in Max Rheinhardt's *Midsummer Night's Dream* (1935). In a later scene

Cicciolina has sex with three rather hairy, dark-skinned satyric men – the juxtaposition of white skin and swarthiness tapping into the 'Beauty and the Beast' fairytale. It is not entirely clear whether the fairytale iconography is an attempt to seduce a female audience as the traditional readers of fairytales, but it may also work to tap into fairytales' heady web of danger, desire and sex. The juxtaposition also enhances Cicciolina's whiteness, conventionally coded as goodness. Her fairytale princess image frames her sexual desire as innocent, even though users of the film may be aware of her predilection for urinating and defecating in her previous films. The contiguity of white (innocence/goodness) and her (dirty) pleasure in anal sex and excretion is perhaps key to understanding the transgressive pleasures that are mapped on to the film and Cicciolina's image. The co-presence of these conflicting, yet fascinating, elements embody a range of repressed and more legitimised sexual economies into one character. Her innocence is coded through her dress, her hair, her high girlish voice and her sweet demeanour towards her sexual partners. In the opening scene she initially carries a white fluffy teddy bear and later a Tiny Tears baby doll. At first glance she embodies the innocent desire of Hollywood stars like Marilyn Monroe whose sexuality was framed by innocence and childlikeness, but, unlike Marilyn's star persona, Cicciolina is never innocent of the gaze and the effect she might be having on the user. Her performance is played directly to the camera as an overtly exhibitionist pleasure. This is the first sign that the 'innocent' label is not so simple as it might seem as innocence and exhibitionism are not conventionally seen as synonymous.

In this first scene the Tiny Tears doll, which is almost life-size, replaces the teddy bear. Cicciolina sits, partly naked, astride a chair, cradling the doll. The framing and composition of the shot associates her with the image of the Virgin Mary holding the infant Christ. In some Renaissance icons of the Virgin she demurely displays a single breast. While this might be read as a sublimation of sexual desire through motherhood as a symbol of nurture, the stainless Virgin of Christian icons is wrought to downplay any overt sexual readings of the image. Mary's image is coded as sublime grace rather than as a proto-page three girl, but perhaps it is the sexual undercurrents of Mary's image that endows the Marian cult with its seductive power.[25] To read this image as sexual is, within the logic of Catholic discourse, perverse. The image of Cicciolina holding a mass-manufactured plastic doll, which might belong to any small girl, can be read to overtly subvert and sexualise the innocence of the Madonna. Further, the full-frontal view of Cicciolina's breasts and open vagina pollutes the chastity of the reference image. The display of her genitals and her seductive gestures and wide smile inverts the discourse of purity that is traditionally assigned to the Virgin. As Cicciolina performs her sweet song, baby doll cradled in one of her arms but not obscuring her breasts and genitals, she masturbates herself with a crystalline-looking dildo. As she does this there are a series of cutaway shots to the transfixed record executive biting his hand to signify his desire. Cicciolina lays the dildo aside and then gently squeezes the doll which begins to wet itself. The water flows down Cicciolina's torso and between her open legs. There follows a medium close-up of Cicciolina's lower torso and she begins to urinate on the carpet. A close-up then allows the viewer to see that the urination is authentic. The song's sweet tinkling tones are analogous to the sound of her urination as well as aurally paralleling the sparkling costume and dildo. The honeyed sounds of the song also hold something abject within it. The song and the costume help to elide the abject meaning of her blatant pissing on the carpet but there is something even more sinister at work – a kind of black magic which turns purity into delicious pollution. The scene ends with Cicciolina calling over the watching record executive and she fellates him. He orgasms very swiftly and his semen drips down her sweet-looking face. She then gently and pleasantly admonishes him for being a 'speedy gonzalez' (like the Madonna, she has the 'ear of understanding'[26]).

There are several contradictions in this scene which are located around the economy of abjection in the nexus of female archetypes – the mother, virgin, fairy queen and scarlet woman. The full flood of Cicciolina's urination is bracketed by signifiers of seduction and can be read as a means of buffering the abject meaning of the scene. By couching the urination within signifiers of innocence, the excess of the action is rendered ambiguous and thereby fascinating, perhaps also uncanny. Unlike Regan's urination on the carpet in *The Exorcist* (William Friedkin, 1973), where the urination is a signifier of psychic disturbance and is calculated to be shocking, here the dual encoding of Cicciolina as both seductive and innocent is calculated to entrance. The fetishistic function of the fairy-tale *mise-en-scène* also works to disavow the abject, 'dirty' practice of pissing on the carpet. I would suggest that this renders the act both uncanny and abject. Its uncanny status, as a way of describing an experience symptomatic of the mechanism of abjection, leans on the delocation of urination from the familiar toilet to the sexual space – tapping into the mixing of sexual and excretory functions of genitals in the child's psyche. It also gently foregrounds the unhomeliness of sex itself by dislocating the homely safety of bedroom sex and aligning it with a 'wild' version that precedes the channelling of sex and gender and, of course, lapsarian shame. In biblical terms she is perhaps more like the Old Testament witch Lilith than the New Testament's Madonna.

The dual coding of Cicciolina (dirty-shameless/innocent) creates an ambiguity which tempers the force of abjection. Abjection is also attentuated through the doll's urination which foreshadows Cicciolina's, creating an association between the innocent, instinctual urination of babies and Cicciolina's wilful, abject act. This works to construct Cicciolina as a 'naughty' girl who has not yet learned the full implications of her actions. The lights that play on the flow of her urine also help to aestheticise it, mirroring the silver slivers of light that catch her sequined costume. Thereby she is given the aura of a naiad, water sprite or siren – luring through her sweet song the unsuspecting record executive to the doom of premature ejaculation.

The combination of seduction with innocence which brackets the act of urination can, however, also be read as enhancing the transgressive currency of the scene. By aligning her blatant act with the image of the Madonna, the act is assigned a sinful perverse pleasure which would not be there were no reference made to Our Lady. This is, therefore, an economy of sexuality that trades on transgression and the forbidden, rather than on innocent instinct. Cicciolina's face and body are coded as conventionally beautiful (serene symmetrical features with high cheekbones, long legs and pert breasts); once the rivulets of urine run down her legs and her face is covered with semen her Madonna-like beauty becomes polluted with the signs of dirty sex and thereby constitutes the ob-scene of soft-focus idealised sex. The presence of signifiers of dirty sex, made all the more prominent through the juxtaposition of beauty/innocence, tap into the potentially deep and disturbing connection of sex and abjection. The full force of abjection in the scene is certainly tempered, but the presence of abject acts in the scene does, nevertheless, subvert the sublime and bea(u)tified ideal represented by the Madonna. Cicciolina is then both beauty and the beast. For a beautiful woman to be shamelessly pissing under the public gaze transgresses the aesthetic and social codings of femininity and motherhood. This transgression is, however, couched within the framework of spectacle and simply works to conserve the transgressive (and conservative) status of the genre and to conserve, through inverse (binary) mapping, the conventions of femininity.

There is a further aspect of transgression in this small scene which works to abject the user, whose diegetic counterpart is the record executive. I would propose that this scene promotes a viewing position which is voyeuristic and passive. Gaylyn Studlar argues that, rather than signifying lack, women on screen can instead signify power (the power to castrate).[27] Cicciolina's silvered sparkling costume and the light which flickers off her costume, the sparkling light being both there and not there, would seem to signify the ghostly trace of the missing maternal phallus. As su phallus is present in the scene and strengthen: that she is a potentially dangerous, castratory f power to magically enslave the Ulyssean record executi cause his sexually incapacitating premature ejaculation confirms her elided castratory power. The executive is the willing victim of Cicciolina's gaze and her siren-song. Her Medusa-like gaze, in the first instance, has the power to harden the penis, but then renders him impotent through premature ejaculation which becomes a sign of submissive defeat rather than triumph. Cicciolina is therefore invested with the tormenting power of a female Tantalus. This is not, then, a scene of the man's sexual possession of Cicciolina but rather his abasement, submission and loss of control. A kind of death which is, as Bataille says, both liberating and terrifying. (Perhaps some male users might disavow the pleasure of loss of control by thinking that if they were in the place of the executive they would command the situation.) Cicciolina controls the gaze and her kindly attitude towards the men in the video is always framed by her domination. She is not, however, coded as a conventional porno-dominatrix, she has no whip and uses no harsh words. As I have already said, 'speedy gonzalez' is seduced by her song, her gaze and her kindly words. He does not control the scene, but instead is 'out of control' (signified by his hand biting, premature ejaculation, whimpering noises). As he watches her masturbate and urinate on the floor, he is transfixed, and it is only at her behest that he is sanctioned to approach her. The opening section of the film works through the excessive pleasures of expectation and awe which depend on the complex mapping of Cicciolina's image and actions through a range of 'archetypal' or mythic signifiers.

The meanings of the scene can also be usefully aligned with the concept of primal fantasy, as delineated by Laplanche and Pontalis's 'Fantasy and the Origins of Sexuality'.[28] This article explores the insistence of fantasy in adult sexuality. Laplanche and Pontalis suggest that there are three primary fantasies, first identified by Freud, which are responses to the child's questions about their origins. These fantasies become repressed through the processes of socialisation and they play an important role in the shape of adult sexuality and desire. They are: the fantasy of parental coitus, of seduction and of castration. The unconscious fantasy of seeing or overhearing parental coitus invests seeing and hearing with a libidinal and transgressive charge and this fantasy underpins many of the pleasures in watching Explicit Sex films (in other words, the desire to see and hear that which is normally hidden or forbidden). In *Cicciolina in Italy* the promise is to show the acts of fucking, fellatio, anal sex and urination. The fantasy of seduction is also present within the film. In general, this fantasy is the product of the child's own sexual feelings which have been assigned an external source. Although a key discovery of psychoanalysis has been that young children are sexual, it is nevertheless the case that childhood is discursively construed as a period of sexual 'innocence'.[29] Because of this and the repression of sexual feelings for a parent through the Oedipus complex, childhood sexuality, to conserve the sense of childhood sexual innocence, must be retrospectively fantasised as having been introduced by an external seducing agent. The fantasy leans on the notion that sexuality is the result of a seduction in which the subject is passive, rather than active. It produces secondary fantasies based on seduction by another. Seduction is not then a sadistic fantasy (this would relate rather to secondary fantasies that stem from the primary fantasy of castration), but instead is a fantasy that relates to a Bataillean loss of control. The film leans on this fantasy of loss of control.[30]

As the user watches Cicciolina as she masturbates and urinates – her gaze directed into the camera and therefore directly at the user – the scene translates through the fantasy of seduction. The diegetic spectator, the record executive, is seduced by her actions – he is rendered passive by the scene and is shown to be so engulfed by her presence that he loses control of himself and is driven to a swift orgasm. Because film itself is akin to the flexible spatial and temporal realm of fantasy, users can then site themselves either with the subject of her gaze, the man, or with Cicciolina's controlling gaze allowing the user of the film to position themselves against their gender coding.

As Cicciolina is not cast in the role of a conventional dominatrix, but rather as a fairy queen who works the seductive magic of sexuality, she does not directly evoke the castration fantasy, but this is, nevertheless, still a reading available to users. If users position themselves with the male gaze here they become abjected because they no longer occupy the place of the controlling, active male. Through the web of the passive seduction fantasy, Cicciolina weaves an enveloping spell around the user. She is the benign fairy godmother (although she is the bad fairy too) who holds and enchants the child. Her spell conjures up a Bataillean yearning for a lost continuity (with all its pleasures and risks); her lulling song and the other signifiers of seduction eliding the risk of identity threatening envelopment.

Cicciolina's blue dress, the baby doll and her face semen-stained/tear-stained (like Tiny Tears, Cicciolina both cries and urinates), resonate within Kristeva's description in 'Stabat Mater' of the Madonna as Mater Dolorosa (Our Lady of Pain): 'under the full blue dress, the maternal, virginal body allowed only the breast to show, while the face, with the stiffness of Byzantine icons gradually softened, was covered with tears. Milk and tears became the privileged signs of Mater Dolorosa'.[31] The man's ejaculate that covers Cicciolina's face condenses tears and milk; and, like the archetypal mothers in De Quincy's essay 'Suspiria de Profundis' (Sighs from the Depths),[32] she is both Mater Lachrymarum, Our Lady of Tears and Mater Suspiriorum, Our Lady of Sighs. The semen/tears on her face, and her sighs, are the signs of her *jouissance*; a self-contained pleasure or *jouissance* that presents a teasing enigma to the user. Her sexual *jouissance* is not sublimated as mysticism but instead bears the traces of the mystery of the (m)other's sexual desire. As the mother's desire is for the child always a curious puzzle the film positions the user in a familiar, repressed, and therefore uncanny, place and we are left with the vexing question: what does Cicciolina want of me? Even though she apparently shows us all, her desire is never made fully transparent to the user because her actions bear the traces of hidden and contradictory desires akin to that of the mother's.

Although throughout the film's opening sequence the user might have been pleasurably identifying with Cicciolina's power to entrance through the web of mythic Circean resonances spelled out in the scene, this identification always flounders because, despite this identification, the user is always ambiguously positioned as her subject, her reader – prompting us to ask, what is the nature of our desire, do we desire to be her or be at her feet? On the one hand the film elicits a sense of mischievous and pleasurable complicity, but on the other, an anguish-bound sense of separateness and discontinuity. The opaque patina of mythic significations that I have identified in the film suggests quite strongly that the transgressive status of the film lies only in a temporary escape from the basic banality of sexual repressed desire and is governed by the desire for continuity with the Other/other. As much as I would like it to be, the film is not particularly subversive, but is rather symptomatic of the heterosexual matrix's channelling function in sex and gender formation.

I conclude by returning to the Lacanian/Laplanchean paradigm that the signification of sex and desire is always staged as an enigma; an enigma supported by taboos and prohibitions, and the solution of which is endlessly deferred. This is why sexuality is always the source of diverse and endless discourse, but is also resistant to enquiry. Sexuality, desire and fantasy are then located within the interstices of structural and dynamic functions of transgression, and through abjection, sex, fantasy and desire will always have a recalcitrant role to play. It is this that keeps desire in circulation, and difference, which is vital to the functioning of the symbolic system, in play. For this queer reader, if there were no law, then there would be nothing to transgress. As Bataille argues, the taboo is necessary to the constitution of culture and sexuality and, therefore, for the meanings and experience of transgression. We might seek, as Bataille says, redemption through sex, but sex and desire will always work to lacerate our sense of a coherent self. Sexual reformers, sexual taxonomists, libertarians or pro-censorship feminists cannot erase the anguish and liberation symptomatic of the sexual 'real' which underpins the representation of sexuality, as ideologically problematic as this may be, in Explicit Sex films. Explicit Sex films carry the abjected traces of sublated desires and it might therefore perhaps be more fitting to relabel the genre of 'Explicit Sex films' as 'Implicit Sex films'.

NOTES

1. George Bataille, *Eroticism* (London: Marion Boyars, 1987), p. 15.
2. Judith Butler, *Gender Trouble* (New York and London: Routledge,

1990), p. 2.

3. Julia Kristeva, *Powers of Horror* (New York: Columbia University Press, 1982), p. 72.

4. This film seems to have gone out under different titles. The copy I have been working from is entitled *Cicciolina in Italy* and is the title I will use in this chapter. The film also seems to have been called *Red Telephone*. Unlike mainstream films, Explicit Sex films often do not carry the date of production or the director in the credits. Anonymous authorship exacerbates their transgressive status. There are, however, some 'auteurs' of the Explicit Sex film genre such as Michael Ricaud, director of *Education d'Anna*.

5. Explicit Sex films depend on the circulation of culturally-specific taboos and concomitant repressions for their transgressive status and their generic coding. Unlike art cinema or softcore, Explicit Sex films promise to show us that which is hidden in other forms of cinematic and televisual representation.

6. Bataille, *Eroticism*, p. 31.

7. This also corresponds to Freud's enquiry into the formation of the psyche in 'Civilisation and Its Discontents' and 'Totem and Taboo'. For instance, 'Sublimation of instinct is an especially conspicuous feature of cultural development; it is what makes it possible for higher physical activities, scientific, artistic or ideological, to play such an important part in civilised life . . . it is impossible to overlook the extent to which civilisation is built upon a renunciation of instinct, how much it presupposes precisely the non-satisfaction (by suppression, repression or some other means?) of powerful instincts. This "cultural frustration" dominates the large field of social relationships between human beings', Sigmund Freud, *Penguin Freud Library Volume 12: Civilisation, Society and Religion*, James Strachey (trans.), 1929 (London: Penguin, 1991), pp. 286–7; and 'We are so made that we can derive intense enjoyment from a contrast and very little from the state of things'. Ibid. p. 264.

8. For example, in the analysis of sex and politics in the writings of Herbert and Wilhem Reich. For a sustained discussion of these texts see Jeffrey Weeks, 'Dangerous Desires', *Sexuality and Its Discontents* (New York and London: Routledge, 1985).

9. Freud's concept of the death drive also expresses a similar idea.

10. Bataille, *Eroticism*, pp. 16, 17.

11. Rather than using the term 'viewer' or 'spectator' I will use the term 'user' to describe the viewer of an Explicit Sex film. This term connotes an active participation with the text which falls into line with the film's aim to move the user's body. In so doing I signal that the processes of reading Explicit Sex films might have a qualitative difference from reading many other televisual or cinematic texts.

12. Importantly, because the representation of these acts are coded as

generically distinct from other mainstream cinemas and broadcast television, their transgressive status is institutionally and aesthetically corroborated.

13. For Hegel, the principle of sublation or *Auflebung* is that nothing is lost and always remains as a part of the whole. In a dialectical pattern the thesis and anti-thesis remain within the synthesis.

14. It is, though, problematic to conceive of any form of sexual exchange as outside of the system as, in a Lacanian reading of the sexual un-relation, sex is always a form of impossible demand on the other. The un-relation is thus subject to the dynamics of exchange in what Hegel called the master-slave relationship, and is therefore always bound into power. The heterosexual ideal of sex as an expression of love often operates as a ruse to disguise this power relation.

15. See Mary Douglas, *Purity and Danger* (New York and London: Routledge, 1966).

16. Kristeva, *Powers*, pp. 2–3.

17. 'Holiness' and 'purity' are meanings that are defined negatively through the process of abjection. 'Purification', for example, is a means of 'decontaminating' the subject from the polluting abjected non-object. The language used here pervades many modes of knowledge – however, the shared feature is that the body or an item closely associated with the body is penetrated or contaminated by the non-object (for instance, viruses, radiation, as well as the more obvious sexual meanings around virginity and monogamy). All these things relate to the integrity of the boundaries of the body.

18. 'Intact' is also used in relation to virginity. The concept and valorisation of virginity leans upon tropes of contamination and pollution of the sexually 'innocent' body. Traditionally, virginity in Western culture is seen as being related to taboos about paternity and can be regarded as operating to 'police' and regulate female sexuality.

19. Kristeva, *Powers*, p. 9.

20. See Barbara Creed, *The Monstrous-Feminine* (New York and London: Routledge, 1993).

21. Sigmund Freud, *Penguin Freud Library Volume 14: Art and Literature*, James Strachey and Angela Richards (ed. and trans.), 1919 (London: Penguin, 1990), pp. 335–76.

22. Freud, *Volume 14*, p. 368.

23. Freud, *Volume 14*, pp. 363-4.

24. Ilona Staller adopted the name 'Cicciolina' for a radio show that she appeared on in Italy in the 1980s. At the time of writing, a debate about the meaning of the word 'Cicciolina' has appeared on an internet newsgroup. Some participants claim it means 'piglet' or 'little bit of meat' (slang for the clitoris), whilst others maintain that it means 'little toy' (which might also imply the clitoris).

25. Kristeva examines the Marian cult in relation to male fantasies

about, and female experiences of, motherhood in 'Stabat Mater' in Toril Moi (ed.), *The Kristeva Reader* (Oxford: Blackwell, 1986). One aspect of the power of the Marian Cult is the sublimation of sexuality within the image of the Virgin Mary. This, she speculates, may be a 'sublimated celebration of incest?' (ibid. p.253). The power of the Marian cult thus relies on the power of sublimated sexuality and fantasy and, Kristeva says, 'Around the time of Blanche Castile (who died in 1252), the Virgin explicitly became the focus of courtly love, thus gathering the attributes of the desired woman and of the holy mother in a totality as accomplished as it was inaccessible. Enough to make any woman suffer, any man dream' (ibid. p. 245).

26. Kristeva, 'Stabat', p. 257.
27. See Gaylyn Studlar, 'Masochism and the Perverse Pleasure of Cinema', in Bill Nichols (ed.), *Movies and Methods II* (California: California University Press, 1985).
28. See Jean Laplanche and J. B. Pontalis, 'Fantasy and the Origins of Sexuality', in Burgin et al., *Formations of Fantasy* (New York and London: Routledge, 1986).
29. Jacqueline Rose explores the discourse of childhood sexual innocence in *The Case of Peter Pan* (Basingstoke: Macmillan, 1992) and in so doing shows the kernel of disavowal that remains in relation to the idea of children as perversely sexual: 'Freud uncovered in the sexual life of children the same perverse sexuality that analysis revealed in the symptoms of his patients and which was expressed indirectly in their dreams. By stating that this perverse sexuality was in fact quite normal to the extent that it could be located in the sexual life of the child, and by insisting, furthermore, that it was only spoken in the form of the symptom because it was a form of sexuality which was to be totally repressed elsewhere, Freud effected a break in our conception of sexuality and childhood from which we do not seem to have recovered' (p. 14).
30. This, for some users, might resurrect the complex feelings around the mother's body which have been repressed through gender formation.
31. Kristeva, 'Stabat', p. 173.
32. This essay is cited in Maitland McDonagh, *Broken Mirrors, Broken Minds: The Dark Dreams of Dario Argento* (London: Sun Tavern Press, 1991).

11

Symptoms of AIDS in Contemporary Film: Mortal Anxiety in an Age of Sexual Panic

MONICA B. PEARL

In so far as AIDS is 'a nexus where multiple meanings, stories, and discourses intersect and overlap, reinforce, and subvert one another',[1] AIDS films display anxieties about sex, sexual identity and disease in general. Paula A. Treichler writes:

The AIDS epidemic . . . is simultaneously an epidemic of a transmissible lethal disease and an epidemic of meaning or signification . . . This epidemic of meanings is readily apparent in the chaotic assemblage of understanding of AIDS that by now exists.[2]

AIDS is a crisis not only of the body but of representation in that the subject of AIDS poses a problem for established representation.

In this chapter, I will look at films that are not self-consciously about AIDS but which I believe reflect a societal anxiety about it. I will be examining the way sexual panic and a new anxiety about mortality and loss – both of which, I hope to suggest, are linked to and arise from the discourse on and fear of AIDS – make their way into a mainstream cinema that in no obvious way seems to be about AIDS. The cinematic genres in which these anxieties seem to be most conspicuously evident are those that dramatically negotiate popular sentiments about love and sex. In what follows, I will look at the romance genre that I call reincarnation films and then turn to sex thrillers, uncovering in each their underlying preoccupations with AIDS-related anxieties.

AIDS is itself a representation: it is the nexus and manifestation of what is traditionally and essentially terrifying about sex and death in Western society. The tradition of terror includes perverse sexuality; death, particularly death that is sudden, unexpected and premature; loss of those whom one loves and believes one cannot live without (that is, abandonment); and debilitation, dementia and loss of control over one's body. Judith Williamson writes:

[S]ex and death are always liable to tear through the familiar fabric which clothes our naked experience – yet these are precisely the events that are also inevitably linked with AIDS: sex as a means of HIV transmission, death as its probable outcome. It is no coincidence that sex and death are events of the body: the point at which we meet, and are a part of, the material world, no longer imposers of meaning on it but imposed upon by its meaninglessness.[3]

There is nothing so terrifying, it would seem, as a vacuum of meaning. AIDS itself, while assumed to be a disease, is actually an acronym for a syndrome that occurs when any number of diseases or conditions are present along with HIV, itself another acronym.

The virus that is thought to cause AIDS is itself meaningless. Williamson writes, 'nothing could be more meaningless than a virus. It has no point, no purpose, no plan; it is part of no scheme, carries no inherent significance'.[4] The cultural anxieties that circulate around AIDS arise from the despair involved in reacting to meaninglessness and trying to construct meaning. One of the ways to respond to meaninglessness is to create a narrative that determines origins and destinations. According to Williamson: 'narrative structures are enormously important to our way of thinking: we like things to have a beginning, a middle and an end, we like events to have a point, to seem to be going somewhere'.[5] Cinema is one way we have to give meaning to what we perceive as meaningless, and specifically to AIDS, as making films is one of the ways we have culturally to give something a story. Movies, besides distracting us from our anxieties, tell us stories that describe – and often pretend to try to alleviate – our anxieties. Some of the questions that AIDS films try to answer are, 'where do terrible things come from?' and 'what have we done to deserve this?' The films try to cure our panicked curiosity about origins and intentions:

A search for sources is a large part of the teleological or goal-directed mode of thinking which characterizes both rationalist/modernist thought, and, of course, all fictional narratives – which, being finished constructs, always *do* have a predetermined goal.[6]

The 'goal' of the narrative of reincarnation comedies, for example, is to recover the proper body – the body one believes one is *supposed* to have and not the body that has been taken and prematurely ravaged.

THE REINCARNATION FILM

Reincarnation films are movies in which one of the characters dies and returns as a ghost, dies and returns in a new body, or does not die but somehow, retaining the same soul or personality, assumes another body. My point about separating these films off into their own genre of reincarnation films is that they are in many ways a response to the emergence of an awareness of AIDS.

There are myriad ways in which death is represented in films, many of which are expressed comically or flippantly. An increasingly familiar genre is the one in which a character is not only given a new chance at life, but given a whole new body. While there have been films like this throughout the history of cinema – *Heaven Can Wait* (Ernst Lubitsch, 1943) and its 1978 remake (Warren Beatty), for example – there has been a proliferation of them in these last years of desperation. These recent films generally play on sex and gender mismatching; that is, the characters revive as the same gender, but a different sex. Their souls are still masculine (for it is mostly men) but their bodies are now female. In some films the person does not even have to die to get a new body – souls are accidentally exchanged, as in *Prelude to A Kiss* (Norman René, 1992), or a soul is sent out in anticipation of a death, as in *All of Me* (Carl Reiner, 1984). Often the new body is temporary – either because the protagonists struggle to retrieve their own body, or because the new body was a spiritual test before the protagonist could get into heaven, as in *Switch* (Blake Edwards, 1991).

Many love or comedy films are made in the mode of fantasy. They tend towards realism only in so far as they exhibit our desire for what realism would be if we had our way and our desires were fulfilled. A 'realist film creates a world which is as recognizable as possible; and audiences understand it by drawing analogies between the world of the film and their own world. They are assisted in this process by the lengths that realist film goes to in order to look like real life.'[7] Reincarnation films contrive an unusual fantasy realism that accepts all the qualifications of the material world, making the transmutation bizarre and miraculous, yet ultimately believable. The films depict fantasy desires fulfilled and then illustrate their disadvantages: we do not really want our fantasies fulfilled with what we think we do (as in wanting a new body and a new chance at life and then wanting the old body back, even if that means returning to prepubescent youth as in *Big* (Penny Marshall, 1988); becoming older, more decrepit and close to death (*Prelude to A Kiss*) or, in fact, actually dead [*Switch*]).

Science fiction and horror have often dealt in the realm of new bodies: frightening growths and permutations, coming back from the dead as a monster, but these body-switching reincarnation films – often comedies – are about hope, not fear. When Amanda (Ellen Barkin) is on trial in *Switch* for the murder of her former male body, we in the audience can understand how everyone else thinks she is crazy, but we, the audience, are always apprised of the true narrative. We are supposed to believe that if we were in that situation we would know the difference and we would believe that our loved one was still really alive, as in *Prelude to A Kiss*. There is a set of new-body movies in which the dead loved one comes back not as a new human being but as a ghost (a ghostly incarnation of his former self). In this case the dead character retains not only his original sex and gender, but his original body, albeit now amorphous and permeable, as in *Ghost* (Jerry Zucker, 1990) and *Truly, Madly, Deeply* (Anthony Minghella, 1990). The primary anxiety in reincarnation films is not fear of what monstrous fate could befall one, as in science fiction or horror films, but the anxiety of resolution: that ethereal love, but also concrete bodies, will be restored.

DEATH AND THE OBSTACLES OF LOVE

I will look at the film *Prelude to A Kiss* in particular because I believe it best embodies the themes that constitute a reincarnation film – that is, it most clearly exposes the subtext of what reincarnation films are yearning for: love that transcends, not just death, but our actual bodies; recognition of the importance of personal identity; and an ultimate desperation to recover one's original body.

The nature of love in film today is that it requires some trial and proof. The central relationship is constituted by discreet sex, fidelity and a conspicuous absence of any desire or behaviour that might be construed as perverse. True love – as manifested in the contemporary romance – is marked by loyalty, which is often determined as sex (or the suggestion or even just the promise of sex) only with your partner, and then some trial of loss and recovery, as in *When Harry Met Sally* (Rob Reiner, 1989) where the two protagonists lose and rediscover each other repeatedly, and *Pretty Woman* (Gary Marshall, 1990) where Vivian must leave at the end before Edward doubles back to reclaim her, to give just two of many possible examples. Recovery in romance can be taken two ways: as finding again, as in rediscovering, and as revival. To revive is to bring back to life, and indeed, that is the agenda of a significant subset of romance films – the reincarnation film: to demonstrate the agonising loss of one's loved one and then to bring them brilliantly back to life.

The theme of lovers separated by death has always been a thematic milieu ripe for melodrama, but natural expiration from illness, and even sudden traumatic accidental deaths, have already been milked for every last drop of melodramatic appeal. Melodrama has, however, now been successfully revived to create credibility for impossible situations, like the transubstantiation of a soul and personality into a new body. The theme of lovers reunited across the threshold of death is an old, familiar and heartrending scenario; in this era of plague – in a time of panic that young attractive virile men or innocent beautiful women are likely to age rapidly and die protracted deaths for no apparent reason – the fantasy proliferates on screen, offering hope and reassurance in the possibilities of not just eternal love across and within the great beyond but the possibility of eternal physical contact.

Love stories are often about mortality. Michael Westlake and Robert Lapsley, in a Lacanian interpretation of cinematic romance, outline the loss and perpetual dissatisfaction involved in cinematic portrayals of true love and the illusion of satisfaction: '[r]omance does not deny that there is a lack, but it claims that it can be made good'.[8] If love amplifies the always instantiated loss of original love then love is always about death, the yearning towards that which cannot be fulfilled: 'romantic narratives are almost invariably concerned with the obstacles in the way of its realization'.[9] In reincarnation films, death or the comparable loss of one's body becomes just another impediment to the realisation of love and the satisfaction of desire in the lexicon of Hollywood obstacles in the course of romance.

Most reincarnation films are romances or turn out to include a love element. Some of them, like *Switch* and *All of Me*, are not exactly tales of love but do revolve around themes of sexual desire and compatibility. Films like *Ghost* and *Truly, Madly, Deeply* are more obviously romantic love stories where death becomes the obstacle to union. Reincarnation films constitute a different kind of romance – not where two people fall in love but (in the case of ghost films) where two people are already in love and become mournfully separated by death. Many of the reincarnation films are either comedies or include a strong thread of comedy. Humour allows tragedy to become something manageable, something we can inspect; 'comedy is an area of expression that is licensed to explore aspects of life that are difficult, contradictory and distressing'.[10] Comedy, it is suggested here, is about as close to tragedy as you can get.

BEING AND TIME: PRELUDE TO A KISS

In *Prelude to A Kiss* Peter (Alec Baldwin) and Rita (Meg Ryan) meet, fall in love and marry, whereupon Peter discovers on their honeymoon that his wife is acting very strangely. Upon their return to Chicago he realises that someone else's soul has become encased in his wife's body and that his wife's soul is somewhere else, in some other body. When Peter encounters the old man – Julius (Sydney Walker) – who now houses Rita's soul, he returns to his apartment to find Julius-in-Rita's-body gone. The rest of the film consists of Peter not only searching for Rita's proper original body but in managing to live together – in love, after all – with Rita's unexpected physical permutations.

The film opens with the reflection of a clock tower upside down, reading near midnight, until the camera tracks up, along a vine, to Peter's watch showing the same hour and then to Peter looking across the water at the tower and then takes Peter's view of the clock tower as it tolls midnight. Visually connecting the clock tower to Peter's watch establishes for the viewer that the film's theme is time and that it will affect Peter personally. It is just after this image of the clock tower that Peter and Rita meet. The meeting at the end of the film, in which bodies and identities are resolved, is set for high noon, and we get a shot of the same clock tower bearing the same time, as though time will return to the moment they first met, and they will rediscover each other. The segue song between the clock tower and when Peter meets Rita is one sung by Brian Ferry called 'The "In" Crowd'. The lyric we hear is 'maybe time will be your window' and in this narrative time *is* the window through which we see and follow the events of the story. *Prelude to A Kiss* is a film about time and mortality, about running out of time, about finding the right (some)body before the clock tolls for thee, and about – as the spinning of the clock's reflection illustrates – the difficulty, despite the relative fluidity of time upon reflection, of turning ahead or turning back the clock. The narration opens with Peter's voiceover, as he walks from his perch on the roof back to the party, musing about the sign on a roller coaster that says 'ride at your own risk' and how it suggests there is no one in control who is interested in your safety and well-being, that anything can happen, and, he concludes, anything can.

On their wedding day Rita asks Peter just before the ceremony if he will love her when she is balding with yellow teeth. He says, of course he will. In a matter of hours (by the time of the reception, although it will take him a week to discover it) she is indeed balding with yellow teeth. When Peter is first alone in the apartment with Julius he cries, 'I'm not equipped for this . . . I'm not attracted to you'. And it is at this point, when he realises he is newly married to an old man, that he quizzes her again on her identity, frantic to establish yet once more that it is she inside Julius's body, demanding the name of the boy she went out with in high school, and cries out again, 'if I could believe you were really here'. Although he manages once to kiss her, embodied as she is as an old man, he is still tormented throughout the film that it is not her and her body, even though it is indeed 'really' her.

In a gesture of congratulations on her marriage, Rita is kissed by an unknown man who has wandered into the grounds of the wedding party. Although neither Peter nor the viewing audience can detect it immediately, Rita and the old man, Julius, have exchanged souls, each now inhabiting the other's body. *Prelude to a Kiss* is a movie about accelerated time and about the ageing and deterioration of the body; it is a film about growing old but also about *sudden* deterioration – the same extraordinary effect that AIDS has upon the body – 'ageing before one's time': suddenly one finds one's loved one, for example, old, deteriorated and often with an unrecognisable personality, due to dementia, perhaps, or simply rage over the premature deterioration and imminent death.

When Peter realises that the Rita in his house is occupied by someone else's soul he rants, pleads, with tears in his eyes: 'just tell me where Rita is', which, taken as a metaphor for a lover's death and not a simple (and infinitely more acceptable, in the world of cinematic possibility) transubstantiation of souls, would easily represent his grief over loss – that headfirst plunge into an inability to understand or accept where one's loved one has gone. (During the wedding ceremony Rita forgets and needs to be reminded of the line, 'in sickness and in health', portending some difficulty in keeping this particular vow.) And, of course, a natural extension of grief, dramatically recapitulated in the reincarnation dynamic, is to see one's loved one in others – in many and rather improbable others. Here Peter has lost Rita but 'finds' her again in the unlikely Julius.

The mechanism that initiates the drama is Julius's urgency, knowing he is dying, to trade in his own body for a young healthy one. At the same time, Rita, about to plunge into a frightening new future, suddenly and sharply desires to know how it feels not to be afraid. These simultaneous longings allow for their bodies to be switched. It is notable that it is precisely the luxury of growing old that is lost to those with AIDS. In this light both Rita's desire to leap into what she perceives as a secure old age, and Julius's desire to be young and healthy, are understandable.

It is difficult given these interpretations not to see the movie as a parable of the way AIDS descends tragically and confusingly upon couples in love, especially as the writer and director (Craig Lucas and Norman René) are the same writer and director who created the AIDS film *Longtime Companion* (Norman René, 1990), the first feature-length movie about AIDS. An interesting feature, in this respect, in *Prelude to a Kiss* is Rita's father's tattoos. They serve, on the surface, as a piece of identification. When Peter wants to be sure that he has found Rita (in Julius's body) he asks her to identify her father's tattoo. Tattoos also serve to represent body identification generally. One is one's skin, this identification suggests; when one is fighting to live one is 'saving one's skin'. Tattooing has been suggested as a form of identification for people infected with HIV; American journalist William Buckley, for example, has proposed that those infected sexually be tattooed on the buttocks, while those infected intravenously be tattooed on their arms, in order to protect those who interact with them.[11] The film is not only offering a parable of a couple living with illness but is also creating a forum for questioning the meaning and effect of identity: that is, how being a certain kind of person determines whether or not you will fall ill or deteriorate before your time.[12] It is also asking what is the measure of mortal illness unto death: the loss of skin, hair, teeth, limbs? What can one lose and still remain, vitally, oneself? The film asks, how much of an individual is her or his body?

Further, *Prelude to A Kiss*, through fantasy, gives reason to the sorts of resolutions at which one arrives when contemplating not only the prospect of death but that *who one is* contributed to that demise. The story of *Prelude to A Kiss* provides an exploration of and resolution to the idea that who one is is intractable, regardless of outward appearance. However, beneath the romantic surface of true love knowing no boundaries lie the ideological problems of outward appearance as an obstacle to true identity: '[w]ith its lack of ideological imagination, the film exploits the very age-ism, misogyny, and homophobia that we expect it to explore: it perverts – that is, contradicts and disposes of – the very proposition of imagining alternative bases of love'.[13]

Although the kiss between Peter and Rita-in-Julius might be shocking to watch, we know he is really kissing his wife and heroically overcoming the boundary of her old man's body. The kiss should indeed be more shocking as an idea (although not visually) as Peter is 'really' kissing Julius, a man. In the first instance, 'because it is a *male* body, figuratively it stands between Peter and the spirit of his wife, and also between Peter and the flesh of his wife';[14] but also, it must be said, because it is an old body. If the body that Rita got herself into was a young, attractive, male body, the problem would then simply be one of gender. The film excuses its potential homophobia by making age and the perishing body the repelling factors. That Peter and Rita learn that Julius's body is dying is crucial to the story as it provides the strong narrative motivation for recovering Rita's body; otherwise, if Rita's body were only different but healthy, Peter would be revealed as a man with good intentions but who could not keep his end of the 'in sickness and in health' compact, a vow that presumably includes, 'in permutations in appearance, sex, or general desirability'.

Another film which exhibits concern over identity and appearances is the mainstream self-proclaimed AIDS film *Philadelphia* (Jonathan Demme, 1993). Andrew (Tom Hanks) exhorts in the camcorder visit to his childhood home 'don't trust appearances', asking the audience to recognise both that his veneer as a successful attorney masks his true identity as a homosexual but also that his identity as a homosexual might conceal his true humanity, his true ability to practise law, for example, or to believe in justice. From the brief survey here it appears that films attempt much more to satisfy the questions and insecurities an audience might have about (sexual) identity than about (sexual) behaviour. They take for granted an essentialism about who we are and do not consider that who we are might be constituted by what we do.[15] *Prelude to A Kiss* participates in the essentialist notion that who we are is based on a core identity – easily reduced to the idea of the soul or a personality – that is both separate and inseparable from the body (Rita is Rita, no matter whose body she is in, but Rita is not satisfactorily Rita until she has her own body back, allowing Peter to ask at the end of the film when Julius and Rita are attempting to switch back bodies, 'where's Rita?' and for Julius-still-in-Rita to point to Julius's body) and largely dismisses the notion that we perform and behave who we are, that we are what we do.

Reincarnation films can be read as attempts to give meaning to what is experienced in our Western culture as the unbearable meaninglessness of the virus that causes AIDS. The general experience of AIDS, as Jan Zita Grover suggests, is that 'AIDS is not simply a physical malady; it is also an artifact of social and sexual transgression, violated taboo, fractured identity – political and personal projections'.[16] Reincarnation films amplify and compound the meanings of the disease and its effects and encourage the creation of fantasies to both probe and provide reassurance for our fears.

Both reincarnation films and sex thrillers elaborate cultural meanings of love and sex, and cultural uncertainties about mortality. In exploring answers to the question posed by Linda Singer, in her book *Erotic Welfare*, 'What is so attractive, at this particular time, about . . . eroticizing the connection between pleasure and danger?',[17] I will now examine how contemporary Hollywood erotic thrillers reflect personal and cultural anxieties about AIDS.

THE SEX THRILLER

By sex thrillers I mean those films in which suspense is the primary feature and in which sex features as a contribution to the suspense or to its resolution. In this category I will examine *Body of Evidence* (Uli Edel, 1992), because it identifies so closely the emerging anxiety about whether one can be killed through an act of sex, and then focus more closely on *Damage* (Louis Malle, 1992), because it best represents the idea abundant in other films of the genre that illicit sex – that is, adulterous sex – is a symbol of mortal infection in the lexicon of anxiety and film representation.

Murder and brutality expand the meanings of safety with regard to sex. In *Basic Instinct* (Paul Verhoeven, 1992), in which safety is a critical concept but a useless term, Gus, Nick's fellow detective, gets angry at Nick in the Country and Western bar for his reckless sex with the prime murder suspect, who allegedly kills men during sex. Nick responds: 'Next time I'll use a rubber'. Nick is portrayed in this film as reckless, willing to 'take risks'. Here is an example of safe sex meaning something wildly different from protection from infection. One type of unsafe sex in other words (which gets very little press) is sleeping with someone you believe to be a killer and who uses methods and techniques in bed recognised to be part of a known murder. In *Basic Instinct* safe sex means not getting murdered.

There are always reasons why not to engage in safe sex, and some of these are both literally and metaphorically pasted up on the screen. Obstacles to safe sex in real life are about education, economy, self-esteem and identity; in the movies the more common obstacles are passion and obsession. So easily does obsession supersede more pedestrian excuses like 'it interrupts the natural course of lovemaking' or 'I suspected he was healthy' or 'there were no condoms in the house', that it makes the day-to-day extra-cinematic details of safe sex or a concern with them seem ridiculous. It is in the films of sexual possibility and sexual enactment that the closer-to-home anxieties about sex and sexual identity and death – usually negotiated around condoms and other means of practising safe sex – are played out in terms of grand passions and obsessions.

LETHAL SEXUALITY: BODY OF EVIDENCE

Body of Evidence expresses the newly-awakened anxiety in the age of AIDS: 'can you fuck someone to death?' The anxiety is expressed in the film by a child, since the adults amongst us are supposed to know better: Frank Delaney (Willem Dafoe), the lawyer for the prime suspect, responds to his son's question, 'can you screw someone to death?', by telling him that it is not something he needs to worry about yet, the implication being that he will have to worry about it one day. The answer in the movie is that you *can* 'screw someone to death', especially as the femme fatale, in the twist of innocence-revealed-as-guilt at the end, is found to have done just that, guilty as charged for having 'fornicated Andrew Marsh to death'.

The plot of *Body of Evidence* is very simple: Rebecca Carlson (Madonna) is accused of murdering her boyfriend for the eight million dollars left to her in his will. The twist is that she is accused of killing him by having sex with him (although the actual elements that kill him are the cocaine slipped into his nasal spray combined with the strenuousness of sex and, particularly, the 'increasingly strenuous sex' that Rebecca Carlson requires). The idea behind this movie is, then, that sex can kill you if you choose the wrong partner.

In its expression of current sexual anxiety, cinema turns falling in love into the risk. Love is the risk factor when it is with the 'wrong' partner and when perversity is involved. Bobby Garrett (Joe Mantegna), the prosecuting attorney, says at the trial, 'Andrew Marsh made what turned out to be a fatal mistake: he fell in love'. Love is expressed as a risk in thrillers, hardly ever in romances. In sexual thrillers the body itself becomes lethal: the prosecuting attorney pronounces alarmingly, 'she is not only the defendant; she is the murder weapon itself'. Her defence is that she loved him and therefore would not have killed (infected) him – a dubious defence indeed.

Like *Philadelphia*, *Body of Evidence* is a film that sublimates the quest for answers to sexual perplexities into the criminal justice system, attempting to resolve questions of sexuality and identity through the pursuit of justice. While Frank Delaney protests in the film that, 'it's not a crime to be a great lay', the court system that *Body of Evidence* cinematically mirrors to examine issues of sexual and mortal misconduct is the same court system that increasingly in the USA makes HIV infection a crime; that is, it is a crime in many states to knowingly infect another person with HIV. Notions of consent are dismissed, as presumably no one would consent to being infected. In sexual thrillers one may consent to dangerous sex but not to sex that leads to death. For death one gets prosecuted, exiled or killed. Cinematic morality is punitive and unforgiving.

ILLICIT ROMANCE (SEXUALITY) AS INFECTION: DAMAGE

The central relationship in a thriller is marked by perversity, infidelity or indiscreet, that is, explicit, sex (as opposed to the discretion required of romance films. It is generally not romantic or based on love).

As films of adultery become more explicitly dangerous and threatening, the more possible it is that the 'other' that defines a liaison as extra-marital, or extra-anything, is conceived as a lethal 'infection' meant to destroy the agent that brings the infection into the family realm, ultimately to destroy the family unit itself. The 'infection' destroys the family not so much because the family is infected by the errant family member, but because the family cannot sustain the stigma – the idea – of infection, and its members must individually absolve themselves, indeed cleanse themselves, of the taint.

In *Damage*, infection comes from outside the perfect and respectable family, first brought in, 'innocently', by the young son in his twenties. The idea of infection is embodied in this film by the concept of the 'other woman', brought into the family by the son but made truly into an other and rendered menacing by the father. This is the way that, not necessarily HIV, the virus, but the *spectre* of AIDS is brought into a family. The fear of AIDS, after all, is to most people only minimally the fear of the actual virus (which so many people know so little about that their fears both outrun and underestimate the actual possibilities of infection) but far more the stigma of what it means to have AIDS, to be in a family of which a member might have AIDS, or even to know someone who does or who might have AIDS.

Anna (Juliette Binoche) is the woman with whom Martyn (Rupert Graves), the son, begins a relationship and brings into the family. While Ingrid (Miranda Richardson), Martyn's mother, is sceptical about and distrustful of Anna, Stephen (Jeremy Irons), Martyn's father and respected Member of Parliament, becomes tormented and obsessed by her and conducts with her a sexually explicit, and often what appears to be a sexually violent, relation-ship. In the end Martyn discovers Anna and his father making love and accidentally backs up over a stairway rail and dies. The family crumbles, Ingrid goes to pieces over the loss of her son and Stephen resigns.

Writing about an early film of sexual danger, *Fatal Attraction* (Adrian Lyne, 1987), Linda Singer remarks: '[a]s the plot unfolds, representations of pleasure are progressively displaced by images of panic, hysteria, destruction and eventually death'.[18] *Damage* exemplifies this cinematic panic in the age of AIDS as its plot emerges from the equation: pleasure equals panic.

Following the analogy of a family 'infected' by stigma, Martyn, the son, is treated at times as a gay son and Anna as his gay male lover. Ingrid, his mother, says 'always nice to meet Martyn's *friends*'. And his grandfather, Edward (Ian Bannen), says, 'is this your new *friend*?' in that way that families allude to a same-sex partner with-out wanting to acknowledge that person's sexual relationship to their child. In the end the son dies – causing his family great scandal and shame – a far from unfamiliar pattern to families that have lost a son or other family member to AIDS. The initial, but brief, image of a stable family 'works to position sexual threat as a force from without, and as a gratuitous, hence unjustified, invasion by the alien or outsider, rather than as a dynamic already operative within the family.'[19]

Anna first appears in black leather when she introduces herself to Stephen. Her first words are 'you're Martyn's father', confirming not only his identity as first and foremost the father of her lover but indicating that this film will be in some important ways about identity, and specifically about identity as connected to family position. The first image of Anna is her entering through a doorway. Indeed, it is a movie of doorways. Stephen and Anna often see each other through doorways, or the audience is invited to observe them through doorways, the absence of such passages indicating less a freedom from constraints than something even tighter closing them in. When Stephen appears at Anna's home for their first liaison, the *mise-en-scène* has Stephen fitted perfectly within a picture frame, indicating that already he is 'framed' for his transgression, his desires, indicating that there will be repercussions and that they are anticipated and already inevitable. The last image we have of Stephen while still in contact with Anna is against the very corner of a picture frame, indicating that he is now 'cornered', barricaded by the consequences that have transpired. The sex in which Stephen and Anna engage in a doorway on a street in Paris is the scene that depicts Stephen's relentless attachment. There is no going back. He has 'crossed the threshold', has corrupted the doorway. Of course, thresholds are symbols of a home, the boundary that creates a home, evident in the post-nuptial ritual of a groom carrying his bride over the threshold of their new home, marking the start of their life together. Stephen and Anna violate this threshold. The very last sequence of Stephen has him in what appears to be the south of France walking through a very large light-filled doorway back to his rustic home. Freedom in this film is not the *lack* of doorways, but passages that have lightened and opened up.

The primary images of the film are not only of doorways but also of staircases. The film opens with Stephen descending a large majestic staircase in the House of Commons. He again descends – in an image that can be taken as an allusion to a descent from respectability into the hell of perfidy and disrepute – after his first sexual encounter with his son's lover. The central dramatic and traumatic image of the film is Martyn's descent over the banister past the winding stairs to his death, after whom, naked, his father runs, leaving his bed of iniquity, descending the winding stairs to hold his dead son in his arms. Stephen's chase after his son depicts his having plunged the depths of ignominy and having brought his family with him. The 'infection' has taken hold and his family suffers the depths of his descent. Stephen's final decline is in his own home, the morning after Martyn's death, when he descends the stairs to tender his resignation from parliament.

Damage is a film that tries to give meaning to infection, a sense to the meaninglessness of the element that breaks up a family. While a sex thriller like *Body of Evidence* reflects our anxieties, a thriller like *Damage* interprets them, tries to give them meaning. Stephen's last words in *Damage*, a voiceover, muse, 'what really makes us is beyond grasping; it's way beyond knowing. We're given to love because it gives us some sense of what is unknowable. Nothing else matters. Not at the end.' Suspense is a condition of aggravating the unknown and the unknowable; to be in suspense is precisely to be uncertain. A thriller exaggerates this 'not knowing', tries to paint it with images that will make sense, tries to excite our fears, not to allay them, but to keep them alive, to illustrate that alleviating them is both impossible and dangerous.

NOTES

1. Paula A. Treichler, 'AIDS, Homophobia, and Biomedical Discourse: An Epidemic of Signification', in Douglas Crimp (ed.), *October*, Winter, 43 1987: p. 42.
2. Treichler, 'AIDS', p.32.
3. Judith Williamson, 'Every Virus Tells a Story: The Meaning of HIV and AIDS', in Erica Carter and Simon Watney (eds), *Taking Liberties: AIDS and Cultural Politics* (London: Serpent's Tail, 1989), p. 70.
4. Williamson, 'Virus', p. 69.
5. Williamson, 'Virus', p. 70.
6. Williamson, 'Virus', p. 71.
7. Graeme Turner, *Film As Social Practice*, second edition (London: Routledge, 1993), p. 156.
8. Robert Lapsley and Michael Westlake, 'From *Casablanca* to *Pretty Woman*: The Politics of Romance', *Screen*, 33 (1) Spring 1992: p. 28.
9. Lapsley and Westlake, '*Casablanca*', p. 38.
10. Richard Dyer, *The Matter of Images: Essays on Representation* (London: Routledge, 1993), p. 114.
11. See Simon Watney, *Policing Desire: Pornography, AIDS and the Media* (London: Comedia, 1987), p. 44; and see also Richard Goldstein,

'AIDS and the Social Contract', in Carter and Watney, *Taking Liberties*, p. 93.

12. The film *Big* can also be read as an AIDS parable, but it is not a film of reincarnation in the way the others are. It is, rather, a film of getting an older body, one's own older body – getting a body, in fact, that is about the median age of those dying of AIDS. This film does not suggest, as the other Reincarnation Films do, that one can better be oneself in one's own body. Indeed, Josh (Tom Hanks) has a fine time being himself, which is what makes him so charming to everyone around him – he is a child in a grown man's body. There is no issue in this story of waning or compromised health. Thirty is about as good as thirteen, this film seems to suggest, with regard to body and health. Everything Josh gives up by returning to his boyhood is promised to him upon growing older; what he gets is a chance to do it all over again, make different choices (or make the same ones again), a fantasy opportunity lost on no individual dying at an unreasonably young age of a disease that there have been no reasonable cautions against, particularly in its earliest years of manifestation.

13. Diane Sippl, '. . . Even As Also I Am Known', *Cineaction*, 33 1994: p. 24.

14. Sippl, 'Even', p. 24.

15. See Judith Butler, *Gender Trouble: Feminism and the Subversion of Identity* (London: Routledge, 1990), for a discussion concerning this distinction.

16. Jan Zita Grover, 'AIDS: Keywords', *October*, 43 Winter 1987: p. 18.

17. Linda Singer, *Erotic Welfare: Sexual Theory and Politics in the Age of Epidemic* (London: Routledge, 1993), p. 179.

18. Singer, *Erotic Welfare*, p. 180.

19. Singer, *Erotic Welfare*, pp. 181–2.

Notes on Contributors

Michele Aaron is Lecturer in Film and Television at Brunel University. She has published articles on erotic thrillers and on homoeopathy and literature. She is currently completing doctoral research on the politics and representation of self-endangerment.

Helen Hanson is a research student in the English Department of the University of Southampton. Her thesis is entitled 'Haunting Images: Reading the Cinematic Body of the 1940s'. She has taught film, literary and cultural studies courses at the University of Southampton and other institutions.

Barbara Kennedy is Senior Lecturer in Film and Cultural Studies at Staffordshire University. She is currently working on a book for Edinburgh University Press, entitled *Deleuze and Cinema: The Erotics of Sensation* based on her doctoral thesis. She is co-editing *Cybercultures* (Routledge, forthcoming) with David Bell and has published work on cyberfeminism and film.

Dr Tanya Krzywinska lectures in Film at Brunel University. She holds a Ph.D. and an MA from the University of North London and has published on pornography, vampires and European Cinema. She is currently working on possession in the Horror film and art cinema.

Kenneth MacKinnon is a Professor in the School of Literary and Media Studies at the University of North London. His articles on Greek Tragedy, on Film and on Sexuality are widely published and his several books include *Hollywood's Small Towns* (Scarecrow,

1984), *Misogyny in the Movies: The De Palma Question* (Associated University Presses, 1990), *The Politics of Popular Representation: Reagan Thatcher, AIDS and the Movies* (Associated University Presses, 1992) and *Uneasy Pleasures – The Male as Erotic Object* (Cygnus Arts, 1997).

Dr Fran Mason is a lecturer in Contemporary Cultural Studies at King Alfred's College, Winchester. He has written on postmodern culture and contemporary fiction, and is currently co-writing a book on gangster movies.

Monica B. Pearl is currently completing doctoral research on AIDS and Literature at the University of Warwick. She is editor and co-author of *Women, AIDS and Activism* (South End Press, 1990) and author of *The Consequences of Desire: Personal Responsibility in the AIDS Crisis* (Cassell, forthcoming).

Dr Julian Petley is Lecturer in Media and Communication Studies at Brunel University. He has written about the Bulger case for *Index on Censorship*, *The British Journalism Review*, *Social Science Teacher*, *Samhain* and *Scapegoat*, as well as contributing a chapter (with Bob Franklin) to *Thatcher's Children? Politics, Childhood and Society in the 1980s and 1990s* (Falmer Press, 1996).

Anna Powell is Senior Lecturer in Cultural Studies and Film at Manchester Metropolitan University. She is currently completing doctoral research in Popular Vampire Texts and Transgression. Her publications include an article on the representation of women in Powell and Pressburger films, 'Blood on the Borders: *Near Dark* and *Blue Steel*', *Screen*, Summer 1994 and 'Tripping the Dark Fantastic: Women's Vampire Fictions', *Metropolitan*, October 1995.

Paul Sweetman is Lecturer in Sociology at the University of Durham. Previously based at Southampton University, his research interests centre around issues of the body, identity, fashion and consumption.

Dr Linda Ruth Williams is Senior Lecturer in Film at Southampton University. She is author of *Sex in the Head: Visions of Femininity and Film in D. H. Lawrence* (Harvester Wheatsheaf, 1993), *Critical Desire: Psychoanalysis and the Literary Subject* (Edward Arnold, 1995) and *D. H. Lawrence* (Northcote House/British Council, 1997) and has written widely on cinema, feminism, Victorian poetry and modern fiction. She writes regularly for the British Film Institute magazine, *Sight and Sound*, contributing substantially to the 1993 collection, *Women and Film: A* Sight and Sound *Reader*. She is now completing a book on Erotic Thrillers for Edinburgh University Press.

Index

abjection, 35, 41, 45, 99, 127, 135–40, 188–209
AIDS, 80, 144, 194, 210–25
Alien, 36

(The) Bad Seed, 92–4, 96, 104
Barker, Clive, *Books of Blood*, 32, 42–3
Basic Instinct, 72, 74, 75, 137–8, 219–20
Bataille, Georges, 135, 188–92, 194–8, 203–6
Blade Runner, 108, 133
Blake, William, 87, 89
blood
  and body horror, 32, 34
  and body modification, 167
  as drug, 143, 144–5, 147, 149–50, 153, 155, 157
  see also vampires
body horror, 32–43, 101
body modification, 113, 117, 125n, 165–87
  as dieting and 'keep-fit', 166, 167, 182
  as scarification, 146
  see also reincarnation films; piercing; tattoos
Body of Evidence, 74, 135, 138, 219–21
Brite, Poppy Z., *Lost Souls*, 143–160
(The) Brood, 35–6, 38, 41, 43, 101
Brooks, Peter, 56–7

Bukatman, Scott, 122
Bulger, James, 103–5
Burroughs, William, 149, 150, 153, 160
Butler, Judith, 51–3, 60
Butterfly Kiss, 67–84

Cadigan, Pat, 108
Cameron, Deborah and Fraser, Elizabeth, *Lust to Kill*, 78
Cartesian discourse, 112, 129, 134, 152
  see also inside/outside; mechanic/organic,
castration, 28, 58, 60, 63, 66n, 129, 203–5
Chariots of Fire, 16
children
  and the Cold War, 94
  and the domestication of horror, 94–101
  as monsters, 87–107
  and sexuality, 190, 200, 202, 204–5, 209n
Chinn, Sarah E., 50–1
Clover, Carol, 37
Crash, 33, 40, 43–6
Creed, Barbara, 35, 38, 41, 45–6, 114, 197–8
(The) Crying Game, 49–66
cyborg, 108–24, 130–41

Damage, 135, 219, 221–4

229